D1504311

# Whither We

# Tend

## A Novel By

## Christopher R. German

"If we could first know *where* we are, and *whither* we are tending, we could then better judge *what* to do, and *how* to do it." - Abraham Lincoln

For My Wife, who believed that a better man could be found

For My Dad, who said, "I Love War"

## Preface

### Christmas with the Major

The terminal was empty except for the half dozen passengers who were arriving from BWI. Gus was just getting back from a job in Fallujah and he wondered where the other four passengers were coming from. They all looked like government employees of some sort, except for the one, an Army private who was in utilities. He, no doubt, was on leave and coming home for Christmas.

Although he had no way of knowing for sure, Gus was certain that no one else on this flight had to fly home on Christmas Eve for a funeral.

He got the message while he was on duty on Monday and was on a plane home by Wednesday. He was tired from the flight, first through Frankfurt, then over to BWI, and now into Bradley. Her wake was happening right now and he wanted to be there but he realized he still had to rent a car and make it down to New Haven by 6 PM. He looked at his watch, 12:24. It was still on Fallujah time, but he was pretty sure he wasn't going to make a 6 PM closing time.

He figured her parents were probably there, maybe some friends from college and of course, the theater. None of her people had anything good to say about him in the good times and they probably were cursing his name right now, for not showing up to her wake. "They were divorced," her mother would say, "but at least he could have shown up for her wake."

Her mother had a soft spot for her eldest daughter. Gus knew how they must have felt when Melissa told her mom that he had left her.

Melissa. Just thinking of the name gave him knots in his stomach. Knots from anger knots from heartache and knots of regret.

Maybe, if he hadn't left her, she would still be alive? She'd probably have hepatitis from drinking so much or the early stages of lung cancer, but she'd be alive just the same. Maybe if her mother had not placated her little girl, giving her the top-notch Ivy League schooling and the BMW for her sweet sixteen? Maybe if she had worked an honest job, like medicine, instead of being an actress, she would have had the strength to overcome her addictions and be a grown-up.

He remembered when she was turned down for the role in Wicked. She said that her career was over and that she was washed up as an actress. He tried to tell her that she could play all sorts of other roles or write or direct, but if she wasn't the lead, she wanted none of it.

That was when the drinking got bad. A year and half of boxed wine and antidepressants took their toll on her body and their marriage. When he came home from his last mission before they separated, he found her sitting on the couch crying at 1 PM, a full glass of blush, and a half-empty bottle of Xanax on the coffee table. The pile of empty boxes on the back deck made him shake his head. They weren't there when he left the week before.

He tried to get her help. He called her mother and told her what he found when he got home. She once again made excuses for her daughter, "she's learning how to live life without the theater," she said.

He went to the Al-Anon meetings with her and drove her to her therapy appointments. She sat in silence at the 12-step meetings and managed to wrap her therapist around her finger the way she did everyone else. He was an easy target, a pill-pushing quack in Milford who had seen her in Mama Mia in 2007. He loved the fact that he had a Broadway star as a client.

The last time he drove her home from the hospital, he knew that was the last time he would see Melissa. The divorce had been final for a year, but Gus was still the emergency contact on her medical forms at St. Raphael's. Her lips were stained from charcoal and the doctor said that her liver function indicated the early stages of liver disease.

"What the hell are you doing to yourself?" he asked, "You're not going to see 40 if you don't quit drinking."

He could see the black stains between her teeth when she spoke, "It wasn't my fault, Julie and Sandra came up from the city and we met for a drink downtown. They forced me to take a shot and after that, I blacked out."

"You don't remember wandering downtown with a bottle of 151, singing the entire score from "The Sound of Music"? When the cops picked you up, you were halfway through your fourth rendition of <u>Do A Deer</u> on the stairs of the Yale Art Gallery wearing only a bra," Gus said.

She began to cry, "Since you left me, I am lost, Gus. I feel so alone."

"Don't try that crying shit with me, Mel, we've done this too many times. Why the fuck did you have them call me? When are you going to change your emergency contact to your parents, or Julie, or Sandra, or anyone else other than me?" he said.

"I meant to have them call my mom, but your number was already in the file and they just called. I'm sorry I bothered you," she said, rolling her eyes.

"You *are* bothering me. You're killing yourself and that bothers the hell out of me. If you could take this the least bit serious, you'd see that is why we got divorced. That is why you were cut from the show and this is why you aren't working anymore," said Gus.

The car slowed at the light and she took her opportunity to say, "Fuck you, Gus," and got out.

He drove slowly behind her as she walked away, yelling to her, "Get in Melissa. It's freezing out and you have no clothes on. Let me take you home."

"No asshole! I don't need you. I'm fine," she screamed back.

The police cruiser pulled up behind Gus and squawked the siren. The officer said on the PA, "Are you okay, sweetheart?" She turned and flipped the cop the middle finger.

Gus loved the look in her eye when she was being defiant and laughed when the cop ordered him to pull over.

He stopped the car and rolled down the window, as he watched Melissa shiver and walk down the sidewalk.

The officer got out of his car and walked up alongside Gus on the driver's side and said, "Relationship problems, sir?"

"No officer, I'm divorced," Gus said, "She is my ex and just got her stomach pumped at St. Raph's. I'm trying to drive her home, but you're more than welcome to take over. I believe she was your guest last night as well."

"Oh, you and she have history?" asked the cop.

"To be honest sir, I think now she has more history with you guys than me," said Gus.

"Why don't you just get her in your car and get home, she looks like she had a rough night," said the officer.

Gus was sick of this conversation and said, "That was what I was trying to do before you pulled me over, jerk off?"

The officer ordered Gus out of the car and he watched her turn the corner and walk out of his life.

When he got the message that she was dead, he wondered if that cop knew that he was partially responsible.

The voice mail came from her friend Sandra. In it, she said that Melissa had left a note saying that her life meant nothing and that the worst mistake she ever made was losing Gus. She downed a bottle of oxy with a bottle of Everclear and was found floating face down naked in her tub by the police doing a wellness check. Her mother asked the cops to do a wellness check when Melissa didn't answer her phone for three days.

Now that he was back stateside, and back in Connecticut, he felt alone knowing that she was no longer there and that he couldn't call her. He hopped on the car shuttle and stared out the window as he watched the sunset. The only trouble he had getting to the car was when an old woman yelled at him for not wearing a mask, saying, "The vaccine isn't here yet asshole, you still have to wear a mask!" He sheepishly pulled the mask up over his mouth and nose and mouthed the words, "Fuck You," behind the safety of the surgical-grade shield.

When he got to the car, he threw his duffel in the back seat and ripped his mask off as soon as he got in the driver's seat. He looked at his watch and it said 12:47. If he hurried, he could make it to the wake.

He sped down I-91 and got to the funeral home on State Street, fifteen minutes before the close of viewing hours. He walked in and saw Melissa laying in a casket and her mother weeping with her father's arm around her back. Sandra and Julie huddled in the corner talking softly beneath masks. A half dozen other people Gus didn't recognize, with masks on, sat in the folding chairs around the room.

The emptiness of the room depressed him. This was the woman he loved and she was leaving this world as lonely as she was when she lived in it. Sandra walked to him as he walked in.

"Hey Gus, did you have a good flight?" Sandra asked.

Julie turned her back on him and several of the faces turned to look at him.

"Yeah, I did. It took two days, but I made it. Sorry, I'm late," Gus said.

"It's okay. You made it," she said.

Gus didn't like most of Melissa's friends, but Sandra could be decent from time to time he thought.

"Hey thanks for letting me know," said Gus, "I can't believe she's dead."

13

"She was so lonely and lost," said Sandra, "I tried to help but there was no reaching her."

Gus said, "may I go see her?"

"Sure- please do," said Sandra as she motioned towards the casket in the front of the room.

Gus walked slowly towards the open casket. He could see the makeup that they put on her face covered her beautiful cheeks and skin. Her hair was stiff and unnatural and he guessed it smelled of hairspray. She looked asleep. He touched her hand and it was cold. A sprig of pine was tucked in her pale fingers to remind everyone that she killed herself at Christmas.

Her mother walked up, wiping the tears from her eyes, and said, "You're late. She's gone."

"Yes I know," said Gus, "She left us too early."

"You know you did this to her," her mother said.

Gus waited for someone to come fetch this bereaved woman, but no one did. He didn't want to answer her.

"You're the reason she is dead. You're the reason my daughter is gone," she said.

Gus said, "I know," and walked toward the door.

He attended the funeral on Christmas day and stood well away from the sparse crowd, behind a tree that stood next to a marker that read "Rose Marie Santiello July 4, 1962 - September 7, 2001."

They sang Amazing Grace and Sandra spoke of her days on the stage and her love of horses. She made no mention of her marriage to Gus. When it was over the family all climbed in cars and drove away. No one spoke to Gus and he made no effort to speak to them.

He got in his car and drove back to the car rental place at Bradley, this time ensuring to have his mask on. He sat in the terminal when he got through security and waited for two hours until his flight began boarding.

He watched the news about the newly approved vaccine and the violence from protests between the Proud Boys and Black Lives Matter activists in Washington D.C. He read an article in Newsweek about the effort to exclude the 106 members of congress because of their support for the Texas lawsuit attempting to overturn the election. Then he watched the end of a Spanish version of It's A Wonderful Life, wishing the airport bar was open.

An older man sat two seats down from him and started a conversation, "Don't you just love traveling on Christmas?"

Gus said, "I dunno. I just buried my wife, think I would rather not travel today."

"Oh, Christ that's hard. Was it Covid?" the old man asked.

"Nah, she ate a bottle of pills and drowned in her bathtub naked," said Gus.

The old man bit his bottom lip and looked at the floor. He looked up and said, "I'm sorry for your loss sir."

Gus thought for a moment and said, "The world lost something in her, I'm sorry for your loss sir."

Before the old man could say anything else, the announcement came to start boarding. Gus gathered his bag and pulled his boarding pass from his pocket. He stopped to look at the setting sun across the tarmac and boarded the plane for DC.

By New Year's Eve, life was back to normal and he was standing guard at his post in Fallujah, humming <u>Auld Lang Syne.</u>

---

<u>Christmas at The Gates</u>

Simon opened the bottle of Browne and poured two glasses. The sound of Christmas music playing in the living room and the golden color of the setting afternoon sun, made it seem like Christmas, even if the usual crowd wasn't coming this year.

His parents were isolating in Palm Springs and Sarah's parents were staying home on the Eastern Shore. Every year since they were married, they had either gone to Maryland or Florida, but this year they were staying home in Stratford and enjoying their first Christmas together as a couple.

This year, they got their first real tree, cutting it down at Jones Tree Farm and trucking it home tied to their roof rack on Sarah's Outback. He hadn't used a Christmas tree stand in years and forgot that he needed to put a plastic bag under it before he brought the tree in.

The leaking water soaked and stained the rug and Sarah shook her head as he walked in with the wine looking at the stain.

"You know, I would give anything if we hadn't spilled that water when we put this tree up," Sarah said, taking the wine glass from Simon.

"I haven't had a real tree in years, I'm sorry that I forgot how to do it," Simon said.

"It's okay, we'll get it out somehow," Sarah said, "at least we have a tree".

Simon and Sarah were celebrating their third anniversary this year, and Christmas was always a second thought to the celebration they shared nine days before. Usually, they went away for their anniversary and would just be arriving at one of their parent's houses right about now.

This year though, they had to forgo the anniversary trip. The tree, the decorating and the cooking were all up to them. Simon kind of preferred it that way.

"You know, this pandemic has a bright side," Simon said, "We've never spent Christmas by ourselves before."

"It's kinda nice, isn't it?" Sarah replied.

Simon had bought a small rib roast that he was going to cook on Christmas day and Sarah was making bacon-wrapped scallops with asparagus for Christmas Eve dinner. Their families had always done these two meals for Christmas Eve and Christmas day because the quick-cooking scallops made it possible to make it to Christmas Eve service at the church and everyone loved prime rib on Christmas day. Since it was just the two of them this year though, Simon had the butcher cut a two rib roast, so they didn't have a bunch of leftovers to throw out.

The two made dinner and ate, finishing their bottle of Browne. They had dessert in the living room and turned on the television to watch the evening news.

The anchor read a story about how conservative pundits like Russ Limburgh and Allen Johnson were saying that the Herzog loyalists should consider sedition if Herzog was going to be denied the presidency. The anchor said that they ought to be jailed for their suggestion and that all Americans should be coming together to celebrate the holidays with the spirit of forgiveness and thankfulness after a year like 2020.

Simon said, "I can't say I agree with sedition, but I also can't say that they don't have a reason for concern."

"What do you mean?" said Sarah, "O'Leary won, lets just accept that and get on with ending this pandemic."

"You know they did rig the primary and who knows what O'Leary did to keep his son out of jail for Burissma. Where there's smoke, there has to be some fire. They're gonna keep investigating O'Leary and his team well into the next year and you know it," said Simon.

"I can't believe you are even considering their side Simon. They are racist assholes who want to overturn a legal election because it didn't go their way!" Sarah said irritated.

"I'm not saying they are right, I'm just saying that they have a point," said Simon.

"And what point is that? That if you lose an election you can just set aside millions of votes and name whomever you want to the presidency or threaten to secede from the Union if you don't get your way?" Sarah said with growing anger.

"I can see you take this very personally Sarah, it's Christmas Eve. I don't want to fight," said Simon.

"You bet your ass I take this personally, I'm a woman. Herzog is a racist bastard who grabs women by their pussies and you want me to understand HIS side of the story?" she yelled.

"I'm not saying that..." said Simon.

"Or he can divert millions of dollars to a wall no one wants, cage immigrant children from parents who cross the border and otherwise be the xenophobic asshole we know him to be?" yelled Sarah.

"No...I just think..." said Simon
"Or his followers can intimidate, and threaten innocent people with weapons at their homes because they didn't like the fact that he lost an election fair and square?" she continued yelling.

Simon was growing irritated by being domineered in this conversation but did his best to try and diffuse the situation.

"Honey, I'm just saying that they aren't all wrong," said Simon.

"Oh like Hitler wasn't all wrong because he was named Man of the Year in 1939 despite the fact that millions of German's followed a dictator blindly resulting in the deaths of millions of Jews, Russians, Americans, English, French, and every other country where he killed people? Herzog is the same man as Hitler, he just isn't as successful. You and all those other assholes who say they have a point or that that orange-haired bastard shouldn't be run out of the town on a rail covered in tar and feathers are just as complicit in the installation of a monster," said Sarah getting up and going to the kitchen.

When she came back she had poured a glass of wine and didn't bring one for her husband.

"Sarah," he said, trying to hold his temper, "I resent the fact that you lump me in with Nazis and racists. You know me and you know what I think, I don't support his racist policies, but I also can't support the Democrats who have rigged the political system ever since they lost to George W. Are we supposed to just turn a blind eye to all the things they have done wrong simply because Herzog is an asshole? That is why they have a point, we can't trust the democrats any more than can trust the republicans and something stinks when it comes to O'Leary. I wouldn't be half surprised if they didn't impeach him in the first six months."

Sarah took a long sip of her wine and listened to her husband.

"Simon I am sorry if you think I am lumping you in with racists like that fat radio hack, Russ Limburgh," she said, "but if you believe for a second the conspiracy crap they are feeding you about O'Leary and Barissma and Hillory's emails and the satanic liberal cult that is taking over the world, then I say you are as much of a shit head as they are."

Simon could feel his temperature rise and the fact that she had not brought him a glass of wine while she so conspicuously sipped hers made him angry. He tried to fight fair but was losing his patience.

"You libtard morons are just as bad those racists fuckers who say they want to secede. You're all part of the same problem, just different sides of it. You take half-truths as fact and blindly follow your almighty media, whether it's MSNBC or Fox News, you're all part of the same problem," he barked at his wife.

All she heard was the phrase "libtard" and the glass flew from her hand. It smashed on the wall behind Simon's head into a thousand shards, that rained down on him soaking him in wine and covering him with glass.

The sound stopped him first and then the feel of the wine on his head stole his attention. He looked at her with incredulity. His jaw dropped and his mouth lay open mid-thought.

She looked at him and her face went pale. Neither could believe that she threw the wine glass and no one knew what to say next.

She got up from her seat and went back to the kitchen. When she came back, she had a sponge and towel and another glass of wine. She lovingly set the wine in front of Simon, while she dabbed his head and picked the glass out of his hair and off his shirt.

He lifted the wine glass and said, "Thank you."

When she had cleaned most of the glass up, she said, "Honey why don't you run upstairs and hop in the shower. Just be careful about the glass and your bare feet."

Simon did as she suggested and went up to shower. He came back down, all clean and free of wine and glass. He saw her cleaning the stain from the wall and the back of the couch.

He saw a fresh bottle of Browne sitting open on the table and two clean wine glasses with a piece of pecan pie with whipped cream slightly melted on top. Next to the table, she placed his slippers where she thought he might like to sit, and on the television played It's a Wonderful Life.

She said, "I love this scene," as George ran down the street in the snow, wishing the old building and loan a Merry Christmas.

Simon said, "I do too. I am sorry for what I said. I never meant to call you a libtard."

Sarah said, "I'm sorry too. But I still think you're an asshole for agreeing with anything those racist morons say."

"If I tell you that it wouldn't hurt my feelings to see O'Leary impeached, will you throw another glass of wine at me?" asked Simon.

"Probably," said Sarah, "so don't say it out loud ever again in my presence."

Simon said, "Okay, good tip. Thanks for the pie."

They watched the rest of the movie and went to bed. The next morning they walked on the beach and enjoyed a prime rib for Christmas dinner in their home together, without a single visitor or family member.

That night when the holiday was ending and a gentle snow began to fall in the backyard, Simon put his arm around his wife and said, "Sarah, this is the best Christmas ever."

## Chapter One

"The restoration of American Democracy is complete. The United States Army has secured all the territories that displayed acts of rebellion following the recall of the presidential electors from the 2020 Presidential race. As such, President Franklin Crawford is asking all volunteers to register in person with their local Patriotic Unity Station at their earliest convenience. There, those seeking to support the cause of restoring services to the affected areas will be assigned a volunteer service. For more information or to find your local station, please go to www.AmericanStatesUnited.gov"

He read the email with a sense of incredulity. "How did we get here? What does this all mean now?" he asked himself. Ever since the rebellion started, strange emails and texts similar to this would show up regularly on his phone. He wondered why we needed a "restoration" when, supposedly, we never lost the Nation.

It had been three years since the emergency election, and Simon was getting tired of the mixed messages he read constantly. One day, the rebellion was just a rumor and a bad hoax, while the next it was going to be the undoing of our American way of life.

It was just like the covid pandemic: One day it was a hoax. The next day we were all going to die. He had no idea what to think, and he hated feeling as though he could no longer trust his judgment. Where was the truth, he wondered.

The general election was just the start of it. The protest and scuffles at the Million MAGA march should have been the first sign of trouble. No one confirmed how many known seditionists were in attendance or how many were actively tracked by the FBI. When they stormed the Capitol Building, they finally started arresting extremist individuals, but no individual or group was ever identified as the leader or organizer. The blame was laid solely on President Donald Herzog and his cronies.

Despite their rhetoric, it seemed that no one took any real notice or considered the white demonstrations a threat to national security until they bombed the bank buildings in Tampa. Oh sure, they rolled out the National Guard for every black lives matter protest and every announcement that yet another cop wouldn't be charged for killing yet another black man. For the seditionists however, it was hands-off, until something big happened.

Thank God for Covid-19, though. If the pandemic hadn't killed a million people in the US already, everyone would have been rioting in the streets when Congress passed the "Highway National Safety Act." I-95 was closed along with every other major highway when the administration said it would help to keep corona from spreading further. They never mentioned it, but it also helped the authorities tamp down the unrest.

Simon didn't know what to think anymore, other than things had most definitely changed.

Now, the police were making daily "keeping the peace" runs throughout the neighborhoods in their armored Humvees. The Navy parked an aircraft carrier off Charles Island, right after the Tampa bombings, and it never left. The only time that ever happened before was when the World Trade centers were hit. This time, the Navy moved in overnight and three years later, everyone just accepted it as normal and moved on.

The local deli flew flags out front and named a sandwich after the ship when it showed up, "The JFK." It was a chicken cutlet with bacon, pepper jack, and ranch dressing on a pretzel roll.

Simon had no idea what a chicken sandwich had to do with a Navy Aircraft carrier or the former President but the local radio jocks spent a week broadcasting about the deli, its new sandwich, and the boat. Soon following, the local McDonald's had a similar version of the sandwich on the menu, and everyone was all jazzed about the "NEW USA," as they liked to chant, with Navy ships parked in their front yard.

Unlike the aftermath of the World Trade Center tragedy, this time there were no freedom fries or other gaudy patriotic outpourings. To all appearances, the swing towards national loyalty was a tacit one, which allowed the Government to move in unprecedented fashions toward authoritarianism and the seditionists to grow "the rebellion," in the quiet undercurrent. Both sides of the extreme fringe, Antifa and QAnon, were already armed to the teeth before the gun ban went into effect three weeks after O'Leary was inaugurated. When that happened they went underground and started organizing online and in the backwoods of places like Arizona and Montana.

By the end of 2022, online groups with names like The Q Republic, The Seditionists, and The Black Reclamation, were organizing and active in all fifty states. Some blew up old cars, barns, trailers, and storage containers on camera and streamed it live from Bumfuckville, USA. They put the videos of their "tactics" on social media sites for the alt-right like QNEWS and Parler with captions like, "Death to Dems" and "Payment for the Steal" to prove their commitment to their ideals.

Others marched and rioted, burning down businesses and blowing up police cars. Conservatives called their side patriots and blamed the libs for their Antifa antics. The liberals called their side activists while referring to the conservative fringe as terrorists. Fingers were pointed in every direction, but in truth, neither their tactics nor their beliefs mattered. Whether they torched police barracks or raided the Capitol Building, they all had the same ax to grind: they hated the Government.

When the protesters who fought so hard to keep Herzog in office, finally banded together with the white supremacist groups, they called themselves the Seditionists. These were the groups that blew up six of the major bank buildings in Tampa Bay. In response to the attacks, Naval ships were moved into American harbors, the Army was ordered into the streets and all of it was to *protect* hometown America. The military occupation of America began.

The Army set up security offices in places like New Bern, North Carolina; Stratford, Connecticut; and Kalamazoo, Michigan. They called them Military-Political offices. They were set up in local municipal buildings, and people were encouraged to report seditious neighbors. They thought that would root out the bad elements.

At first, it bothered Simon, but he, like everyone else, accepted it after learning that either Antifa or a group of white power extremists bombed Tampa. The general public was never told exactly who did it, just that they were the "seditious fringe."

Three years later, the mixed messages from the media and the emails from the Government made Simon wonder what he wasn't being told and what was really going on. He started questioning everything.

Looking back, he couldn't remember a time when the military wasn't in town hall, although he knew it wasn't always so. It truly bothered him that he could not remember what life was like before. "New normal becomes *normal* so easily," he thought.

Finally reading the last of the morning's messages, Simon stuck his phone in his pocket and pulled the toast out of the toaster. The coffee was ready and the sun was just starting to come up, melting the frost on the windshield of his truck. He thought to himself, "I'm still gonna have to scrape that shit off before I head out."

Simon owned an insurance agency and liked to get there before the traffic got too bad. Since they shut down I-95, traffic was diverted to all the local roads. This made getting to his office on the northside of town a real bitch.

He shoved the toast into a sandwich bag and poured black coffee into his travel mug. Simon knew he would have time to eat his breakfast at one of the thousand red lights he would encounter on his way to work.

Pulling on his gloves and his puffy green coat, Simon grabbed his coffee and stuffed the toast into his pocket. He walked across the crunchy frozen lawn and down the driveway to his truck. He beeped the door to get it open. The beeper made no noise.

"Shit" - he thought - "the battery died again." He stuck the key in the door setting off the car alarm, waking the entire neighborhood as well as his sleeping wife inside. She jumped out of bed and stuck her face in the window.

He looked up sheepishly from the driver's seat and shrugged, holding up the dead car beeper for her to see through the frosted bedroom window pane. He mouthed "I'm sorry" and stuck the key in the ignition to shut off the alarm.

The truck roared to life and the heat kicked on, blowing freezing air right up his nose. Simon turned the heater dial off and reached over to the passenger floorboard to pick up the scraper. He remembered throwing it down there after going through the exact same ritual yesterday.

"Winter driving is hell," he thought to himself.

Simon got back out of the truck and looked up to see if his wife was still glaring at him through the window. He guessed that she must have returned to bed and envied how warm and comfy she must be. Three more days until the weekend and he could stay in bed with her and be warm, happy, and rested.

Thanks to the February sunrise, the scraper chipped the thin sheet of ice off the windshield with ease. Back in December, he would have had to do this in the dark, but the longer days meant Simon could at least go to work in the sunlight, and scraping ice wasn't such a chore.

With the windshield clear and the truck starting to blow warm air from the heater, Simon turned the radio on and listened. He forgot for a moment that he could no longer listen to NPR. Funding cuts had killed the public radio station at the end of last year when he listened to the farewell episode of Morning Edition.

The static on the channel where his favorite radio station had been, made him wonder once again, what the hell happened to the world he knew? He switched over to satellite radio and heard an old Bleacher's song he loved and his concerns quickly faded to the back of his mind.

Simon threw the truck in reverse and backed up the driveway and onto the glistening road. Apparently, the sand truck wasn't coming this morning, and the town was going to rely on the sun to get rid of the black ice today. Come to think of it, he couldn't remember the last time he saw a sander or, for that matter, a garbage truck or even a school bus. Budget cuts seemed to hit the municipal services first.

He backed into the road and then slowly drove down the hill to Main Street. He kept it under the speed limit, seeing how icy the roads were. He was happy that he left the cinder blocks in the bed for extra traction.

The roads were still pretty empty at this hour. Simon made it through the intersection, past the pharmacy, and donut shop without much trouble while enjoying the song on the radio. The cop car that sat in the gas station parking lot with the lights on gave him pause as he cruised through the light, mid-sip with his coffee in hand.

Once he passed it, though, Simon could see that the cop car was empty. It was just there to keep the appearance that cops were watching. So he bumped his speed up to 35 MPH. He pulled the bag from his pocket, slid a piece of toast from the bag. He felt a drip of butter land in his lap.

"Damn it," he said to the steering wheel, "Not again."

When Simon arrived at the office, it was empty. No one had arrived yet. The parking lot had not yet thawed due to the shade from the storefront, and everything was still coated with a thin layer of frost. It looked quite pretty, like some holiday card he sent his clients, but he knew it would be slippery for the ladies when they got there.

Simon opened the door to the office, grabbed the bag of salt, and spread it over the walk in front of his office and in the five parking spots that were reserved for his employees and his customers in the strip mall parking lot.

When he was done, he went inside and flipped on his computer monitor, and waited for the rest of the staff to arrive.

Simon scrolled through the emails, reading again the message he received from the government this morning. Everything else looked like spam or customer inquiries which he would leave for his assistant to sort through when she got in. He then turned his attention to the voice mails and finished his cup of coffee.

He glanced, once again, at the butter stain on his pants and thought maybe he should try to wash it off in the bathroom before anyone got there. Before he could finish the thought, Marion walked in and shook the cold from her coat.

Always a step ahead of him, she said, "Did you see that email from the feds this morning?"

"Yup," Simon said, "do you think they actually 'restored democracy' this time?"

"No way in hell," she said with a wry sideways smile.

The two often chatted politics in the early hours of the day, before the phone rang and billing calls were made. It gave them a sense of normalcy when so many things weren't normal anymore.

Amy, the office assistant hurried in, just as the silence was returning to the office. "She blows in like a hurricane most mornings," Simon liked to say. Amy's energy disrupted the morning silence and her voice sounded shrill against the sound of computers warming up and the humming of the water coolers.

Neither Simon nor Marion liked her that much, but Amy answered the phone and made copies. How much did they have to like her to do that kind of job? Amy swung her coat around the back of her chair and with that the office began to buzz with a new day's duties.

Simon lost track of time and before he knew it, it was lunchtime. He offered to run up to the corner to get sandwiches, but Marion said she brought yogurt today and Amy was waiting for her boyfriend to "slip away for lunch." Amy often "slipped away" for lunch when her boyfriend was in town. Simon thought that "slipping away" meant a midday quickie in the car after turkey on rye, but he would never say anything to her about it.

Simon shrugged and said, "Suit yourself," as he put on his jacket and jingled his keys in his hand.

When he stepped outside, the air was much warmer than it was when Simon got to work that morning. Most of the frost had melted into a damp residue that filled the warming air. Days like this meant spring was on the way and he thought that if it warmed enough this afternoon, the spring peepers might be out again that evening.

The weather was getting warmer daily, and the wildlife was feeling the brunt of it. When Simon was a kid, spring peepers didn't usually come out until early April. Here it was, the second week of February and there was plenty of ice this year, but not a trace of snow anywhere in New England the entire season. The spring peepers were already calling and Simon thought, "this just isn't right."

The scientists said four years ago that we were on the brink of environmental collapse, but the Rebellion seemed to put that on the back burner for the Crawford administration. If O'Leary had served all four years, he might have done something, but when they recalled the electors six months into his administration, the priorities all seemed to change.

When Crawford took office, he made it clear that his top priority was putting down the Rebellion and stomping out the online activists. "He must have forgotten that his predecessor said that climate change was a top priority," Simon said to himself.

When Herzog finally admitted his loss to O'Leary, Simon and the rest of the country hoped that things would get better soon. However, when it became clear, just a week after O'leary's inauguration, that you had to be wealthy or over 75 to get the vaccine anywhere in the world, it was clear nothing would change.

The Pandemic would continue to kill. The rich would get richer and the poor would get poorer. Health care would still be unaffordable and the planet would still be on the precipice of environmental collapse. Nothing had changed in twenty- five years, why would it change just because we put a Democrat back in the White House?

Simon was still hopeful, even after all the early signs indicated that the status quo would remain, that the Constitution might win and normalcy could return under a moderate Democrat.

It took them two months into the new presidency to indict O'Leary's campaign manager, with much pressure from Herzog and the seditionists. The O'Leary surrogate was only the first of many to sing like a canary about O'Leary's involvement. One by one, the Dems went to prison. O'Leary had to resign after his impeachment, which overjoyed much of the country because everyone ultimately wanted his younger, Asian female VP in the first place. She took over when O'Leary was impeached and that's when they blew up Tampa.

Multiple online extremist groups coordinated the Tampa attack, which was nothing more than a fleet of commuter buses full of fertilizer and propane tanks strategically staged in front of bank buildings. The Feds for some reason never saw it coming. When credit was finally claimed, a group called "The Seditionists" with a capital "S," said they would bomb every major city if they didn't recall the election and try again.

The Sedontionists fancied themselves warriors, after storming the Capitol with automatic weapons and ranting about demonic pedophiles on social media. It was at the same time that the Feds busted one of the radical racist groups who supported Herzog and who was cleared of involvement in the bombings, that Frank Crawford stepped in from obscurity.

Franklin Crawford was an Afghan war vet, who worked in green technology setting up solar farms in the Midwest. It was rumored that he moonlit for the security firm Dark Pond before getting into politics. The people of Iowa took a liking to him when he started a Mayoral run in 2021. He surprised everyone when he backed out of the run in protest, when the Party elites were found to be stacking the deck against his GOP opponent saying, "I won't run in a rigged election." That protest got him a blip on CNN but made the shell shocked voters of Iowa, still reeling from the realization that yet another election was rigged, swoon for a little honesty, and a pile of integrity.

The Iowan Democrat Governor, seeing a political winner in his midst, appointed him as a replacement to fill the vacated Congressional seat, after the incumbent was killed in a car crash. He jumped on the National stage at the O'Leary Impeachment trial with a speech about the evils of a corrupt Nation, and it was *his* suggestion that they recall the electors from the 2020 electoral college and repoll them to make up for the fraud perpetrated by the Democrats.

The impasse came when the Democrats would not allow Herzog back on the ticket. They said that just because they failed at convicting him at his second impeachment, even after he left office, he was still unfit to be President despite having the votes in the Electoral College. The Herzog loyalists refused to allow any of the former O'Leary camp on the ballot citing similar complaints. They compromised for the common good, having both parties nominate a new candidate.

The only social democrat and senior senator from Vermont, Eugene Greenbaum announced Crawford as his man for the job in his retirement speech from the Senate, citing Crawford's progressive agenda and his green technology background. As it was, no one trusted the Dems anymore and Greenbaum was the only politician anyone respected.

The Republicans were all but bankrupt after four years of Herzog trashing the GOP. When they discovered that a Republican PAC for Senate Minority Leader Mack McCortle funded the bombings of Tampa, the Republicans finally went defunct. McCortle, not only acknowledged his PAC's involvement but tried to defend the role that it played in the bombings live on CNN. At the joint session to investigate the bombings following that interview, the entire Congress, both sides and houses, walked out when Senate Minority Leader McCortle took to the dais. The Minority Whip Kelly Grim led a mass resignation of Republicans that was live-streamed from the steps of the Capitol building. That left only Crawford with the funding and the backing to take the Presidency.

They de-emphasized Crawford's work with Dark Pond in the ad hoc primary they held to find a new candidate to run. Hillory tried in vain to get back into politics, in light of the post mortem Republican presence and a brief bounce back into the spotlight that was created when her husband and former President suffered a heart attack. The Democrats ran her again in their nominating session, as they had run out of other viable candidates, but she was booed off the stage and into political obscurity. When it was clear the Dems couldn't find anyone else to run, Greenbaum and the Socialists seized the moment and the process and put Crawford on the ballot.

In the general election, however, the party used Crawford's Dark Pond experience to sell people on the idea that Crawford could protect them from Online fringe terrorists. The only conservative who could muster any kind of backing at all was some Mormon senator from Utah who ran as a self-funded Independent and won the popular election by nearly 3 million votes. The somewhat moderate conservative didn't do as well in the electoral college with only 237 votes, so President Franklin "Frank" Albert Crawford was sworn in on June 17, 2022.

Crawford's first official act was to classify anyone who supported Herzog as a "seditionist" and termed their activities as "rebellious." This caused a huge battle with the ACLU and he alienated most of the conservatives who still had the nerve to call themselves conservative, but the safety of America was paramount. At least that is how Simon saw it.

He wasn't a huge fan of either candidate in 2020, but he listened to the popular outcry and voted for O'Leary, the way everyone else did. He was quite happy to see O'Leary resign and even happier when

Greenbaum climbed back on stage and told the world to vote for Crawford.

It wasn't that he thought O'Leary was a bad guy in the Obama years, but he didn't like how the Democrats gamed the process both in the 2016 and 2020 elections. Greenbaum was the rightful winner both times, or at least that's what Simon thought. He most assuredly won the 2016 primary, and if Herzog hadn't screwed up the pandemic response so badly the Dems wouldn't have tried to rig the primary again in 2020, screwing Greenbaum once again.

He thought the primary process was a sham. The Democrats always knew what was best for us and that was supposed to justify how they rigged the process to put the anointed candidate in the general. When they finally proved that O'Leary and the Democrats rigged the electoral recount and the senate runoff in Georgia, Simon said he would never vote Democrat ever again.

It wasn't that Simon was liberal or conservative. He hated government excess but thought everyone deserved health care. He was certain the Government was behind 9/11 but didn't believe that the political elites were trying to control the world population with chemtrails and demonic pedophilia. Most of all, Simon prided himself on being moderate and that was the one thing Crawford wasn't.

Crawford could have been a great guy in another time, Simon thought. In the days of outright rebellion and with everyone eyeballing everyone else for being a seditionist though, he thought having a Dark Pond guy in office was just electing the polar opposite of Herzog. Why was everything so extreme these days?

Crawford supposedly had a talent for digging up the bad guys and taking them down with very extreme prejudice. They loved to tell the story during the campaign about how he was the guy who took Zaman Al-Hassin in Tikrit when the US was still hunting Arabs in the middle east. Crawford wasn't the guy who gave the order to kill Al-Hassin, but actually, the guy who climbed into his room in the dark and stuck the knife in his ear. People said his nickname in Dark Pond was "mean mother fucker" and Simon worried about a guy like that as President.

When he got into office, Crawford started by ordering the withdrawal of forces in the Middle East. When the economy tanked in 2022, he said we couldn't afford to be the world's policeman anymore. That was when he drew down US forces from the rest of the world positions and started using the military to control the troubles at home.

After Tampa, the Military took control of cities like Seattle and Miami. That was when the political arrests started happening. Entire groups of protesters were rounded up and sent to prison under charges of sedition. It was rumored that when the federal prisons were filled with domestic terrorists, the Military set up camps on BLM land in Arizona, where they held domestic terrorists awaiting trial as they had in Guantanamo.

The backlog was three years out for trials, but so many Americans got fully behind the cause to root out domestic terrorists, that no one cared.

Mother's called on their sons, sisters called on their brothers, neighbors called on neighbors. All you had to do was say that guy had a MAGA hat and he was on a bus to somewhere to be dealt with.

Three of Simon's former neighbors had disappeared since Crawford took office. Truthfully, he hadn't known them very well. Their short conversations were only in passing when taking out the trash or collecting the mail but he never heard them say anything good about Herzog or his supporters. They were hauled away just the same.

The only good part of this new normal, if there was one, was that everyone was much nicer now. Up until and immediately after the election, people were getting mean. They threatened to kill each other online and that anger spilled over into real life. People started fistfights in the church over who won the election. Hatred, anger, and fear turned into random gunfights in the streets.

It all changed when you could call and have anyone hauled off for just the *suspicion* of sedition. People started speaking with a lot more care and compassion for their fellow man, both online and in person.

Simon knew he didn't like what he was seeing in the US now, but he knew as long as no one said anything bad about him, it wasn't his problem and everything was gonna be okay.

That's when the car slammed into the side of his truck.

He was so deep in thought that he failed to notice the light change on his way to get lunch and the SUV slammed right into him as he crossed the intersection. There is a lot to be said for the build of his truck and that of the SUV because neither driver was injured. The jerk who got out of the SUV didn't see things that way.

"What the FUCK are you doing ASSHOLE!?" the other driver screamed as he climbed from his crashed SUV.

"J-J- Jesus, are y-y-y-you, you okay?" stammered Simon.

"Yeah I am fine, asshole, but my car is trashed, you better have insurance," the other driver barked.

"I am an insurance agent," Simon whimpered, "I have a business right down the road and was on my way to lunch. Jesus, I'm glad you're okay."

"What the fuck were you doing?" the other driver said rubbing his neck, "You drove right through the light. You're lucky you didn't break my neck."

Simon said, "If you want, I'll call an ambulance. Here's my card with my info on it." He handed him a business card that read:

Simon Gates
*APT Insurance*
Owner/Agent

(203) 555-3179

They could hear the sirens now of the responding officer in the distance.

"I don't need an ambulance, I took bigger hits in Fallujah. You're lucky we didn't both turn into a ball of fire," the other driver said with a sneer.

Just then the police car pulled alongside and Officer Mike Krajewski climbed out of his car. "Gentleman what happened here?" the officer started as he eyed the damage on both cars and the growing line of traffic on each side.

The other driver yelled, "this asshole ran a red light and I hit him."

Simon, now getting tired of this driver's attitude, said, "Officer, I don't know what happened, he just came out of nowhere and hit me."

The officer walked around Simon's truck and looked at the damage and then walked over to the SUV and peered in the window. The SUV driver's face changed quickly when he saw the officer look inside.

"Sir, can you tell me what's in this bag on your front seat? Is that a book?" the officer asked, peering in the passenger side of the SUV.

The other driver said, "it's just clothes and some of my papers, officer. I'm heading out of town. In fact, I need to get going. I think my car is fine, can we just chalk this up to no-fault and get out of the way of traffic?"

The officer lifted his shoulder to key his radio mic to call for backup. Simon didn't see it happen but heard the shots as the angry driver fired two shots into the police officer's forehead, killing Officer Mike Krajewski. He then turned the gun on Simon and said, "I'm gonna stay in touch, I'll see you later."

He climbed back in the badly damaged SUV and started the motor. The tire rubbed against the smashed-in bumper as he drove away and Simon collapsed to his knees in shock.

Almost immediately, a dozen police cars and ambulances were on the scene. Simon was lying with his face pressed into the road in handcuffs, looking the dead officer in the eye as he peered from underneath the blood-soaked sheet on the roadway.

Simon's face hurt from the sand and pebbles on the pavement and he thought he would stop breathing from the knee pressed into the back of his skull. The officer on Simon's back talked nonchalantly to his peers about the weather, while an old lady who was sitting in traffic in a burgundy Cadillac tried to get their attention. She stuck her head out the window and yelled, "Officer! Sir, you're arresting the wrong man."

The officer got up off Simon's back and walked up to her and said, "Were you here, ma'am? Did you see what happened?"

She said, "Yes I did. That man on the ground got into a car accident with a very dangerous man who used plenty of foul language. He was the one who pulled out a gun and shot that officer on the ground over there. Like I said...you're arresting the wrong man."

The officer said, "Are you sure? Did you see it all?"

"Yes," she said, "I saw the other man who drove away shoot the officer."

He directed her to pull off to the side of the road and began to take down her information as a witness. He turned to the sergeant and said, "Sarge, that guy didn't do it. Take the cuffs off and let him up, will ya?"

The sergeant came over and picked Simon up off the ground and said, "Geez man, I'm sorry," dusting the dirt off of Simon's shirt and face. "Let me put you over here for a few minutes while we figure out what's what."

Simon, who was crying from seeing the officer shot and the pain of being smashed into the pavement, said, "Can you take these handcuffs off, so I can call my wife?"

The sergeant reached into the wrecked truck and picked up Simon's phone from the cup holder. He said, "Here you go, fella. I'll put this in your pocket so you can call your wife when we release you from those cuffs."

Simon sat on the curb for two more hours before the sergeant came back and released him from the handcuffs. He had stopped crying and wanted a drink of water desperately, and asked, "When can I go?"

The sergeant said as he removed the cuffs, "It won't be much longer, you can call your wife now and tell her to meet us at the station."

She didn't pick up on the first try, so Simon dialed again. This time she picked up and said with annoyance in her voice, "What's up Simon? I'm busy at work."

"Sarah, I had an accident," Simon said, "A cop has been killed."

"Killed, what do you mean Simon?" she asked.

"The police officer who responded to the accident was shot in the head by the driver of the other car and then he drove off." Simon heard the words coming out of his mouth, but couldn't believe he was saying them.

"My GOD are you alright?!" she yelled so loud that the officer standing beside him heard her.

"I'm fine," said Simon trying to quiet his voice, "I just have to answer a few questions I think, and won't make it back to the office today, can you please call Marion and tell her. Also, can you pick me up at the police station later?"

The officer beside him interrupted, "we'll give you a ride home when you're done. Tell her not to wait up."

Simon said, "This could take a while, Sarah. I'll call you when I'm done." Before she could answer, Simon hung up the phone.

He sat down on the side of the road and the smell of the newly budding skunk cabbage burned his nose and eyes. Being out of the sun, he felt the coolness of the winter still emanating from the earth beside the road and he wondered if Officer Mike Krajewski had a family and if they knew what happened yet.

He wondered why the guy did what he did? Why didn't he shoot Simon as well? He wondered why things happened the way they did.

The sergeant came back over and asked him where he wanted his car towed when forensics was done with it. Simon said, "I always work with Breezy Point, can you have them pick it up?"

"You've done this before?" quipped the sergeant.

Simon smiled and said, "I'm in insurance."

The sergeant said, "Okay I get it. You've had a rough day. Why don't I drive you to the station and get your statement? Then we'll take you home. Alright?"

Simon agreed and climbed in the front seat of the cruiser, next to the officer. Fifteen minutes later, they were at the station. He walked inside, with the officer directly behind him, pointing the way to go.

The statement lasted three hours and he was forced to answer awkward and seemingly unrelated questions about his life and his political beliefs. "Do you have any loyalties to Donald Herzog or any of his supporters? Do you think that President Crawford is doing a good job?"

He was confused by the questions and wondered what they had to do with a car accident and a dead cop. Simon stopped the interview and asked, "Sergeant, I haven't had an accident in a while, but what does any of this have to do with the accident?"

"We think Officer Krakewski's killing was politically motivated. The other driver was a known seditionist. You may be on his target list now," said the sergeant, matter of factly.

Simon squirmed in his seat and said, "how's that? It was just an accident?"

"The plate that Officer Krajewski radioed back before he was shot was registered to a John Newsome, a former Herzog loyalist and a member of a known online hate group, we believe. We've notified the Army and the FBI. They will be here later today to investigate. I've taken your statement, but they may want to ask you some questions in the days ahead. Are you planning on leaving town at all?"

Simon said "No," and handed the officer his business card. It was the same card he handed to Newsome- if that was his *real* name. Simon extended his hand and said "This is my office and my personal cell is on the back. Anytime you need anything I am available."

The sergeant thanked him and offered him a ride home, but Sarah was waiting in the hallway outside when they walked out of the interview room.

She ran towards him and hugged her husband. They held hands as they walked out of the police station.

"Let's talk when we get home. I'm beat," Simon said as they walked towards her Prius. They climbed inside and went home.

## Chapter 2

He didn't say much on the drive home and she didn't ask very many questions. The events of the day wore on both of them. He saw a man get killed and she spent most of the day worrying her husband would be taken away.

That was the way people thought now. Any interaction with authority could be the last time you were ever seen, and his wife had no illusions about the fact that he had brushed with death today. She just didn't know the full extent - yet.

Simon wasn't sure if he should be more worried that he was on the government radar now or that a rebel combatant had his information. He had no idea how to tell his wife his dilemma, so instead, he sat in silence.

When they pulled into the driveway, Sarah blurted out, "What the hell are you thinking? Say something!"

He didn't know where to begin. He didn't know what to say. He just knew he was scared and had no idea how to tell his wife that he may have put the two of them in grave danger because he wasn't paying attention while driving.

Simon breathed deep and said, "Can we go inside first, I need a drink."

They got out of the car and walked slowly up to the front door. They noticed the door was slightly ajar and the hall light was on. That was not the way it looked, normally, when they came home and after the day Simon had, he wanted to run far and fast away.

Simon mustered all the energy he had left and kicked the door in. The swinging door knocked the vase off the hall table and it smashed in a million pieces with water flying everywhere. His wife, shocked at the display of aggression in her normally docile husband, screamed at the sound of smashing ceramic.

When they stepped inside, other than the smashed vase, nothing seemed out of place. The TV was still in the living room, the laptop still on the desk. No one had rifled through any of the drawers and it didn't look like a break-in at all.

Sarah said, "Great, you broke my mother's vase for nothing."
Simon replied, "Let me tell what happened today, and then you might understand. But first I need that drink."

He walked back to the kitchen and pulled a bottle of Tanqueray out of the freezer along with two ice cubes. He placed the bottle on the counter and grabbed a glass from the cupboard and threw the ice in the glass.

Unscrewing the cap he said, "I don't know how to say this, other than just saying it, so here goes." He paused to fill the glass with gin and dribbled a little from the overfilled glass as he drank its entire contents in one gulp.

"I saw a cop get killed today by a rebel operative and I gave him my business card."

"WHAT?" she said. She reached into the cupboard and grabbed a glass for herself. While she normally never drank gin, she mirrored his behavior and drank down her drink in one swallow. She then bent over the kitchen sink and vomited.

It was all clear and came out just as cold as it went down. He looked at her dry heaving over the sink and realized why he loved her so much. Her flair for drama matched his.

Simon said, "Had I known you would take it so well, I wouldn't have worried so much about how to tell you gently."

She spit one last time, pulled her long brown hair back and turned to him, and said, "Don't be a smartass. What the fuck happened?"

He proceeded to tell her about the accident and the SUV driver who was such a jerk at first. He then told her about the gunshots and being handcuffed face down. He told her that the other driver made sure to tell him that they would see each other again before he drove off. He continued about how the cops told him that the other driver - the cop killer- was a known rebel organizer.

By the time he had finished the story, the bottle of gin was gone and they had started on a bottle of red wine. They moved their conversation to the living room and sat on the couch, looking into each other's eyes. "What? I don't understand," he said, "is why the door was open when we came in?"

Sarah, now visibly shaken and thoroughly drunk said, "Maybe he came to check you out and realized you were just a boring insurance guy and no threat to the rebellion? He was probably walking around here when we were at the police station and he knows all about us now?"

The thought thoroughly scared Simon, but the fact that his wife thought he was a boring insurance guy hurt his feelings. Equally drunk he replied, " What do you mean I'm boring?"

Sarah realizing what she said, trying to back peddle, said, "you're not entirely boring, you did witness a murder today." Reminding him of his day, slightly sobered Simon and brought him back to his worry.

Simon, not wanting to get into an argument about the fact that his wife thought he was a bore, said, "It's time for bed. Let's go." Sarah agreed and wandered up the stairs, while Simon checked all the doors.

He locked the front door and shut off the front hall light. He then went around to the slider in the back and put the bar in the jam to keep it from opening. He then went to the French doors that overlooked the herb garden on the side of the house and noticed his business card tucked in the handle. He _was_ there.

Simon yelled up to his wife who was half-dressed and passed out on the bed, "Honey, he _was_ here." She didn't hear him. She was passed out drunk and in his state, he didn't see much use in waking her. He brushed his teeth, swirled some mouthwash and took two aspirin with a pint glass full of water, and passed out next to her on the bed.

When they woke in the morning, they both had massive hangovers and called in sick to work.

He remembered seeing the card in the door. Simon told his wife that he tried to wake her and tell her the night before, but that she had already passed out. With no energy to worry and a banging headache, they took showers, dressed, and donned sunglasses. They called the police to tell them about the card, and the open front door.

The sergeant from the day before said that he would send over a unit right away and within the hour, four police cars were in their driveway with canines and forensic gear.

They dusted all the doors for fingerprints and used the dogs to sniff around the house and yard for any kind of trace of the man. By the time they left, it was late afternoon and the two were ready for bed again. They regretted calling the police. The cops found no evidence. Instead, they used every chance they had to ensure that the middle-aged couple were not rebel sympathizers.

Simon handed her a glass of ginger ale and some saltines on a plate and said, "Honey I think we seriously ought to reconsider the next time we decide to call the police."

"Why is that?" she said with a sarcastic tone, "you don't want to be accused of being seditionist while reporting a crime again?"

They chuckled at the irony but both felt strangely relieved that the cops didn't find a reason to arrest them. For a period there they worried that the police were not on their side at all but rather looking to take down everyone. They were irritated by the fact that they might be considered enemies when in the first place they were the ones that called the authorities for help.

It occurred to Simon again, at that moment, that things seemed to change so much in such a short period of time.

They grilled pork chops and drank bloody marys for dinner. They watched Netflix until 9:30 when they decided to go to bed after having such a rough night before. He locked the doors and paid special attention to the French door handle where he saw the card the night before, shuddering for a second to think that that man had been his home.

The next morning was Saturday and when Sarah's alarm went off, he pulled the covers over his head and went back to sleep for another half hour. By the time he woke up, the smell of coffee filled the house and he could hear his wife on the phone with her mother at the kitchen table.

"He didn't tell me what he was doing when he crashed," Sarah droned to her mother, "all I know is he was distracted and ran a red light and that's when that bastard hit him."

"Of course, we have insurance, he's an insurance guy, Mother," she continued with her mother. Her voice took on an annoyed yet caring sound when she talked to her mother and he could tell right away that she had already told her mother too much.

As he walked into the room, he could tell the questions were coming from her mom rapid-fire now and she was getting increasingly annoyed with each one. "No Mom, No Mom, Yes Mom, No Mom, I don't know Mom. Kiss dad, I love you, Goodbye. Good By Mom, Mom GoodBye. Tell Dad I Love him too. B-Bye, Mom. Bye...He is standing right here Mom, ... B-Bye," and with that, she punched the button and the call was over.

"You told your Mother," he said dryly rubbing the sleep from his eyes. "The coffee is still hot, pour a cup and sit down, I want to talk to you," she replied.

He dutifully grabbed a mug from the cupboard, poured a black cup of coffee, and walked toward the table. Pulling out the chair and setting the cup on the table, he said, "what's up?"

"I'm worried," she started, "I don't trust that we are safe here with this rebel guy running around and I don't want to call the police ever again."

"What do we do, quit our jobs and move to Canada?" he said, half kidding and half-serious.

"It's too cold in Canada," she said, "Besides it would take us months to sell the house."

Sarah was the practical one in the pair. Only she would consider it necessary to sell their house before running for their lives. Everyone else would just pick up and go. It was her pragmatism that kept them on the path to success, he thought. It was one of the reasons he asked her to marry him.

This was a second marriage for both of them. He married while he was in his mid-twenties to a Catholic girl who was dead set on having a dozen kids. He later learned that kids weren't in the cards for him by any kind of conventional means as he had a low sperm count. She divorced him and married a guy who started a family with her within months of her new marriage and last he heard, they were at three and counting.

Sarah, a dental hygienist for a local practice, was three years Simon's senior and a mother of one girl from her first marriage from whom she was estranged. Her ex-husband was abusive and loved to play mind games and caused a chasm in their relationship. Her daughter was now grown with a family of her own and couldn't see her way clear of her father, to have a relationship with her mother again.

Simon felt heartbroken for his wife's loss and wished he could give her another child to make up for it. Ultimately, however, the two agreed that they were well beyond the child-rearing years and even if they did get pregnant, it would likely not work out well. They said it was all in God's hands and to this point, God had kept them childfree and so it was.

"Well if warm weather and a realtor are necessary to save our lives from a crazed killer," reasoned Simon, "you call Estelle over at Remax and I will start packing for Mexico."

She didn't laugh and rolled her eyes at him and said, "Will you be serious Simon, this is not a joke."

His phone was still on the charger from the night before and he realized at that moment that he had not checked it after he woke up.

"Where are you going, " she said annoyed, "we're not done."

He had a habit of walking away in the middle of conversations, which she had complained to him about many times. "I'm not walking away, I'm just getting my phone. I have an idea," he said.

She took a long pull on her coffee cup and swallowed the complaint she wanted to sling at him.

He returned to the table with his phone and opened the screen to find that he had received a text message. He clicked on it and read it aloud to her,

"Want to join the fight for a Free America? Want to help us beat the rebels back and keep our streets safe? You can join the effort by volunteering today to help your local Patriotic Unity Station. Reply to this Text with your name and zip code and a representative will call you ASAP!"

She listened intently and wondered what he had in mind. He was 44 years old and twenty pounds overweight. How could he join the Army? There was no way she was going to let him go to war.

"I got an email about this the other morning," he said quietly, "I wonder if I helped them with their Patriotic Unity stuff if I could get a little protection from the Military?"

She looked at him like he was insane, but spoke deliberately, "Honey, I love you. You're in your 40's and you sell insurance. Do you actually think they want you as a volunteer to fight the Rebellion?"

"Enough with the boring insurance guy shit," he wanted to say, but he realized that this would not help his case. Instead, he said, "I don't know, but I'd be willing to find out."

She wasn't used to him being reasonable when he wanted something badly so when she saw him dial his exuberance back, she was impressed. "Well if you're just looking she said, "send them your info and let's talk."

He typed his name and zip code in reply and hit send.

He got up to get another cup of coffee and started to tell her about his desire to join the Coast Guard when he was a kid. The phone rang. It was a local number in his caller id and so he picked it up.

"Simon Gates here," he answered.

"Yes Mr. Gates, this is Lieutenant Altieri of the Third Mechanized Division stationed here in Stratford. We are running the local Patriotic Unity Station here at the Reserve Center off Nichols Ave by the Big K Supermarket. I got your text message and wanted to see if I could schedule some time for you to come in and look around? We need all the volunteers we can get and would love to give you a personal tour of the station."

Simon was a little overwhelmed by the call as he never really expected to hear from anyone.

"I'm sorry," said Simon, "I just started my second cup of coffee and I'm not as sharp as might be at 11 am, could you please repeat that for me?" he swiped the speaker button on his phone and a man's voice with a slight southern accent came through for Sarah to hear.

"Oh, of course, sir, I am Lieutenant Altieri of the Third Mechanized Division stationed here at your local Patriotic Unity Station. We need volunteers like yourself to help us win the cause for freedom and I wanted to invite you down for a tour of the facility."

Sarah's eyes opened wide and a look of amazement came across her face. "Would it be okay if my wife joined me for the tour?" asked Simon. "We are both very interested in this effort."

Sarah waved her arms back and forth and mouthed, "NO" to her husband who recovered quickly saying, "I mean I don't know if she will want to join me, but I just want to know if she is welcome to?"

The Army officer said, "By all means Mr. Gates, every citizen is welcome to help out in our fight for freedom and we would love to welcome your lovely wife down here if she would like to join you."

"Great, I'll ask her when she gets home," he smiled broadly at his wife, "What time and where?"

"Well sir, I will be here all day if you would like to come down?" said Altieri, "How does 1400 sound?"

"Sounds great I'll be there and maybe my wife will come too." Simon eyed his wife who was shaking her head no.

Altieri said, "Very good sir, I will see you then," and hung up the phone.

Simon looked at his wife and who buried her head in her arms laughing. "What are you laughing at," he said indignantly.

"Nothing," she stammered as she looked up with her cheeks red from smiling and eyes welling up with tears. "I just can't see you in a uniform with a buzz cut."

"I'm not getting a buzz cut, I'm just volunteering in these fucked up times to see if I can keep us alive a bit longer. I don't appreciate your attitude."

Sarah realized that she had pushed a little too hard and Simon was a bit fragile after the last two days. She calmed him down saying, "Honey, relax I'm just kidding. I didn't mean anything by it and I think your idea may work. I'll even go with you to look at the place if you want me to still?"

Simon realized he had been outmaneuvered and said, "yes, that would be great. I'm sorry I yelled."

With that, they took showers, got dressed, and went to get breakfast.

They walked into the diner where a dozen booths were filled and the smell of syrup and coffee hung heavy beneath a layer of grease. An older woman with thick curly dark hair flecked with silver, chewed a piece of gum loudly as she rang up a check for three large men who stood in a group by the dessert case. She looked up at Simon as he held the door for Sarah and said, "Sweetie, you can sit wherever you like."

They took an empty booth in the middle aisle at the far end of the restaurant, that still had creamers from the previous guest, sitting at the edge of the table. Within seconds of them sitting down, a tall thin blond woman with tattoos down one leg and up one arm and thick eye makeup walked to the table with a pot of coffee and two cups and said, "Would yous like coffee?"

Sarah nodded on behalf of both of them. The waitress pushed the pile of creamers that were on the table together with a few more from her pocket towards the couple after she filed two cups with black coffee.

"I'll be right back to take your order," said the server, "the menu is on the board."

Simon still hadn't gotten used to the no menu rules left over from the pandemic. He never understood how menus could be that much of an infection vector unless someone sneezed directly on them? As it was, it seemed everywhere had a menu board now and menus were a thing of the past.

Squinting he said to Sarah, "what should I get, I can't see it?" Sarah was his visual translator for the menu boards at all their favorite restaurants. He was supposed to wear glasses but stopped when he was a teenager and refused to admit that he was now in his 40's and glasses were pretty much a rite of passage.

Sarah said, "you always get the corned beef hash when we come here with a poached egg, potatoes, and fruit. You don't need to read that on the menu, you should know that."

He agreed and when the waitress came back he ordered what she told him he would order and she got a Belgian waffle. They ate while they made very little conversation as Sarah had a habit of listening to other people's conversations in restaurants. "That man over there, with the blue shirt, talking on the phone," she would say, "he is having gallbladder surgery next week. And that girl over there, the one with the nose ring, she thinks she's pregnant."

He was always amazed at how well she could hear a single conversation through a crowded room and her amazing ability to read lips when she couldn't hear exactly what people were saying. He half expected her to pull her hair back behind her ear and hear that sound effect from The Bionic Woman, "Na na na na na" when she did it. She wasn't bionic, she just had an amazing gift for observation.

It was her observation that keyed her into the conversation she heard from the back booth. Two men were talking quietly about a car wreck where "the hawk wrecked his SUV and shot a porgie." Porgies were garbage fish that the locals like to catch and eat and it was the use of the word that caught her attention. Porgies lived in the sound and had nothing to do with SUVs.

She listened in more intently and completely ignored the last bites of her waffle. Simon was all too happy to eat them off her plate and she allowed him, as it kept him quiet as she could hear more if he wasn't talking. She made mental notes that they were talking about driving to Gettysburg and that "The Hawk" would meet them there. If she heard what she thought she was hearing, they were safe for now. She knew she had no way of knowing for sure, but didn't like the fact that these guys were talking like this in her vicinity.

When they walked out she took note of their clothes and their weight and shape. She noticed one was a dirty blond with a forearm tattoo that looked like a Navy tattoo. The other was slight and had a dark brown mullet under a red trucker cap. He wore a teamsters jacket and big black combat boots.

When they paid the bill and got to their car, Sarah said to Simon, "did you hear that?" She always asked him if he "heard that" and he always said something about her having the hearing of a cat. She rolled her eyes and said, "those two guys in there that looked like truckers, they were talking in code I think, and I think they knew the guy who hit you." He didn't doubt her for a second, but didn't pick any of that up and didn't want to admit it so he said, "Jesus what should we do?"

Sarah said, "I don't know. I don't think they saw us, but if I am right we will see them again. I'm gonna keep an eye out for them."

The breakfast turned to brunch and when they were on the road the time was 1:30. They had to be at the station at 2 PM and so Simon suggested they head up there now just in case traffic was bad as normal.

They were in luck on this Saturday afternoon and made it in ten minutes. They pulled into the parking lot of the Army base and noticed the overgrown hedges and the rusty old Army trucks in the back. It didn't look like an Army base they had ever seen, but this was just a reservist base they figured and maybe that's why they needed volunteers.

There was only one other car in the parking lot and the place seemed abandoned. Simon pulled the Prius between the faded yellow lines on the cracked pavement and got out to walk towards the door. A young good-looking black man in a freshly pressed military uniform waited for them at the door.

When they reached the door, Simon stretched out his hand and said, "Are you, Lieutenant Altieri?"

The man said, "Yes Sir," and held the door as they walked inside.

## Chapter 3

When Simon entered the main room, the smell of disinfectant and time made him think of that battleship he toured in Fall River last year. He figured that every military installation must smell the same and this one looked like it was built at the same time as the old WWII battleship.

The walls were painted with a yellow ochre color that reminded him of separated mustard in the bottle- the thick and chunky part at the bottom with all the vinegar on top. Clearly the last time this place was open, people were allowed to smoke inside the building.

The desks were scattered about the place in a ramshackle sort of way and the drawers all seemed empty and unused. There was one office with a light on and a plant in the window and he assumed that belonged to the Lieutenant.

He even thought he eyed a Commodore 64 in the corner that he recognized from when he was a kid, but other than that, the age of information had not reached this office as of yet.

The Soldier invited him to have a seat in his office and when they went in, the officer pulled a chair from the corner and invited Sarah to sit down first. Simon took a chair from next to the door and slid in next to his wife across the desk from Lieutenant Altieri.

A warm smile came across his dark face and it didn't quite fit with his starched shirt and the row of ribbons spread out across his breast. But he had a soft warm voice like that of butter melting on a warm day.

Immediately, it occurred to Simon that he liked this man and respected him thoroughly due to the collection of colorful ribbons he wore on his chest and his affable nature. Simon wanted to wait for the soldier to speak first, but couldn't help himself and blurted out, "What is that one for?" pointing to a ribbon on the soldier's chest that resembled what he thought was the gay liberation flag.

"That is the Army Service ribbon," Altieri explained. "I got it for completing my officer training." He corrected himself," I mean I received the medal for completing my officer course."

Turning on his recruiter personality, he smiled and began, "Mr. and Mrs. Gates I am very glad to meet you and so grateful that you could meet me on short notice like this." said Altieri, "As you can probably tell from this place, we are in need of some help."

Mrs. Gates stopped him right there and said, "my husband is the volunteer, I am just here as moral support."

Altieri said, "That's fine Mrs. Gates, may I call you Sarah?" She nodded and he continued, "We are hopeful that everyone will want to do their political duty, but were not recruiting here, just asking for volunteers."

Simon broke in, "What exactly is it that you want us to do?"

Altieri got very serious and said, "Mr. Gates, we are at a crossroads in the military right now. The rebellion has not only depleted our forces over the last four years but has also depleted our confidence. The desertion of 2021 left us severely short-handed when nearly half the standing forces decided to side with the rebellion. Our recruitment numbers are way down and we are trying new means to fulfill old roles. A gentleman like yourself with a degree and a business background could go a long way to helping us properly staff this and other units and help us win the hearts and minds of America once again, which is the real war we are fighting."

Simon was a little shocked to hear how blunt the officer was being about the situation and asked, "I thought we had taken all the rebel-held territories and we were on the way back to normal?"

"Simon," said the Lieutenant, "I don't think things will be normal for quite some time."

Sarah and Simon were both a little taken back by the implication of what the soldier was saying. "So you're saying we are at war and we are not winning?" Sarah asked after a long moment of silence.

"No, ma'am. War requires an act of Congress. Did you hear about that police officer who was shot over on River Road the other day?" asked Altieri.

"Hear about it? I was the guy who got into the accident with the shooter," Simon said.

"Well then, you know the rebellion is walking everywhere among us," replied Altieri, "and they are willing to kill to make their point."

A shiver ran down Simon's spine. He couldn't escape the reminders of that horrific day. He felt like he might never get away from that driver of the SUV.

"Well, that is one of the reasons why I am here," said Simon, "The guy who did the shooting came to my house and the police didn't seem to be all that concerned with finding him. More to the point they seem to be looking at us for some reason."

"Simon, you have to understand," the officer explained, "the authorities are suspicious of everyone and everything right now. They are not all bad, but the rebellion has infiltrated the police forces, the Military, the Government, and who knows where they are planning to strike next. That is why we are setting up these unity stations. If the people start defending their home towns, then we can win this battle and save our country."

This wasn't what Simon was expecting to hear when he walked in, but the more he heard, the more he felt he was in the right place. Simon pushed a little harder, despite the obvious discomfort of his wife sitting next to him, "what would be required of me if I volunteered?"

The Lieutenant's eyes lit up and he said, "We have received special authorization from Congress to allow civilians to train, work and live in our barracks if they would like to. You will take on the role of an *actual* citizen-soldier, where we will train you with weapons, provide you with a uniform, offer you access to the PX, and all other base amenities such as medical and dental. The only thing is, you won't get a paycheck."

"Will I have to quit my job?" Simon asked hesitantly.

At that, Sarah turned to her husband and looked at him like he was crazy. She was too much of a good wife to call him out in this conversation but her skin was crawling at the thought of her husband joining the Army. She pressed Altieri for details and asked, "Are you expecting him to fight and you're not even gonna pay him?"

"Sarah, You probably don't remember how the reserve used to work, but let me explain it to you if you want to know."

Sarah lost her father in the cold war over Germany and had at least a dozen other family members since the American Revolution, who went to war to fight for America. She kept this fact to herself most times but wanted to say, "My family has bled more for this country than you will ever know." Instead, she said, "Oh yes please Lieutenant, can you please explain it to me?"

She decided with that last bit of mansplaining he was decidedly smarmy and she didn't like him.

73

The officer continued, "I would love to ma'am. The reserves kind of petered out three years ago when Crawford cut the reserve budget in favor of beefing up the active-duty forces. What we used to do is offer citizen soldiers a chance to serve where service members would serve one weekend a month and two weeks a year?"

Altieri said. "Well this is kind of like that, but because you are in your hometown and we aren't paying you, you can come and go as you please and the only requirement to be in good standing is ten hours of volunteer service per week. For most of those ten hours, you will be working out, doing drills, and getting in shape and stuff. So kind of like, think of it as a gym membership- with a uniform. You, Sarah, can do all your shopping at the new PX when we build it."

Sarah was not the cook in the relationship and hated shopping. She was certain this man was a total asshole now.

Simon on the other hand got excited at the idea that he could wear a uniform and get in shape. He was 44 and getting a little doughy around the middle. He loved to play war as a kid and always wanted a set of camo gear with combat boots. Most of all, he wanted to serve his country after high school but his sinus surgeries kept him from being accepted, so he went to college instead.

Sarah chimed in with her dry sense of humor, "So if there is no fighting, how is this different than the boy scouts?"

Altieri laughed at that comparison and said with a little more enthusiasm than anyone in the room was comfortable with, "the boy scouts don't train with weapons or learn how to blow things up!"

Simon had been to one too many scout campouts as a kid where they did just that. He snickered thinking about his times on the shooting ranges and the campfires he started with homemade napalm made from gas and Styrofoam cups. He caught himself and decided to keep those memories to himself.

Sarah did not see the humor in the comment but was far too adept at awkward social moments to say it out loud. Instead, she said, "Simon, I think I need a ginger ale?"

That was code in their relationship for "get me the hell out of here" and Simon knew it. He was too excited to keep hearing about playing soldier that he ignored it, and let Altieri run down to the kitchen and grab one from the vending machine. He knew he would hear about this later, but to his wife's credit, she smiled when she took the beverage from the Lieutenant and said thank you.

Simon said cautiously, "I have to be honest with you, one of the reasons this sounds so good to me is I am worried that I might get some trouble from that driver who was part of the rebellion and I don't trust the police to protect me. I was hoping if I joined your outfit, that the Army might offer me some protection from that guy."

Altieri thought for a moment and spoke deliberately, "Simon, if he wants to get you, he will get you whether you wear a uniform or not. But I can tell you when you are in this station, you are safe from everything that has to do with the rebellion because this is the one place on earth where I know the rebellion is not at."

Despite the poor grammar, Simon felt better just hearing that statement. He knew he was going to do this, but he needed to speak to his wife first. He asked Lieutenant Altieri if he could think about it over the rest of the weekend.

Sarah knew what he was thinking and tried one last time to pick a hole in the idea. "If this place is so safe, why is no one here? Why does it look like a relic from the 1940s and why is the Army looking for a 44-year-old man to join its ranks?"

Altieri knew she wasn't sold on the idea before she ever asked those questions, but thought he had the man sold. He turned directly toward her in his swivel chair and looked directly into Sarah's eyes.

"Sarah I am going to say this as diplomatically as I can. Our Country is in a tough spot right now and we need to pull all the stops out to save it. My orders are to enlist the support of the community, regardless of age, race, creed, sexual orientation, or religion, and develop a local defense force to protect this town and this community. Your husband is an upstanding member of this community and while he is a bit older than our normal recruits, we would like people like him and you to take part in this effort so that we might reach into the hearts of our community and fight the rebellion on a whole new level."

She didn't know what to say to that. He seemed quite earnest in his conviction and she felt a bit of pride that he wanted to enlist her husband's support. No one had ever called either of them upstanding members of the community.

Simon saw that these words had hit their target and thought it better to quit while he was ahead. He said, "Lieutenant, I want to thank you for taking the time to speak with us today and we have a lot to talk about. I think my wife and I would like a chance to confer and I'll give you a call Monday when I get into the office. If that is alright?"

The Lieutenant agreed and walked them to the door. He waited in the doorway as they got into their car and didn't turn away until the car was out of the parking lot.

Simon blurted out as soon as they reached the street, "what do you think honey? Is this not cool or what?" He sounded like an eight-year-old with a new gaming system, but she wasn't going to take his excitement away from him. It sounded like the nation was in far worse shape than anyone disclosed in the news media and if this worked, they might just be part of the way to fight the good fight.

Simon's mind was bouncing from idea to idea- "How the hell am I gonna run an obstacle course? I haven't done a push up in years? Do you think I will have to shave my head?"

Sarah drove home and didn't bother to interrupt Simon.

He spoke the entire way back to their house and didn't realize for a second that his wife had not said a word until they pulled in the driveway. It was well past 3 PM now and the sun was starting to set. The sideways light showed delicately through her long brown hair.

His attention was taken from her lovely brown hair when he noticed the tears falling down her cheek. "Why are you crying?" he asked. She couldn't speak and he could see she was having trouble swallowing.

She shook her head, turned off the car, and got out quickly without looking at him. He followed her up the drive across the lawn and up the stairs to the front door.

Once inside she ran to the couch and buried her face in a pillow. He sat down next to her on the sofa and gently rubbed her back and whispered, "please tell me what's wrong?"

She was sobbing now and having difficulty catching her breath, but managed to get the phrase out between sobs, "I'm scared."

His heart stopped for a moment when he heard her say those words because he was scared too. They didn't know what was next, they didn't know what would be coming for them and they didn't feel the safety they once thought was theirs forever.

The idea that America was falling apart at the seams seemed like a commonly held belief since Herzog's election in 2016. The four years of lying and hate, the battles over race, the pandemic and then the recall of the electors, the arrival of the military, and now, he was almost joining the Army to fight for America in her worst hour of need. America wasn't the country he thought it was anymore and he didn't remember when it died. How could he possibly have been so giddy about wearing an Army uniform when all hell was breaking loose?

He got up from the couch and looked out at the last rays of the winter sun. He heard his wife's breathing begin to return to normal and he became very thankful for all he had. He thanked God for his wife and his home. He thanked God for his business and the fact that he had a few dollars in the bank. Despite the understanding that he needed to be thankful for all he had, Simon wanted to cry at the loss he felt, knowing what he was about to do.

He cleared his throat and said, "can you talk now?"

Sarah bobbed her head yes and swallowed hard. "I don't know what came over me," she said, "I just couldn't hold it together any longer."

"Hey, I understand completely," Simon said, "I think I was getting a little too excited. Just now it occurred to me that we are going to war."

It's not that the country hadn't been in a state of war going back to the second Bushe administration, but it seemed now that he was thinking of doing this thing, he was going to be dragged into a war he didn't even know was happening until a few hours ago.

Simon took a deep breath and turned to look back at Sarah. She was no longer crying but looked exhausted and spent. He took a step towards the couch where she sat and the movement pulled her from her trance.

She said, "Simon, I don't want you to go to war." He chuckled under his breath at the thought of him going to war and was sure she was being dramatic. Simon replied, "I don't think it will ever come to that. But I am just as frightened as you are that something is coming."

"This is something different than anything that has ever happened in our lives. The Army is different, the police are different. Hell, even the town is different." Sarah continued as tears began to well up in her eyes again. "I don't know when it happened, but the place we once called home is now at the edge of civil war and it scares the hell out of me. It scares me even more that you are going to start playing with the people who are fighting that war and I don't want to lose you."

The dire terms Altieri used about the crisis the military was facing and the violence he witnessed the other day during the car accident linked up in his mind and the bigger picture became clear to him. Maybe she was right, maybe the war was coming. His face lost the grin and he sat down next to his wife on the couch.

He took her hand and pulled it close to his thigh and squeezed twice. Unable to speak, she responded with two squeezes and added a third. He replied with three squeezes and mouthed the words to her, "I Love You."

She threw her arms around him and sobbed, "I love you, too. I just don't want to ever lose you." He whispered back, "I don't want to get lost," and touched her cheeks with his hands. Feeling the warm salty tears in his dry palms, he pulled her face close to him and kissed her mouth as gently as he could.

She kissed him back and a familiar rush of emotion and pressure pulled them both from their minds and into their bodies. The couple knew each other's warmth and wanted to run from these horrible feelings of fear and loss.

He rose from the couch and took her by the hand up the stairs where they spent the last moments of daylight hiding from the world under the covers together.

They must have fallen asleep because when Simon woke the room was dark and cool. The street lights were casting shadows along the dresser and the pile of clothes on the floor. He rolled over to wake her but realized he was by himself and that she had somehow managed to leave the bed without waking him.

He climbed from the bed and reached to untangle the pile of clothes on the floor. In the dark he joked, is this her shirt or mine? Struggling to cover himself and ward off the cool evening air, he walked downstairs where he could smell garlic and wine and hear a pan sizzling in the kitchen.

He walked in behind her making no sound with his socks on the hardwood floor. She was wearing only a cooking apron and the sight of his wife bearing herself so freely and provocatively made him smile.

He reached around her and startled her only slightly as he bent over to kiss her neck and say hello."Whatcha Makin?" he asked playfully.

"Poison," she said with a deadpan look on her face, "want some?"

Simon laughed and said, "Ooh That's my favorite."

He walked to the cabinet and pulled out a bottle of wine and asked her if she would like a glass? She said, "of course" as she removed the chicken breasts from the pan and ladled the wine and butter and garlic over the pasta and broccoli she had already plated.

They ate dinner and drank the entire bottle of wine without ever mentioning the day's events or the thought of the world raging outside. After dinner, they caught up with the show they were binging on Netflix this week and opened a second bottle of wine for dessert.

When the show was over and the wine was gone, she climbed the stairs to get ready for bed and he checked the doors and turned off the lights. The normal evening was just what he needed and he was thankful once again for his wife and his life. He stopped in the kitchen to drink a glass of water and pop two ibuprofen in his mouth prophylactically for the morning. He refilled the glass and grabbed the medicine bottle and walked up the stairs where he offered the water and meds to his wife who was mid-flossing. She said, "you're so smart" and drank down the water.

They fell asleep without any tossing or turning and the night was quiet and solemn. They woke on Sunday and took a walk on the beach taking advantage of early spring weather and global warming. And then got donuts and hot coffee at the donut place by the beach.

Sundays were his favorite and they enjoyed the peace and beauty of the day of rest. It would be the last quiet Sunday they would know for quite a while. War was coming on Monday, whether they knew it or not.

## Chapter Four

The trees were blooming a month too early or so he thought as he walked out through the glass doors of the hotel. The warm air didn't feel anything like the Februarys he remembered as a kid and he was pretty sure that even this far South, spring usually came much later.

He heard a voice call out to him just as the doors closed behind him and it was the girl behind the counter in the lobby. He spun around and stuck his head back in the door and said, "What did you just say?"

"Oh sir, I am sorry," said the young woman behind the counter. She was just coming out from the office when she saw the doors closing behind the man and remembered her training, "I was just saying have a great day and thanks for staying at the Courtyard Marriot of Gettysburg."

"Oh yes, thank you. We'll be back," he said, removing his head from the door and turning before she could say anything else.

Gus was not the sweetest of men and could be construed as downright rude in most cases. It was dismissive conversations like this that gave that impression or so his ex-wife told him. He almost regretted not being a little more friendly to the young women behind the counter. She was just being professional.

He harped on the lack of professionalism in America these days. He remembered the days when service with a smile was the rule and the customer was always right. Now, you were lucky to get a smile when some kid at the McD's gave you cold fries and flat coke.

He was almost always irritated by something these days. This morning, he was irritated that he had to deal with a rental car and then have to deal with the events of the past week. "If the Goddamned cop had just minded his own business," he thought to himself, "I wouldn't have had to shoot him."

His old knee surgery bothered him as he walked across the wide empty parking lot of the hotel, overlooking the stand of newly budding trees. He could hear the traffic on US-15 behind him and waited for the kid to finish the paperwork for the car.

"Are you done yet?" Gus complained to the young Hispanic man who was scribbling information onto a clipboard.

"Almost sir, I just need to get your credit card expiration date. It didn't come through on the system last night."

"What do you mean you need my expiration date? They told me this was all set?" Gus shouted. He went from simmer to burn so often these days and the kid was scared by the rapid intensification of the situation.

"I-I-I just need a month and year to put in this box," stuttered the 19-year-old kid with acne and a cheap windbreaker that read, Just-A-Buck-Car Rentals on the sleeve, "my boss will need it to process your card."

Gus figured it would be a problem if he caused any trouble as he traveled back for debriefing and realized this kid would be a problem if he didn't get the situation in hand right away. He said, "Oh if that's all you need, why didn't you just say. May of 2025."

The kid scribbled down the info and offered the clipboard to Gus to sign. Gus signed it, "George Soros" and took the keys out of the kid's hand. He beeped the white Kia and opened the door and climbed in. He was gone from the hotel parking lot before the kid even got back into the cab of the flatbed.

"They call this The Lincoln Highway," he thought, "What would Lincoln think of the fact that we're on the verge of a second civil war?" The fact that the Resistance chose to do debriefs at a VFW at the edge of the Gettysburg Battleground was a symbolism that even Gus couldn't help but catch.

Born on the day that Nixon announced the end of the Vietnam War, Gus grew up with the idea that America was losing. He was born Augustus Spiros to a retired Navy pilot and his trophy wife on the shores of the Chesapeake Bay at Annapolis. His father took more interest in 5-martini lunches and golf outings with Spiro Agnew than being a father. His mother found her solace at the bottom of a bottle of valium. His laissez-faire upbringing and sense of self-reliance gave Gus confidence to declare that he was a spartan. He joined the Army at his first chance.

Gus enlisted on his eighteenth birthday. His dad drove him to the recruiter's office, saying, " You're no Navy man so you might as well join the Army." He went to OCS two years later and enjoyed the life, with its clear cut boundaries and order. In the 1980s, the Russians were our enemy, the United States was the good guy and we all worried about nuclear war. It was a comfortable balance of fears and it appealed to Gus.

When Clinton and Reno shot their way through Ruby Ridge and the FBI killed all those people in Waco, he decided things were heading in the wrong direction. The Government was just getting too big and spending too much time telling us how to live. The balance of fear he relied upon in his youth, became muddled and unclear. He resigned his Army commission and went to work for Dark Pond.

When Crawford took over as president, Gus felt he had no choice but to move to Utah. He wanted to go off-grid and parked his trailer as far from civilization as he could get. He found a pristine cliff in the mountains of Utah on BLM land and tried to escape from the world.

*The Plan to Reclaim America* wasn't a manifesto or anything like one at first. He read a story on Facebook one morning about the damage the Black Lives Matter activists wrought and how it compared to the damage of the Herzog supporters, and something inside him snapped. He started writing. He wrote about how he would change it all, the military, the health care, the cops, the economy, the politics, the Constitution, all of it.

*The Plan* started with getting the various forces for change under one tent as Gus liked to call it. Piles of people scattered here and there with weapons and Gadsden flags were never going to have the critical mass needed to properly undermine the forces that held power. They needed organization and structure. They needed a commonly held belief that they would all pledge to fight for. But most importantly, they had to give up the race war.

Gus insisted in his writing of *The Plan*, that they give up the white supremacist's propaganda and develop an all-inclusive strategy. It didn't do anyone any good to be calling black people and brown people names when we all took a bullet the same way.

He thought that aspect of *The Plan* would have been a deal killer, but to his surprise, most of the people who read it, weren't about white pride half as much as they were about hate for what they believed to be a corrupt Government and a love for a lost America. Oh sure, there were white supremacists, but by and large, the people who were fighting weren't racists. He realized that they used that propaganda to develop a linkage between the members and amp up the energy of their following. When they had proper guidance, they all seemed to adopt the idea that race-baiting was non-productive.

Eighty-two pages later, he ran a spell check and posted it to a message board under the title, *The Plan to Reclaim America*. The gun dealer in Albuquerque told him that a lot of people watched that board, but he was shocked when people started reading it. Within a day, it was viewed more than 20,000 times. Then he received the email from John, inviting him down to Tampa.

The Seditionists were not soldiers at all, but an online group of men and women who followed Qanon and all agreed that Herzog's presidency was stolen. They met through online social platforms for the alt-right, and message boards like TheDon.win and 4qun. They connected at various liberal demonstrations and conservative rallies. They cheered at the pro-Herzog rallies and taunted the crowd from the periphery at the BLM protests. They agreed to unite to continue Herzog's work when Herzog left for Argentina.

They had been on the fringe and going to events organized by the Tea Party Movement since Obama. When Herzog took office and platforms like Parler and Gab made communication much easier, they began to mobilize. After Herzog was shafted by Pence during the Electoral college certification and they got pushed back at the Capital takeover, so many of them got arrested that they decided to start an off-grid community in the Arizona desert at Kingman, where freedom still prevailed.

The Seditionists organized as a fighting force in Kingman, but it wasn't until Hawk emerged with his *Plan to Reclaim America* that they would fully fledge into, "The Resistance."

Travis Coville and John Eustace, from Arkansas and Maryland respectively, got their start in the Tea Party. They emerged as the first leaders in Kingman, organizing the online group, and seeding the idea of blowing up the bank buildings in Tampa.

In truth, it was their first organized campaign and a miracle that they had been so successful. John and Travis had never even met Jim and Joan Justice or the Vasich family from Ohio before they joined together with the online group in Tampa. The fact that they managed to get all those commuter buses filled with explosives and parked them in Tampa without getting caught was astounding.

Gus flew back into Tampa to meet John, just after he and the other seditionists hit the bank buildings. Gus didn't like seeing so many civilians killed but believed the action had leveled the playing field for the Resistance. That's why Gus decided to join their convoy headed back to Kingman when he was invited.

They were nice enough to swing through Utah and allow him to pick up his trailer. When he arrived with them at their base camp in Kingman, *The Plan* was set in motion and he got the moniker "The Hawk."

The call to Gettysburg and the killing of the cop were troublesome. He worried that a debate about the necessity of killing the officer could again ignite diverging ideas. It always seemed to go that way. Gus hated the idea of once again rehashing previous arguments about white supremacy. Would this set things back and reignite the race debate? Was that why they summoned him? He had hoped that the issue was buried back in Kingman, but for some reason, people could never get over the fact that race was a nonstarter. If they were heading back to the gutter, he would be back at square one and all because of some pain in the ass cop and an asshole behind the wheel.

He hadn't planned on shooting the cop and wished the cop had never looked in the car window. He also wished he hadn't left *The Plan* on top, because if the cop hadn't seen that, he could have just played it off as a common accident. The nosey cop had to look and when that happened, he had to go in for the kill. Thankfully, the guy he hit never saw anything other than his face. And if he had to, he was willing to button that loose end up as well

He tore out of the accident scene in such a hurry that at least he hoped no one else got a good look at him. The other guy was so dumbfounded that he probably couldn't even ID him in a lineup. The whole incident took less than three minutes before he drove off. In all likelihood, no onlookers saw anything usable. Even the plate was linked to a made-up person, so he felt quite certain he was in the clear. He was just worried he told himself.

He drove the damaged truck to a safe house in Bridgeport, where a flatbed took it down to the meeting in Gettysburg. When he pulled into the VFW, he saw the truck sitting in back behind the dumpster and wondered if any of the local cops had gotten any word about the shooting up in Connecticut. He figured someone would question a wrecked truck eventually, but who knew which cops were on their side and which ones weren't. He hoped John and whoever else was inside knew which side the local authorities landed on.

Parking the car, he was surprised to see so many people. The trucks were lined up on both sides of the street and they were parking on the lawn outback. People were lined up outside the door and milling about the front lawn like this was some VFW dinner for the Jimmy Fund and not a collection of resistance operatives who were supposed to be in hiding.

At least no one was wearing a MAGA hat or dressed like a stormtrooper. He liked these Seditionist people, but he thought they took unnecessary chances. They weren't happy with the risk he took by shooting the cop either and that was why they summoned him to this meeting. He hoped he had not done serious damage to the cause, but would soon find out.

As he walked up to the front door, the crowd parted and he heard low voices say, "That's The Hawk." One woman with attractive, yet weathered features, standing by the front door stepped in his way and said, "Did you really kill that cop?"

Gus looked back over each shoulder and slunk his head low and said, "there are people here," she laughed and said, "Relax, you're among friends, Hawk. This is the New America."

She extended her hand saying, "I'm Gayle. My husband is inside. He wants to speak with you."

He thanked her and walked in. The smell of dust and stale beer-soaked in the heavy drapes and the stain of twenty-year-old cigarettes still hung in the air. The hall was filled to capacity, but the sound was eerily quiet. Those who talked did so in a whisper. At the front table sat five large men in camo gear sipping coffee and mumbling out of the side of their mouths to each other.

Gus recognized the man in the middle of the table as John Eustace and thought he might know one of the other gentlemen, but couldn't place his name. John and Gus had become friends while in Kingman and it was John who read *The Plan* online and invited Gus to join them in Tampa.

John spoke first. Everyone stopped whispering and listened. "Hawk, it's great to see you, come on in."

As Gus walked toward the table, one of the crowd members slid a folding chair into the side of the folding table and John said, "Have a seat, we need to talk."

With that, the room cleared and all three hundred people filed out the door leaving the five men and Gus sitting alone in the hall.

"Hawk, do you need a drink?" said the man sitting next to John.

He hurried to the kitchen window and poured coffee for Gus in a styrofoam cup.
He handed it to Gus and said, "do you need cream?"
Gus shook his head and simply said, "Black is better."

John said, "That's Evan with the coffee. This is Tanner on my right, Jason and Jeffrey on my left. You haven't met these guys before, but they came along with their friends and joined us down in Kingman after you left."

"Where's Travis? I figured he would be at this table?" asked Gus. John shook his head and said, "They got him in Oklahoma. His wife and kids are outside."

That news set the jaws of every man at the table and a dark mood came over the group. Gus said, "Jesus man, I am sorry for your loss. What happened?"

"State Police pulled over his camper just outside of Oklahoma City on Highway 40 west," John explained, "They shot him as he was reaching for his ID."

"My God, what is happening to this country?" asked Gus.

"They're getting scared," said John.

"But you didn't come all the way down here to hear about fallen brothers, did you Hawk," John asked, "You've been doing a little work for the cause yourself, haven't you?"

Gus stiffened and answered in as direct a manner as he could manage with five men staring at him. He fully expected to be dressed down and ejected from the room. "It was an unfortunate event and I wish to hell I didn't have to do it, but that guy came out of nowhere and I didn't have time to stop. If that cop had just minded his own damn business..."

John interrupted him, "You did what was right. I wish Travis had shot first, and he might still be here."

The other four men nodded but said nothing. Gus was shocked but started to relax.

He continued, "I don't think anyone could make me from the accident. I see you got my truck outback? Are you worried that it might get noticed by the law?"

Tanner spoke for the first time and said, "The law is on our side round heah. Your truck and you are safe."

Tanner sounded like he was from Maine, thought Gus, and nodded to the down-easter turned soldier.

"So what do we do now?" asked Jason who sounded like he was from Georgia or maybe the Carolinas.

John replied, "Well the truck is totaled, but Hawk is alright. So I think it's all good for now. The question is how do we get them back?"

Gus asked, "Get them back? For what?"

John answered, "For Travis."

Gus measured his words and replied, "I think that we need to let things settle a bit. They have no idea who I am, the truck was registered to a fake name. I killed the cop before he could figure out who I was and the guy who hit me is a scared little man who buried his head when the shots were fired. But I have my eyes on him, just the same."

Tanner getting back into the conversation said, "Our channels in law enforcement sawr an APB out for the truck and a person matching your description in connection with a shooting in Connecticut. You're safe heah, but I have no idea how long."

Gus replied, "Yeah they might know what I look like, but they don't know WHO I am, and since the truck is here, and they have no way of finding out. Our only concern is the insurance guy and he is a non-issue...currently."

Taking over the conversation, John said, "We have a dinner planned and a few days to get to know each other. Why don't we table this discussion for now and think about it? We can reconvene after dinner tonight."

The five other men agreed and the room began to fill with people once again. The first person to approach Gus was, once again, Gayle - this time with her husband Tanner next to her.

"So you came up with *The Plan*? That's what got us down heah," Gayle asked.

"Yes, I wrote it one night when it all hit me kinda hard and posted it to a chat group," answered Gus, "Then John invited me down to Tampa after they took down the bank buildings."

Tanner jumped in, "Wasn't that amazing? When Gayle showed me what they did and told me about your plan, I knew I had to join up. They took down Bank of America, Wells Fahgo, Citizens Bank, SunTrust, and like four more. All the bahstards who have been screwing us and the economy for decades."

Gayle apologized for her husband's excitement saying, "It's not that we enjoyed seeing all those people die, but the symbol of seeing all those rich bahstards going down in flames with their buildings felt like a step in the right direction, don't you think?"

Someone handed Gus a cup of beer and he sipped it as he listened to Gayle and Tanner.

He didn't want to support the violence either but saw their perspective. Americans on all sides had been struggling since before the 1970s to get by and it was getting worse every year. People were dying because they couldn't afford medication. Making enough to feed a small family and own a home was a joke. The American dream was an antiquated notion that the media came up with to keep the poor working menial jobs. How did anyone not see that at some point the people would rise up?

When they did rise up, did anyone believe that only military targets and fortified government buildings would be targeted? It was just a matter of time before the giant banks were put in the crosshairs and from this conversation, Gus now understood why they decided to hit the banks.

Gus asked the Maine couple, "How did all these people get here? Who are they?"

Gayle, who spent her morning wandering around the crowd and taking stock answered. "Most of these people are from the State Militias, but a few others like us, just came because we agreed with the idea."

"And what is that idea?" Gus asked.

Tanner took his turn to answer, "The Country has become a police state. It has become an Oligarchy, It has become a walk through the pahk for the haves and a slow slide off the cliff for the have nots." Gus recognized the words Tanner was quoting back to him from his writing.

"Ah, so it sounds like you read my book?" asked Gus.

"Nah, my wife told me that. She's the reader. I just liked how she said it," Tanner continued, "In 2018, I lost my boat in Hurricane Florence. I got an emergency SBA loan that bankrupted us and then the bahstads foreclosed on my house. All we had left was the trailer. We drove it out west to live on public lands, but they kicked us off saying that we were freeloaders. The ranchers could make all the money they wanted with their cows out there eating up the land and drinking all the water, and shitting everywhere, but we as Americans who paid for that land couldn't stay on it for more than fourteen days? That was when we went to Kingman and met John. I'm sorry to say I never met Travis. He died before I got there."

Gus felt bad for Tanner and Gayle. It seemed the whole crowd was in one way or another in the same situation as Gayle and Tanner. He could understand why they voted for Herzog in 2016 and he could understand why they voted for him again in 2020. The America they worked for never worked for them and they were sick and tired of it.

It occurred to Gus that he was getting very hungry and the smells coming from the grills and the kitchen were making him ravenous. He asked Gayle, "That food smells amazing. Is there any way I can try it?"

Gayle grabbed his arm and led him up to the kitchen window and called in, "Joy, I need a plate for this man STAT. He's dyin' of stahrvation out heah."

Joy handed Gus a plate filled with roast beef, coleslaw, potato salad, baked beans, and cornbread and said, "You eat that and when you're done, refill at the grills around back. We got burgers, dogs, and fifty barbecue chickens on the rotisserie out'n the side of the building."

He stopped and looked at the mounded plate of food and tried to get Joy's attention before she ran back into the mass of people undulating in the kitchen. He tapped Gayle on the shoulder as she was talking to another woman about mayonnaise and asked with embarrassment, "I didn't bring any cash with me, how do I pay for this?"

Gayle laughed and said, "You just keep writin' and fightin', we'll take care of feeding you."

Gus sat at an empty table and put his plate and beer down in front of him. He took the first bite and realized that the last time he ate was nearly two days ago, just before the accident. The meat and potatoes filled his stomach and the beer made him feel a bit light in the head. "Jesus," he thought to himself, "I should have eaten something before I drank that beer."

A middle-aged woman sat down next to him with pretty blue eyes set in a deeply worn face. She reminded him of a photo he saw of a woman with her two kids in a photograph from the Great Depression. You could tell she was pretty as a young girl, but time and hard living had worn her smile away and left wrinkles where the laugh lines should be. She spoke and said, "You are the founder of this, aren't you?"

Gus nearly choked on his cornbread when she said that and reached for his beer to wash it down. "I don't think so, who told you that?" he asked.

She replied, "I heard a couple of people talking when you were walking up to the building. They said you're The Hawk and you came up with the idea for all this."

Gus said, "I wrote a book about this, but I wouldn't call myself a founder."

Just then a small girl walked up to the table and asked if he was going to eat his coleslaw. The woman said, "Amy don't do that. We have plenty of food back in the trailer."

Gus looked over at the woman and said, "she is more than welcome to it if it's okay with you?"

The woman said, "No sir. We have plenty of food at home."

Gayle was watching the conversation. She stepped in and said. "Ma'am, the food here is provided by the supporters of the Resistance. Please grab a plate, we have so much. May I please get you and your little girl a plate?"

The woman, realizing that she was fooling no one and said, "My husband and son are just outside, could I get them some food too? We can all eat off the same plate."

Gus was silent in this exchange. It crushed him to think perhaps that this woman hadn't eaten for an even longer time than him.

Gayle showed a look of understanding, grabbed the woman and her daughter by the arms and led them to the front, and said, "Let's get a plate for each of ya. Tell me, what's your name, sweetie?"

The little girl took Gayle by the hand and said, "My name is Amy Lynn Miller."

Gayle smiled and said, "Well Amy Lynn Miller, what does your brother like to eat?"

Gus finished his plate and drank down his last sip of beer and went outside for some fresh air. The smoke from the chicken rotisserie smelled amazing, but he felt as if his stomach might burst.

He sat under a tall oak tree and enjoyed the spring breeze while he was people watching. He couldn't be sure but thought that the crowd had doubled in size since he arrived.

He looked up the road and on both sides as far as he could see, there were trucks and campers lining the road. He noticed in the woods behind the building at least a few dozen tents and awnings had been pitched and people ambled between them with beers and weapons. He laughed to himself and thought, "Were it not for the presence of automatic weapons, one might have mistaken this for a Grateful Dead concert."

He saw John eye him from a group of people who were chatting by a bus that was parked out front. He started walking toward Gus.

By the time Gus stood up, John was within speaking distance and said, "This is pretty amazing isn't it?"

"I'll say," replied Gus, "where did all these people come from? There was what, like 30 of us at Kingman?"

"They came because of what you wrote, Gus," said John, "your plan has tapped into the hearts of Americans from all walks of life who have been disenfranchised by the Government. You put into words what we all were feeling and it has formed us into a force to be reckoned with."

The idea that something he wrote could move masses intimidated the hell out of Gus. He worried that if the wrong people read it, there were people that would start looking for him.

He didn't want to seem afraid to John. "How did everyone read it? I thought I just posted it on the message board," asked Gus.

This was where John had to admit his ignorance. "I have no idea how it got out there, but Evan knows what he's doing. I gave it to him and he must have shared the hell out of it. He posted that you would be here and I think everyone wanted to meet you."

"But how do you know we can trust all these people, we barely know any of them. How do you know they aren't moles?" asked Gus.

John got very serious and said, "if anyone is a mole here, they will be dead by morning. We have eyes everywhere."

As John said that, a police cruiser from Gettysburg PD pulled onto the lawn. Several men shouldered their weapons and a hush came over the crowd. Tanner walked over to the car window and began talking with a smile. The crowd relaxed and the men lowered their weapons.

Gus could not hear what he said, nor could he see the officer inside, but they appeared to be friends.

When a man in civilian clothes got out of the car, he and Tanner shook hands. They walked side by side to a line that stretched around the corner to the chicken rotisseries. Gus looked past the men in line and saw a truck unloading porta-potties behind the back and an ice truck where a team of women was unloading bags of ice into the kitchen back door. He thought to himself, "for a thrown-together event these people had a ton of organization."

He turned back toward John and said, "Tell me about Tanner."

John began, "Tanner and Gayle drove with us here from Kingman. They came from Maine where he was a fisherman who fell on hard times. They lost their house and business in 2018 and moved out west to live in a trailer."

Gus interrupted, "yes they told me that, but how did they find you?"

"Oh well, they came to Kingman when they were rustled off BLM lands by the feds," said John, "They set up their trailer a few lots over from where we were. They had been there a few weeks when he came over one night with a case of beer and said his wife told him he should talk to us. We invited him to sit down and he has been with us ever since."

"What about Jeff and Jason, who are they?" asked Gus.

"They are from North Carolina, I think," answered John. "They pulled into Kingman the same week as Tanner. They were friends back home and traveled around with their trailers making YouTube videos with their families for a while before coming to Kingman. They both are hunters and have a nice collection of weapons."

"Alright," said Gus, "then let's finish the table, who is Evan?"

John laughed, and said, "Why is he always last? He is from New York. He had a job as a stockbroker and bought an Airstream with his wife after the market went sour in 2008. They set out and lived in Michigan for a while where they had a little girl and off-gridded on a farm that they leased or something like that."

He took a swig of beer, swallowed hard, and continued, "Then they traveled out to the Dakotas for a few years and their baby died from pneumonia. After that, he separated from his wife and went to live in New Mexico for a while before moving to Kingman. He just started hanging around us one day and I decided that I always wanted to see inside one of those Airstreams, so I asked and he let me in for a tour. He has been here ever since."

"So that is the five of you," said Gus "and I make six. I know I didn't bring all these people here, did Evan do it?"

"Evan is a genius with that online stuff. You should see the set up he has in there." said John, "I think he has his own satellite up in space. He plugs that Airstream in and can get TV from Shanghai and send videos to Guam on a secure line. It's all over my head, but when he read your plan, he said he had to tell the world about it and so he got to work."

John continued, "Jason and Jeff had their network of people who they came to know while traveling. Their YouTube channel was called the "Traveling Rednecks" or something like that. The two families traveled something like 300,000 miles between Mexico and Canada before they shut down the borders. They must have invited their followers to this thing and that is where all the trailers came from I think."

"What happened to the Seditionists?" Gus dug further.

"Well, you know what happened to Travis in Oklahoma," John explained, "His people eventually all landed with us in Kingman. The two militia groups from Michigan and Ohio, what were their names?"

Gus helped, "Justice and Vasich?"

"Yeah, them," said John, "Jim and Joan Justice were their names, right? Well, neither group could make it here, but they said that they would be in touch. I kind of got the feeling they weren't all that big on *The Plan*, so I didn't push it. Last I heard, they were back up in Michigan training together. What was that last Militia we had in Tampa, can you remember their names?"

Gus didn't remember their names either but could recall that he wasn't a giant fan of their politics. He told John, "No I don't remember them, but they also seemed a bit too 'white power' for me."

John said, "Yeah they didn't quite get where we were heading with this, but they were good people as I recall. Never heard from them again after Tampa."

"So what is going to happen at tonight's meeting?" asked Gus.

"Well, we're gonna find out who we all are and develop some marching orders I would think," explained John, "You stirred up a bit of a hornet's nest with that cop shooting last week. The people want action now and you lit the match that started a fire burning."

Gus had eaten so much and enjoyed the afternoon so thoroughly, he almost forgot what happened to bring him here. He still wished he hadn't had to shoot the cop, but with so many people supporting him for doing it, he was almost ok with it now. John cracked another beer and handed one to Gus and said, "Cheers brother."

---

That evening when the sun started going down, the grills were turned off and the hum of RV generators filled the air. Upwards of five hundred people had gathered in the hall with the six men who were at the table earlier in the day at the front, plus the man who got out of the police car.

A bull horn sat on the corner of the table and the temperature was rising every second that passed, with the mass of bodies packed in the tiny hall. A dull murmur rose from the crowd as the seven men conferred quietly at the table before starting the meeting.

John rose from his folding chair and cleared his throat. The room went silent except for a few ceiling fans rumbling. "Welcome to The Resistance" John bellowed without the help of the bull horn. The room erupted with cheers and applause and the windows rattled from the sound.

Five minutes later the crowd quieted and John continued without the bull horn, "You all came from pretty far away places to get here tonight. Did you get enough to eat today?" The crowd erupted again and this time John grabbed the bull horn.

"I gotta use this thing or I won't be able to speak in the morning," John joked with the crowd. The crowd chuckled and the men behind the table smiled.

"Tonight," John started with feedback from the bullhorn deafening the room, "We have a few things to talk about and few decisions to make. First up, there are a lot of you here and we need a few ground rules to keep us safe and happy. I'm going to ask Detective Horowitz of the Gettysburg PD to talk to you about how we are going to manage over the next few days. Detective..." and with that, John handed the bull horn to the officer.

"Hello y'all, I'm Gerald Horrowitz, a detective on the Gettysburg Police Force." The crowd politely clapped.

"You all have the authorities of this town a little bit worried with as many of you that have shown up. We estimate that there are at least 5000 people here right now with more on the way. We need to watch the traffic and sanitation of such a large group. You all seem to have brought your generators, so we're not too worried about the electric, but if you all start dumping your holding tanks in the sewers or digging pit latrines in the woods, it's gonna get nasty real quick. Accordingly, porta-potties and a mobile dump station were delivered earlier today and they will be maintained daily by McSorley Sanitation from Bonneauville. Please use the proper facilities for sanitation. Bill McSorley is a friend of ours and he has pledged to make this thing as safe and clean as he can. You can help him by doing your part.

"As for water, we are on city water here at the VFW, but we only have one hose spigot. When your water tanks on your RVs run out, we will ask you not to use the spigot, but will have a water truck arriving across in the field tomorrow and will be here each day from 9 am to 5 PM. Bring your RV over to him and fill up or if you are camping and are hauling water, you can also go to the truck for potable water.

"I have also been asked to address food while you're here. The supermarket is just down the road, but the VFW ladies have suggested that they will be providing free meals to all attendees for the balance of the meeting. This is free to all, but if you have the means to help offset the cost of feeding such a large crowd, they are accepting cash contributions at the main tent which is being set up outside the kitchen door.

"Finally, we ask that all weapons be kept on safety for the duration of this event and while you may carry openly at this event, we ask that you do so in an as safe and proper manner as possible. No child under the age of 12 is to carry a weapon and we ask that all sidearms be holstered at all times. I have an agreement from the mayor that he will not ask the police to enforce any town ordinances while this meeting is underway and I just want to reassure you that the police force in this town is friendly to this cause. Thank you."

The Detective handed the bull horn back to John and John said, "Alright, if there are any questions about any of what Detective Horowitz just said, the detective and I will be available immediately after the meeting at the main tent by the kitchen door until 10 PM. Now let's get to the true purpose of this meeting with what I hope will be an ongoing discussion for the duration of the next few days, where we may all come to an understanding of our next steps to further this cause."

John continued, "This is the first time we have all come together to discuss *The Plan to Reclaim America* and I am very happy to tell you that the author of that plan that has brought us all together is right here. Please, could we have a big round of applause for The Hawk?"

The five hundred people in the room and at least a thousand people who had assembled at the windows and around the building erupted again in cheers and applause. Gus stood, removed his hat, and lowered his head to the crowd.

John tried to speak over the crowd but was drowned out by the excitement. When the cheering finally stopped and composure returned to the room, John spoke again and turned to the Hawk and said, "I think that shows you what the people think of your book, don't you?" The crowd launched again into cheers.

The pattern continued for the next hour with cheers and applause coupled with short blurbs from John and his bull horn. By the time the clock read 9 PM, the crowd was exhausted from celebrating and John's voice had all but given out.

"Alright folks," said John, "I think that is enough for now. We're going to break into groups tomorrow to discuss ideas and come together again in two days to finalize a strategy. All are welcome to attend the breakout sessions and we will have a schedule of sessions posted by 0600 at the main tent. With that, I think we should all try and turn in for the night. Remember questions about living arrangements can be made until 10 PM in the main tent and I am told breakfast will be served at 8 AM with coffee available in the main tent at 6:30. Have a good night and be safe."

When John put the bull horn down, he sat down and the room began to empty and the murmur of the crowd diminished. By half past the hour, the room was empty except for Hawk, John, Jeff, Jason, Evan, and Tanner sitting at the table. Evan spoke first and said, "I will take care of the breakout sessions schedule and post it online. I think I would also like to take minutes of the discussions so I can post them to our message board as well when we are done."

John said, "That sounds great Evan, thanks. Who wants to be in charge of facilities and ensuring people are handling the sanitation and water regulations properly?" Jason and Jeff both offered their services for facilities management. Tanner agreed to continue developing government relations and dealing with Detective Horwitz. That left John and Gus to begin developing a strategy to implement *The Plan* Gus had written.

John closed the conversation when he said, "Today is Saturday. By Monday the war will have started. We've got a lot to do this weekend."

The men walked out of the hall together and shut off the lights.

## Chapter 5

Simon opened his eyes and for just a moment he forgot the events from last week and the weekend. He forgot that this wasn't a normal Monday. He forgot that he wouldn't have a truck to scrape, a driveway clear of ice, phone calls to make, coffee to drink, and the series of usual Monday chores to complete.

It wasn't until he wandered down into the kitchen and smelled the coffee, that he remembered a whole new set of chores to complete today. He had to get a rental car, he had to call Altieri and arrange an inauguration into a service that he didn't fully understand. He had to face a world that scared him to his core. It wasn't a normal Monday by any measure and all he wanted right now was to head back to bed.

Sarah broke the silence and said, "The coffee is still hot. I put some nutmeg in there the way you like."

"Thank you, my sweet," he responded, wiping the blurred vision from his eyes.

He sat at the kitchen table, holding his coffee, and stared at the blinding sun pouring through the window. He enjoyed, for just a moment, the pain it caused, as it burned his retinas.

"Are you gonna call Altieri today?" asked Sarah.

"Yeah after I get to the office," said Simon, "I have to pick up the rental car over in Bridgeport first. Can you give me a ride?"

"Yeah," said Sarah, "but we're gonna have to leave early, if I am going to make it to work on time. We have an 8:30 patient this morning."

Simon said, "Get in the shower first, I will only take five minutes getting ready."

Sarah left the room and he could hear her footsteps going up the stairs. He swiped his phone open and saw that he had a text waiting for him. It was Altieri confirming a phone call was coming today. He typed back, "Yes sir call you at 10."

He then called Marion on her cell and left her a voicemail. "Marion, it's Simon. I have to run over to Bridgeport this morning to pick up a rental car and then I will be in the office. I'll explain everything when I get there, but we are going to have to make some changes for the next couple of months. I need to talk to you about what's going to happen. By the way, I have a 10 AM phone call with the Army. I'll explain that too."

He ended the call and swiped over to check his Facebook feed and a memory popped up on his notification. He clicked on it. It was a post he shared from November 4, 2020. He wondered why this showed up today, but he must have commented on a post from a friend who shared a meme that said, "I'm confused, does the second civil war start

Tuesday or Wednesday and will we need to stockpile toilet paper for this crisis as well?"

It was a strange reminder of where it all started and an even stranger time to show up on his feed. Herzog's refusal to concede, the weeks of waiting to see if he would, the threats of violence from Herzog and the alt-right. Then the daily hearings in Congress about the "irregularities" in the election and the discovery of the Democrat fraud, the O'Leary resignation, the recall of electors, and then, the election of Crawford. It all started with this memory and it showed up today- how did Facebook know?

He cleared the memory, instead of sharing it, and slid his phone across the table. He swallowed his last sip of coffee and went upstairs to shower.

When she came down, Sarah smelled like flowers and the room had the sense of the woman throughout. There was something about the smell of a fresh shower and a new day that he loved when he kissed his wife goodbye. He so rarely got to enjoy this, because he usually left before she got out of bed. Today he wanted to, no he needed, to sleep in. In doing so, he got the chance to drive with his beautiful wife when she smelled so sweet.

He donned his coat and rushed outside to warm up her car and melt the thin sheet of frost that covered her windshield. She would be another few minutes, as she packed her purse with assorted items and prepped the travel mug with coffee to fuel her Monday morning. Simon sat in the driver's seat and waited for the seat warmer to come on.

Eventually, Sarah came walking down the driveway to the car and Simon beeped the automatic doors, so she could climb in the passenger side. She got in and he asked, " Do you want me to drive?"

She nodded yes and took a sip of her coffee. The steam from the coffee fogged her side of the windshield and he turned up the defroster joking, "you're steaming up my windows." She smiled, but he could tell she was in a decidedly foul mood.

They drove the few miles toward the car rental agency and arrived. He leaned in to kiss her as they walked around the front of the car to exchange positions. She stopped him, looked him in the eye, and said, "Simon Gates, I love you. I know you are stepping into something I don't like today and that you feel that you have to do it. But you better not get lost." Simon was a little shocked by her directness, but recovered without skipping a beat and said, "I promise- I won't get lost."

He kissed and wrapped her in his arms and whispered to her, "I love you."

She wriggled from his grasp and said, "You better, Mister," and climbed in her running car.

He began walking toward the car rental office and she honked at him. He jumped slightly and turned to see her laughing hysterically. He waved at her, feigning annoyance, but laughing. He proceeded toward the office.

The process of renting the car was easy for the insurance agent. He was familiar with the paperwork and his office had rented at least 100 cars from this agency in the last year. It was kind of strange being on the other side of the equation. This time, as a customer instead of being an agent. He knew Manny though, and the people at the car rental place. They made the process easy.

Before he knew it, he was driving out on the road in a new silver Ford Explorer with warm tan leather interior. He felt a fear of driving, that he hadn't felt since he first started driving when he was sixteen and took his father's car to the convenience store for eggs. He remembered the sound of the SUV crashing into him last week. He tried to remember the face of the man, who got out of the car and started yelling at him.

The sound of the two shots fired at the police officer echoed in his mind. He winced, hearing them again, but remembered that he wasn't paying attention when it all started. He pulled himself back to driving and chided himself for drifting out of consciousness. It was a habit he was going to have to quit, now that he was ...in his new situation, whatever that was.

The short drive to his office went even faster today, despite the traffic. He could only creep at a few miles an hour most days, due to the shut down of the major highways. Today, he filled the time taking in the details of the drive in a way he had never observed before.

He noticed the rusted white van parked at the edge of the tire place parking lot. He noticed the blown out portion of the fluorescent sign in the Chinese delivery place's window. He noticed the man selling newspapers under the stoplight at the corner of the intersection and the Connolly Construction truck towing the payloader three cars in front of him. These were details of life in America that he had never paid attention to before and were he watching he might never have run the red light and avoided meeting the man in the SUV.

His thoughts left him when he realized he was pulling into his parking lot and saw that Marion and Amy were already there. He noticed the time. 9:30. That would only leave him 30 minutes to talk with the ladies before he had to call Altieri.

He turned off the car and walked across the still-icy parking lot. He wasn't there to scatter the salt earlier that morning and thought, "I'm going to have to find someone to do this if I am not here every day."

Opening the door, Marion and Amy both met him at the door and were buzzing with questions about the car accident and shooting. He had forgotten that he hadn't talked to them since the accident and hadn't been to work since it happened. He stopped them and said he would answer all their questions when he got a chance to take his coat off and get settled.

He made sure to thank them for all their hard work, they did while he was gone and wanted to arrange to have lunch with them both today in thanks. He walked back to his office. It seemed like an old home he hadn't seen in years.

His coffee cup was clean and upside down on his desk blotter on a paper towel. Seeing it, he realized that he forgot to wash it when he left for lunch last week and Marion must have cleaned it for him. His plant was dry though and wilting. He immediately picked it up and took it to the restroom to give it a drink.

When he came back to the office, Marion followed him in and leaned against the office door. She said, "Well you've had the weekend from hell, haven't you? When you didn't come back from lunch immediately last week, I began to worry."

"Yeah It was quite a new experience, my first homicide," said Simon. He glanced over to the clock. It was 9:58. "I have to make a call right now. I'll explain it all at lunch. Can you call and have something delivered to the conference room for us at noon?"

Marion agreed and stepped out of the office.

Simon picked up his phone and noticed that he was slightly out of breath. He was nervous and his palms were sweating. He dialed the number and it rang three times before Altieiri picked up.

"Good morning, this is Lieutenant Altieri. How may I assist you?" answered the Army officer.

"Lieutenant, this is Simon Gates, we had a call scheduled this morning."

"Ah yes sir, how are you doing?" replied Altieri, "Glad you called. We have been busy since we saw you on Saturday and this is going to be a big week. A transport just arrived here with office equipment, and all the stuff we need to make this place function. When you come back it will look like a completely different place."

"Great," said Simon, "I can't wait to see it. I wanted to check in with you now that my wife and I have had a chance to talk. She is very nervous about how things will develop, but I'm ready to go. I wanted to see what the next steps might be?"

Altieri said, "We had a new order come down on Sunday afternoon. As I think I told you, this is a very new program and things are changing daily. The directive came from the division that all new volunteers will be invited to participate in a three-week indoctrination at their local regional intake center. We will give you a three-week all-expense-paid vacation where you will learn to be a military man once you sign on as a volunteer. I know we didn't mention this in our last conversation, but I thought you might enjoy it? What do you think?"

Simon didn't expect to hear that and immediately thought, "How can I get away for three weeks now?" Another thought came into him, "How would Sarah feel about this?"

"Wow," he replied, "That sounds exciting. I'm sure my wife will find that interesting, too. Where would I be heading?"

Altieri said, "We have a training center up in Massachusetts where we put all our recruits through medical and indoc training. You'll receive your uniforms and all your necessary gear up there and they'll teach you about how we do things in the Army. I will email you a list of suggested personal items that we give to recruits so you can have what you need when you head up. You will train with a new platoon of volunteers. We will all meet here and head up by bus when we have the numbers we need to get this program up and running."

"Wow that sounds pretty cool," replied Simon, "Can I speak to Sarah about it and maybe come by on Wednesday and start the paperwork?"

"No problem, by Wednesday we should have this place humming and a better idea of the schedule. It will be a perfect time to give you an update," said Altieri, " I'll expect you Wednesday morning if that works for you?"

"Yup that works great, how does 8 AM work?" replied Simon.

"0800 it is," said Altieri, "see you then."

The phone went silent.

Simon sat back in his chair and wondered how he would explain this Sarah. She would not be happy, but then again, he wasn't sure she would be upset either.

## Chapter 6

When Gus got back to his hotel, his mind was buzzing with ideas. The day had been one of such comradery and togetherness, that he wanted to share this experience with everyone. The girl at the front desk was no longer there but was replaced by a young black man with short hair, a pencil-thin mustache, and thin wire frame glasses. His name tag read, "Jamal."

Gus walked up to the counter and said, "Excuse me, Jamal, I just wanted to check that I had a reservation for tomorrow night?"

The night counter agent looked surprised when he heard his name mentioned, especially from an old white guy like this. Jamal asked, "What room are you in?"

Gus said, "236."

Jamal typed in the computer and eyed the reservation and said, "Yes sir, I have you checking out on Wednesday actually? Will you be leaving us early?

Gus hadn't realized that they wanted him to stay so long but was thoroughly impressed with how organized John and Evan were.

He replied to Jamal, "No I guess I am staying on until Wednesday. They just didn't tell me."

Jamal realized he was talking with one of the people from the thing that was going on at VFW. He wasn't sure how to approach the subject as he knew that they were not people to mess with. He instead said, "Did you have a nice day sir? Were you out at that event by the VFW?"

Gus did not normally make small talk. He was still riding high on the day's events though, when he answered Jamal, "Jamal, have you ever landed in a place that you just knew felt right? Do you know who we are over there at the VFW?"

Jamal laughed and said, "I drove by there and I didn't think that was the right place for me at all. Lots of guns and not so many faces like mine."

Gus laughed and said, "Yeah I am sure we were a sight from the road. Did you get a look at where everybody came from? There were license plates from states all over the Nation and we were working on something pretty big. Have you ever been part of something bigger than yourself, Jamal?"

Jamal dropped his eyes and said, "I'm just a night guest services agent who lives in his mother's basement."

Gus asked him, "How old are you? You look like you're about 25."

Jamal said, "I'm 24 but people always think I look older."

Gus chuckled a little under his breath and said, "You're young, What's your plan? You're not gonna work as a night desk clerk your whole life, right?"

Jamal said, "I planned on going to basic training next year in the Army if I can figure out how to care for my kids while I'm gone. My Moms says she refuses to watch my babies if I am going to run off to war. My girlfriend left me just after my second baby was born and now the kids are mine, but we live with my Mom and she watches them while I am working."

Gus asked, "Do you have any schooling?"

Jamal said, "I graduated from high school and spent two semesters working towards a business degree at the community college, but I had to drop out and get a job when my girlfriend took off."

Gus felt inspired. He felt ambitious and next he did something that he had never done before.

"Jamal, I just left a meeting where we fed the poor, we saluted the flag and we did what America was supposed to do, care for each other. How does that sound to you?"

Jamal wasn't sure how to respond, and so he put his professional face back on, "Sir, that sounds lovely. I am glad you had such a wonderful day."

Gus pushed further, "No, what I am saying is it sounds like you're having a tough time. So many others like you are having a tough time too. What if we all worked together to take back our Nation and reclaim it so that it worked for all of us. That is exactly what we are trying to do over at the VFW with all those guns."

Jamal laughed and forgot himself for a second and said, "I saw a lot of guns and rednecks today? Is that what you call caring for each other?"

Jamal immediately regretted saying what he said and was prepared to make apologies if he needed to.

Gus laughed and said, "I guess that I could see that if I looked through your eyes too, there weren't too many non-white folks out there, were there?"

"Let me be straight with you," Gus leaned on the counter, "We aren't the most diverse group of people- *yet* -and I wish I could change that. But we are working to make a better America. If you wanted to help us work on our diversity and build a better America, I am pretty high up in that group and could help make that happen ."

Jamal said, "It's my experience, guns and white people don't mix well together for people like me."

Gus could understand his hesitation. He could understand his fear and his caution. He tried to explain himself, but felt he was overplaying his hand and didn't want to seem too forward. "I just mean if you wanted to come by and check it out, I could help you meet some people and show you around."

Jamal sensed he was talking to a good man, but learned a long time ago, that it was better to keep your mouth shut. "Thank you, Mr. Soros, I do appreciate your offer, but I am doing my best right where I am at."

Gus heard the door slam and all of sudden felt incredibly tired. "I get it, if you change your mind, you know where I am staying for the next few days. You know how to reach me." Gus turned around, walked toward the elevator, and went up to his room.

When he got to his room, he opened the door and went in. The air conditioning had been left on all day and the room felt like a meat locker. He opened the window and the unseasonably warm February night air poured in the room. For a second, he thought it might rain right there in his hotel room.

He pulled back the sheet, undressed, and fell asleep.

When he woke, the sun was just rising and the warm night air had turned to a crisp morning breeze. The room felt even colder than it had the night before. He was half-naked and freezing. His muscles ached and his battle scars burned. He rubbed the shrapnel scar on his knee and the scar where the bullet went through his shoulder and willed his limbs to respond.

When he could move, he shut the windows and turned the heat on to 90. He climbed into a hot shower to finish the reanimation process.

When the feeling returned to his extremities and he could move normally again, he dressed, walked down to the lobby where the smell of coffee, powdered eggs, biscuits, and gravy stirred his hunger. He helped himself to toast and yogurt. He squirted a cup of black coffee into a paper cup and sat down to read the complimentary newspaper. The cable news drummed in the background.

A news story caught his attention on the back of the front page about a new program that the military was rolling out called "Patriotic Unity Stations." The article explained that civilians would be asked to volunteer to serve a few hours a week at local stations around the country in the old reserve facilities that were abandoned when the National Guard was disbanded. The units would be trained as regular military, but unlike the reserves, they would not be paid. They would essentially be a replacement for the reserves and would serve as volunteers.

The story intrigued Gus. Why would the Military need to replace the reserves when they just eliminated so much of the military a few years back? Was the Government worried about an attack? Were they planning on using the Military to take over the US even further?

His thoughts turned to his plan. What if they implemented a similar volunteer fighting force for the Resistance? What if they trained the people who were coming to Gettysburg to fight as one unified force instead of a bunch of militias? He talked about creating an Army to fight to reclaim America in *The Plan*, but he didn't talk about how the force would be recruited. This could work and made a lot of sense, he thought. He decided this would be one of his main talking points at the meeting today.

When he looked at his phone. The time said 0814. He was running late. He needed to move if he was going to make it to the VFW on time.

He dumped his plate in the bus pan and hurried past the front desk out to the car. Jamal wasn't there but the nice girl who spoke to him yesterday was. He noted her name today, "Michelle." It was a nice name he thought and said, "Have a Great day, Michelle- I'll see you later." She didn't have a chance to respond but was taken by the change in the man's tone from the morning before.

## Chapter 7

Simon walked into the house and could smell dinner cooking. Sarah beat him home this evening. He stayed late to talk to Marion and Amy at work.

The lunchtime team meeting at noon turned into a six-hour planning session for the agency. They developed a plan for the year ahead where he would take some time off and start shifting some of the operational roles to Marion. This was not something he had planned on tackling today, or for that matter, ever, but the way he felt, it needed to be done.

He wanted Marion to take care of all day to day operations concerning client inquiries, management, and new policy acquisitions, while she worked to become a licensed agent like him. She would begin studying immediately to take the exam and get her insurance license. They thought Simon could help her with the process when he was around. Amy would take charge of all billing, policy administration and would begin searching for an office assistant immediately.

Simon would retain ownership of the agency, and work as his schedule allowed. He explained to them that he wanted to put serious effort into the Army and figured he could cut his hours down at the office to do so. As long as he worked 40 hours a week, he would be compliant with his contract. Now all he had to do was get Sarah to sign off on the plan. That was the part that scared him.

Marion and Amy did not envy the task that lay ahead of Simon. They spent a full hour coaching him on how he might break the news to Sarah. "Make sure you tell her that you're doing this because you love her," were the parting words Marion screamed across the parking lot as he pulled away.

He did love Sarah, with all his being. He _was_ doing this because he loved her. He was doing this for so much more though, he told himself. He decided he was doing this because he loved his country, he loved his home and he loved his life. All those things seemed in jeopardy at the moment. He had spent the last two days talking himself into it and he was now getting quite excited, he just didn't know how to tell his wife.

He didn't tell Altieri this, but after thinking about it, he wanted to get started immediately. That is of course if Sarah said it was okay.

Walking into the kitchen, he could see she was pan-frying a steak. He loved the way she fried a steak, with way too much butter, a touch of garlic and rosemary, and a slight char on the edges with a blood-red center. How she could char the outside without overcooking the inside, was a skill he never seemed to manage to learn. He knew no one could fry a steak like Sarah.

She was already halfway through a bottle of their favorite cab sav, Browne, and he almost felt hurt that she cracked the bottle without him. That was their wine. They served that wine at their wedding and that was a wine they reserved for every special occasion since that magical winter wedding. The fact that she had uncorked it and imbibed half of it, cut him to the quick. There was no way however, he could bring up this hurt, given the dagger he meant to present to her later that evening.

She bent over and pulled a steaming dish of creamed spinach from the oven. She threw the loaf of French bread in and turned the oven off. "Dinner will be ready in five minutes," she said, "get yourself a glass of wine and put some music on will you?"

He wandered to the cupboard and pulled a large burgundy glass from the shelf and blurted out, "Hey Google, play John Prine." They loved John Prine and the google device replied, "Here's a station called John Prine Radio on Pandora." The soft tones of an acoustic guitar began to play. It was immediately recognizable as, "In spite of Ourselves," the only song Google ever seemed to play to start with when they asked her to hear the artist.

He walked next to her and picked up the bottle of Browne and walked to the table and sat down. She laid out plates and linen napkins with a fork on the right and a knife on the left. He poured the glass and watched the woman dart from the fridge to the stove to the table a dozen times.

When she sat down, she was out of breath, but the smell and the sizzle of the steak made his mouth water. He bent his head and folded his hands and said the blessing, "God is Great, God is good...." When he finished, he raised his glass and said, "To my love, Cheers." She smiled and offered her glass to tap with his. Next, he cut into the steak to see if she worked her magic once again. She did, it was cooked to perfection.

He cut a big bite of steak and swallowed it with a sip of the dark red wine, letting it wash over his senses. It felt good he thought and he was almost ready to broach the subject but decided to savor the moment just a bit longer before the battle began.

Sarah fired the first shot, "So, how was your day?"

He swallowed the last bit of steak mixed with wine and tried to soften his counter-assault with an apology. He said, "Sorry I'm late, I had to speak to Marion and Amy about a few things that happened over the weekend and our meeting ran long."

"I bet," she said, "Did you talk to Altieri?"

She wasn't the type to beat around the bush and he knew that but grew fearful when she belayed all conventional preludes to marital war with an unprovoked forward assault. He took one last bite of the steak and a swig of wine before answering her.

She could see he was stalling now and knew she wasn't going like what he said next. He decided that a diplomatic de-escalation made more sense. "What? Just say it," she said.``

Realizing he had no defense and could only risk more bloodshed with a counter-assault, he decided to dispense with the pleasantries and offer his full unabashed surrender. "They started a new program over the weekend for volunteers," he began, "They want me to do an indoctrination for three weeks at a regional training center up in Massachusetts. I want to do it"

"WHAT?" She slammed her glass down, breaking the stem as the bowl tipped onto the table. Thankfully most of the wine was already in her, but the last drops stained the linen napkin.

Realizing that his surrender was stayed and war was averted, thanks to a self-inflicted shot brought about by inebriation, he said, "Watch it-- don't cut yourself."

He gathered the pieces of glass and got up from the table to take them to the garbage, thankful that he had avoided a full-on battle with his wife. She used this opportunity to take his wine glass and drank down the balance.

When he got back, he said, "Hey, that was mine"

She laughed and said, "the keyword there is _was_. "

With the tension of the moment broken by the spilled wine, he offered reconciliation.

"So I take it you're not completely upset?" asked Simon.

It was refused.

"NO. I hate this idea and I hate the fact that you are even asking me. I hate that asshole Army guy and I hate that this country is having another fuckiing civil war over an asshole president who should have never been elected in the first place. I hate all of it, but if you want to do this, I won't be the kind of wife that tells you, you can't. You're a grown man and if you get killed, I will never forgive you. But I love you too much to tell you what to do in a thing like this."

Simon said, " Hey Google Stop....HEY GOOGLE...STOP." The music went silent.

He took her hand and looked her in the eye and said, "I love you... You're drunk, but I love you."

She rolled her eyes and said, "What did you expect? You're telling me you're going to war? Do I have to be sober to hear that news?"

Simon said, "No, you don't have to be sober, but you do have to get me a new glass of wine."

She got up from the table and went to the cupboard and got him a chardonnay glass, as the last burgundy glass that used to be his, was already on the table and full of her wine.

"We have to get better burgundy glasses," he smiled and chuckled.

"Yes," she said, "With thicker stems. Maybe we'll get plastic ones next time."

They both knew plastic would never work. They loved their glass and would have to be more careful with the next set, if they ever got to share a bottle of Browne again.

## Chapter 8

Gus stepped out into the bright sunshine from the tent where he had been talking all morning. His eyes had taken a moment to adjust, but he was pretty sure that there were even more people there now. The field behind the building had trailers parked for as far as the eye could see and both sides of the street were lined with trucks and RVs.

The last two days were astounding. Evan reported that the organization had raised $12 million through private donations from individuals online and received a $60 million pledge from a Texas Cattleman's Association in just the past 24 hours. The groundswell was happening and people from all over the world were paying attention to this impromptu gathering at the edge of the First Civil War battlefield.

By default, because no one else had the know-how, Evan became the secretary of the treasury and the minister of public information. As a former financial analyst, he had the skills to keep the books and the know-how to send out a message that could avoid the eyes of the media and the federal authorities. He also had no problem fundraising from wealthy donors.

Tanner made sure that the local cops kept all inquiries about the huge event on the down-low and developed a line of communication with law enforcement around the country. They figured that the cops would know where all the abandoned military assets might be and he had a knack for finding sympathetic ears within the law enforcement community.

When the government pulled back on the military, they told the public that they were consolidating and beefing up the Army and the Navy. But when they did, they pulled back so fast that they did so in a matter of days. The Air Force, Marines, Coast Guard, and National Guard were all shut down in such a quick fashion that the Department of Defense failed to properly clear out and secure installations on their retreat. That meant that millions of dollars of former US military equipment and property were left unaccounted for in garages and abandoned in warehouses around the nation and was ripe for the picking. In many ways, it reminded Gus of the fall of the Soviet Union.

Jason and Jeff worked as an amazing organizing team. They had the fleet of trailers obeying all sanitation orders and a particular talent for getting messages through the trailer fleet using CB radios in a matter of minutes.

A black helicopter flew over on Sunday and the crowd got nervous. Several weapons were raised before Jason and Jeff got a message for everyone to stand down and stay inside. By the time the helicopter landed, they figured out that it was a billionaire from Arkansas who heard about the meeting online and wanted to see it for himself.

The helicopter, and the fact that it was almost shot down over Gettysburg, scared everyone in the newly appointed Resistance Cabinet enough to ask that all weapons be sequestered for the remainder of the event. The Cabinet, a collection of the six men who were responsible for the organization which included themselves plus

John, Evan, Tanner, Gus, was impressed with the control that Jason and Jeff showed for the trailer fleet.

Another billionaire who lived in Montana offered the organization a 600-acre tract of land near the Fort Peck Indian Reservation where the equipment could be stored in an abandoned online shopping warehouse that was built right after the pandemic began. It was decided that Jason and Jeff would be responsible for securing the abandoned military assets and deliver them to the site in Montana and when the meeting concluded, Tanner would lead a group of volunteers to the site to begin making it ready for delivery.

John was responsible for making a national organization and taking care of the daily operations of the meeting. On Sunday at 1800, he was placed under 24/7 protection and officially elected as the provisional President of the Resistance. He spent most of his time in the main house and that meant that anyone who went inside had to have a security badge and was thoroughly vetted by Tanner and his staff.

That left the military organization to Hawk. He had a knack for military thinking, they decided, from the tone of his plan. He also had more military experience than anyone else in senior leadership because of his time as an Army officer and his subsequent work as a military contractor at Dark Pond. His willingness to use violence to achieve goals, like shooting the cop, also lent to the fact that he might know how to make a bunch of families of off-gridders, trailerites, and former Militia into a formidable fighting force.

When the meeting was over, Gus was told that he would travel down to Florida where yet another billionaire supporter named Travis LaPierre bought a former naval airbase that had been publicly auctioned through the GSA. When all flight duties were turned over to the newly reconstituted Army Air Corp, the Navy gave up all its airfields. Mr. LaPierre bought it to build condos but said they could use it to start an Army while the environmental hurdles were being cleared for development. Gus thought it was a great spot where they could start inducting recruits.

Now that Gus was done with his first meeting of the day, he was shaking his head at how far they advanced and worried that someone must be seeing some of this. The money, the attention, the people. He wondered if at any minute a team of federal agents might descend on this place and start shooting.

There was a certain fact though, that there were more automatic weapons here, locked and loaded and ready to deploy than most military bases around the country right now. Crawford decimated the military with his cutbacks and his consolidation of power, so much so that even the Taliban didn't take the US Military seriously anymore. If America had fallen from grace in the Herzog years, it was now on skid row in the Crawford years.

That morning, Gus had been leading a session about training techniques and organizational methods called "Turning Families Into Fighters." Tanner's wife Gayle, a former teacher, had a ton of insight into how they might use teaching methods to get the trainees up to speed. She had attended every session that dealt with military training and Gus decided she was quite an asset to have on board.

Gayle also had excellent training in hand to hand combat and small arms fire from her years working on the down-east coast of Maine as a fisherman's wife. More than once she had to square off with another boat crew to save her pots and keep the cash from her haul in her pocket.

The lobster blight hit just before the storm took their boat. It became a dog eat dog world in the fishing industry of Maine. When the last lobster was hauled and the industry officially declared dead, she was almost grateful that the Lord had taken their boat and got them out of there before she or Tanner were killed.

Gayle stepped out from the tent just after Gus and said, "My Gawd it's a beautiful day, can we do the rest of these sessions outside?"

Gus agreed by saying, "I'm not sure what the rest might think, but you got my vote."

Just then, the lunch triangle rang and the camp seemed to come alive. Bodies poured from the trailers along the road and in the backfield. The tents that were set up for the break out sessions streamed with people walking in lines up to the main tent for lunch. Gus had no training in crowd estimation but guessed there had to be at least ten thousand people all sitting around this tiny little building on the edge of a battlefield. Surely a park ranger at the historic site must have seen something and called someone, Gus thought?

Tanner walked over and kissed his wife on the cheek. "How was the morning session, love?" he asked his wife.

She said, "Hawk is a whiz at this training stuff and I think we got some great ideas to share with you all later. This was so much fun. How'd you do?"

Tanner said, "Well I tried to speak with the National Park Director for Gettysburg, but it turns out he was furloughed last June due to budget cuts as well, so the park is unstaffed right now. So I asked the Chief today and he agreed that as long as we don't show any weapons, we can spill over a little further on the adjoining field to the south. He just wants to make sure we don't block any traffic lanes or do nothing violent and I agreed, so I think we're okay."

"Tanner," Gus asked, "how many people do we have here, do you think?"

"Oh at least 9,000 at this morning count," replied Tanner, "By now it could be up to 12, you should ask the people making hot dogs they would know bettah."

The smell of beef roasting filled Gus' nose as they rounded the corner to the side of the building where the rotisseries were. The old guys were cooking sides of beef for tonight and they had ten full sides of beef cooking over the pits. He said to the couple, "How am I supposed to eat a hot dog when they have that cooking?"

Gus, Tanner, and Gayle all got in the same line and waited 15 minutes until they were handed a plate with two hot dogs each. Gus asked for some salad and chips and Gayle asked for some potatoes and beans. Tanner ate his hotdogs with ketchup and no sides.

They sat down together at a newly built picnic table under an oak tree and talked quietly while they ate. A young black man walked up to the table and said "Excuse me, Mr. Soros?"

It was Jamal and Gus recognized him immediately.

"Mr. Soros!" cried Gayle, "who goes by that name in this place?"

Gus stood and extended his hand to Jamal and shook it saying, "I do. This is Jamal, I invited him down here to meet a few people and get to know us."

Tanner kept his seat and nodded at Jamal.

Gayle looked at her husband and stood up offering her hand, "Hi Jamal, please forgive me, that is not a name I am familiar with for this guy. I'm Gayle."

Jamal looked uncomfortable and asked, "I'm sorry, did I get your name wrong, sir?"

Gus laughed and said, "No you didn't. I just go by that name when I am not on duty. My real name is Gus, but everyone here calls me Hawk."

"Oh... so then what should I call you?" asked Jamal with suspicion in his eyes.

"Call me Gus," he said, putting his arm around the young man leading him away from the table. "So you came!? I bet this feels kinda weird to you?"

"More like scary," said Jamal.

"That makes sense. Jamal, please let me introduce you to The Resistance," he said looking all around. "You are a personal guest of the Provisional Field Commander and I am at your service."

Saying his new title out loud made Gus feel a little awkward. This wasn't some cookout with 10,000 friends and a bunch of weapons. This was for real, a force, an army in the making, and they were all part of it. Jamal's stomach dropped when he heard that because he felt he just wandered into something he wasn't sure he wanted to be a part of.

Gus saw the fear in Jamal's eyes and wanted to put his mind at ease and said, "Jamal, you are our guest right now, you haven't done anything wrong."

That didn't assuage Jamal's feelings much at all. Gus broke the awkward moment and suggested, "Why don't we give you a tour, and maybe you will feel a little better? Jamal, come with me."

The two walked toward the main building where Gus started to explain the foodservice and the layout of the camp. He offered him lunch and walked with him through the food line, with much interest from the onlookers. Gus paid no attention, but Jamal struggled to get down two bites.

Jamal asked, "how many people are here?"

"We think about 12,000," said Gus.

"Where are they all from?"

"Well," said Gus, "Everywhere. There are at least 43 states represented here and more recruits are arriving every hour."

"What are you guys doing?" asked Jamal.

"We're creating a force to take back America. And all these people want to be part of it."

"Wow. That's pretty cool. When did we lose it?" Jamal remarked.

Jamal tried to be polite but thought he may have erred in coming here.

"The America you know isn't the nation we once knew. We're gonna fight to get back to what it used to be," said Gus.

"How will you win?" asked Jamal.

"Now that's the tough part, isn't it?" replied Gus.

They walked further into the rows of campers in silence. Jamal felt uncomfortable with the stares from older white faces carrying weapons. He felt too young, too poor, and too black for this crowd.

When they got about halfway down the first row, Jamal asked Gus, " Why did you invite me here?"

Gus stopped and looked the young man straight in the eye and said, "Because if this is going to work, we need you. We need smart young people like yourself to join in this effort. We need everyone in this nation who isn't a middle-aged white person to stand up and fight if we are going to win. This isn't just *our* battle or *our* future, it's yours and your kids as well. "

Gus continued, "There are a lot of white faces here, I know, and that may be very intimidating to you. The history of this group is one that wasn't too welcoming of young black men not so long ago. But America is not about the old white people running things forever. If the last two elections taught us nothing, there are a lot more of you, than us. I wrote a book about how to make something like this work and a key part of the plan was to get the young men and women of this nation, like you, involved.

"When you told me about your interest in joining up, and I spoke to you about your future. It occurred to me that you and your family's future is pretty limited. Most people like you realize that they have a pretty limited future under this current system. I think I can do you one better than the Army if you want to fight for a living.

"I need a bright young man like you to serve as my chief of staff and personal assistant as I build an army to reclaim America. I need some help making this a place where everyone has a fair chance to become somebody. I need a young black man to be by my side and I think you are the right guy for the job, even though we have only talked for a few minutes. I get a good feeling about you, but the truth is, I have a lot less to lose by offering you this job than you have by taking it.

"I can't guarantee success and I can't guarantee it will be easy" he continued, "but I can guarantee that I will be there to help you along. So I invited you here. Now I have said what I need to say, you don't have to answer now and you don't have to stay. If I've worn you out already, your welcome to go now. But at least let me buy you a beer and give you a chance to talk to a few people first?"

No one had ever spoken to Jamal like that before. No one ever laid it out to him like that. He wasn't getting anywhere in his current job and his kids had even less to look forward to in the United States. He felt like he was always playing catch up and wasn't ever gonna get ahead.

151

He knew he was just as likely to get killed walking on the sidewalk, because of the color of his skin, as he was in a warzone. That's why he wanted to enlist in the Army, but even if he did get in, how would he pay for his kids and mother? His boss talked to him like he was a moron and his Mom only ever lectured him. His teachers gave up on him a long time ago and he never knew his Dad. He liked Gus and he liked the idea that Gus took an interest in him, even if he did have an agenda. He said, "No I'll stick around for a while longer, I don't have to be to work until 9,"

They turned around and walked back toward the main house.

As they walked, Gus told him about John and how he was the new president who ran the organization. He talked to him about the plan to take all the trainees down to Florida. And he told him about the equipment they would be collecting around the US that had been abandoned by the Military. He stopped just before they reached the far end of a line of RVs at the end of the road and put his hand on his shoulder and said, "I do want to trust you, but if I find out I can't, it isn't going to end well."

Jamal's face went pale. He wasn't sure if this was a threat. He said quietly, "So you mean I have to say yes or you'll …."

Gus stopped him and said, "No. I don't need a yes or no right now, but I do need to make sure that what I am telling you won't make it back to the wrong people."

Jamal pulled away and said, "I'll keep my mouth shut Gus, I promise. Don't hurt me." His ears began to ring and his palms were sweating.

Gus smiled and said, "I won't hurt you, but I had to say it. You want to get that beer now?"

Jamal wasn't sure what would happen, if he said no to the beer, so he nodded yes and began walking back up the street.

"Where are you going?" Gus asked, "we're at my place right here."

He stepped up to a newer-looking trailer that read "Outback," on the side and pulled the unlocked door open, and said, "Welcome aboard." Jamal walked inside and the cool dark interior made him see spots after the bright sunshine. His head was hurting and his heart was pounding.

He stepped toward a couch and Gus slipped behind him and opened the fridge. He pulled out two long neck Budweisers, popped the tops with a church-key he had on the counter, and offered one to Jamal. Jamal took a long sip and felt the cold beer cool his dry mouth and hot throat. He swirled the beer in his mouth to rid the cottonmouth he was suffering from since Gus had threatened him.

Licking his lips with the cool wet beer, he asked, "Gus, May I sit down?"

Gus was just downing his beer and swallowed hard and said, "By all means, have a seat on the couch."

Jamal began to feel a little better, as he felt the beer begin to calm his nerves. When the ringing stopped in his ears and his eyes adjusted fully to the darkness, he asked, "Gus, so what would I do if I joined up with you guys?"

Gus hadn't thought that through yet but liked the idea that this young man would be beholden to him. "Well, I got to drive down to Florida and set up a camp for recruits. I need help with the administration of it and someone to help me keep things in order. I think we could offer you a bump in pay and grade if you said yes. The virtue of a wartime promotion is you get a lot higher a lot faster. How does the chief of staff for the provisional Field Commander sound on your resume?"

"What would I be paid?" asked Jamal.

"It's just like any other job," said Gus "you'll just be working for a start-up business with a few million dollars in the bank. How does $1000 a week sound?"

A steady job with a decent paycheck was sounding better and better to Jamal. "What about my mom and my kids?"

"You will travel with me where I go," explained Gus, "so I will cover all your living expenses, and you can send your money back home to them if you want? We can help you set up a checking account and all that if you need help?"

Jamal was getting a debit card from his employer currently for his pay that he gave to his mom to use and had never had a real checking account before.

"I have never had a checking account before, that would be great, could I buy a car if I wanted to? I get the courtesy van to work most of the time and haven't been able to get a car yet?"

Gus wondered how a man this age had never had a car or a checking account before but felt happy that he could help the man become a better man. "You can do whatever you like with your money, but you'll be traveling with me most of the time and so you can use my car. You'll have a uniform to wear and will have a place to sleep and eat every night so you won't have those expenses either. So you really could have a nice car and also help support your family."

At this idea, Jamal's face lit up and he smiled brightly.

"So this sounds good to you?" Gus asked.

"Yes sir, this sounds awesome" replied Jamal, "how do we get started?"

"Well we shove off for Florida tomorrow," said Gus, "Things are going to move pretty fast from here on in. Can you handle that?"

Jamal said, "I have had days when five guests wanted to check out and another five wanted to check in all at the same time. I can handle it."

"Good," Gus said, "then go home, pack a bag with the bare essentials and come back when you have said your goodbyes. Don't tell anybody what you're doing. You just got a better job offer and it starts tomorrow. Is that clear? What are you going to tell your Mom?"

"I don't know, just that I got a new job and I have to move to Florida to do it. When will I be paid so I can tell her that I will take care of the kids?"

Gus reached into his pocket and pulled out a wad of hundreds. He counted ten off onto the coffee table and put the roll back in his pocket. He picked up the stack of money and placed it in Jamal's hand. "Give $900 of this to your Mom for the kids and keep $100 for yourself." he said, "Tell her you got an advance on your pay and that you will be paid $1000 per week and that you will set up a checking account where she can access the money every week."

Jamal's eyes went wide as he said "$1000 a week, that's $52,000 a year?"

"Yes, you're working for the Provisional Field Commander's staff," said Gus "there are some benefits to that. Now get out of here and be back here at 0600, that's 6 AM tomorrow. Do you understand?"

Jamal stood at attention and said, "Yes sir"

"Welcome aboard, Jamal," said Gus, "We're going to be doing some very big things."

156

## Chapter 9

Tuesday came and went without much fanfare. Amy found three people to interview and Marion made an appointment to join a test prep service for the insurance exam. Simon went through his office looking for anything that he wanted to take with him. He packed a bunch of pictures and the plant in the morning then slowly put each one back in the afternoon. There wasn't anything he wanted to take home and he was hoping to come back soon.

He was going through old emails when a new one popped into his feed. It read, "Official US Army business," in the subject line. He saw that it was from Altieri. He opened it with great interest only to find it was the list of suggested items for recruits to bring to indoc that Altieri said he would send over. He read it out loud,

"10 white tee shirts
10 boxer or brief-style undergarments, white. No bikini-style undergarments permitted
Personal Toiletries and a shower bag
A journal
Cell phone charger and cell phone
A 4-inch roll of masking tape....

What the hell do we need masking tape for?" he wondered.

He reached into the supply closet and pulled out a roll of two-inch tape that they had kept there for mailing packages and yelled, "Amy I have a list of things I need to get for indoc, can you run to the store for me, if I email you this list?"

While he was in the closet, he heard the phone ring. He fumbled over himself to get to answer it.

"Simon Gates Insurance, this is Simon," he answered, just catching his breath.

"Simon, Lieutenant Altieri here from the Stratford Patriotic Unity Station. How are you today?"

"I'm good, how can I help you? We're set to meet tomorrow morning right?" Simon said while he forwarded the email to Amy and typed, "already got masking tape," in the subject line.

"Yeah about that, we have to speed up the process," Altieri said, "we have ten volunteers from around the state ready to report into Springfield tomorrow, can we count on you to join us?"

Simon hadn't planned on shipping out so soon, but couldn't think of a reason to say no, other than his wife.

"Can I check with Sarah?" he answered, "I don't think it's a problem, but I want to check. Most likely you can count on me to head out tomorrow if that's what you need?"

"Great, I hope you got the list I sent you?" replied the soldier,

"Yes sir, I did. Looking it over right now," said Simon. He thought about asking what the four-inch tape was for, but Altieri interrupted the thought by asking,

"Can you report in tomorrow at 0600, that's 6 AM for civilians?"

"Yes sir, I will see you then," Simon finished, "Goodbye for now."

He hung up the phone and yelled, "MAAARRIIIIOOOONNN!"

She came running in and said, "What is it? What's the matter?"

"They want me to report tomorrow at 6 AM," whined Simon, "If my wife doesn't kill me, they are going to at Zero Dark Thirty."

"Welcome to the Army Mister," said Marion, "remember you're doing this for a good cause"

"Yeah, Yeah, I know," said Simon, "Amy, change of plans, can you run to the store today?" Putting his hand on his forehead, he continued saying, "I'm just gonna have to get up at 0430 to be there in time for 0600 as Altieri likes to say."

Marion laughed and went back to her desk.

At quitting time, the two women walked into his office and caught him playing Candy Crush on his phone. He had nothing else to do and didn't want to go home and face his wife.
Marion had tears in her eyes.

Amy started talking and said, "Simon, we are going to miss you, but we will keep the lights on here I promise." She placed the bag of items he asked her to buy on his desk.

Marion stifled back the lump in her throat and said, "I am going to kill you, right after your wife does if anything happens to you."

He laughed and said, "Nothing is going to happen, I am going to Massachusetts for three weeks then coming back to work on Nichols Ave? It's two miles from here?"

"I know, I know," said Marion, "but this is scary and I am worried."

In truth, he was worried too, but there was no way he was going to let them know it.

When everyone left and the office was quiet, he wanted any kind of noise to get his mind off of what was coming. He decided to go home.

He put on his coat and got in the rental car and drove home. It occurred to him on the way home, "what am I supposed to do with this car?"

His car wasn't supposed to be fixed for another two weeks. Simon figured he was going to be knee-deep in Army mud then. He texted Marion and told her that the car would be over at the unity station whenever his truck was ready and asked her to arrange to get it back to the rental place. She replied right away with a thumbs up.

The traffic was horrible tonight. That was something he looked forward to missing in the coming weeks ahead. It felt like it was taking forever to get home to his wife. He didn't want to tell her, but he also wanted to spend every moment he had left with her as well.

Simon didn't know what would be happening on the other side of his indoctrination but worried that the pace of things was increasing. On Saturday, he was thinking about joining a volunteer force. By Tuesday, he was shipping out for three weeks and leaving the life he had taken years to build. What did they know that they weren't telling him? What would he learn when he got to Massachusetts? But most importantly, would his wife ever forgive him?

He wailed on the horn and the man in front him flipped him the bird. The road was packed with cars and no one was moving. He looked at his phone. The time said 6:15, less than 12 hours until he had to report in. He could feel his anger building and he envisioned pulling his truck onto the esplanade, driving over it, and turning around to go the other way. He would never do such a thing, but he wanted to.

Just then, a police car came whipping up the wrong side of the road. His mind immediately flashed back to the car accident and the shooting. A panic set inside him. He could feel his heart begin to race. His pulse quickened and he became short of breath. He felt trapped in the car and trapped in the traffic. He wanted to get out and run far away and never come back.

He wanted to pull a gun and shoot that guy before he shot that cop. He wanted to stand up for his rights and beat something to a pulp all at the same time. He was scared and angry, all at once. All he wanted to do was be at home and hug his beautiful wife.

When he could no longer see the lights of the police car, the traffic started moving again. There was a broken-down truck up ahead that stalled the traffic. He envisioned walking up to the truck and pulling the guy out. He saw himself beating the man unconscious and putting his teeth on the curb. Then he saw himself stomping on his neck and seeing the blood mixing with the gutter sand and trash.
Simon began to realize that his fingers hurt from clenching the wheel so hard. He released the pressure in his hands. They were white and painful and he felt like the skin under his knuckles was about to bleed.

"You're losing your mind, asshole," he said out loud. Maybe a little music would calm his nerves, he thought. He put on the classical station on the satellite radio and a pleasant piano sonata inspired him to take a deep cleansing breath. Just then the car behind bumped into him.

It was just a nudge and he could tell there was no real damage, but Simon went red line. He slammed the car in park and threw open the door. It was dark and the red brake lights lit the rage on his face, so he looked like a Warner Brothers cartoon with smoke coming from his ears. "Mother Fucker, what the fuck do you think you're doing? This isn't even my fucking car?"

The person behind the wheel was a young girl and there was a driving school sign lit up on the roof. He immediately realized he was verbally assaulting a teenager on a driving lesson and he felt horrible.

He waved to the young girl. He could see the horrified driving instructor trying to calm her and stop her tears. Simon climbed back into his rental car. He had never lost his temper like that before in traffic and he wanted to die from embarrassment.

When he got the parking brake off and settled himself in the driver seat, the traffic ahead of him had cleared. He gassed it and took off. He sped home dodging cars and whipped into his driveway where his wife was just getting out of her car.

She closed her door as he pulled into the driveway. He threw it in park, ripped off his seat belt, and ran to his wife, leaving his keys beeping in the ignition and car door open. He grabbed her with all his strength and buried his head in her warm dark hair.

She joked, "I had a messy cleaning today, you might not want to do that..." Something was wrong she could tell.

"Honey, what's the matter? Are you OK?" she asked

He was sobbing in silence and she could only tell by the struggle he was having getting his breath. She held him tightly and said, "It'll be okay. Breathe."

He was hyperventilating.

"Feel my breath and breathe with me," she said trying to calm him. She breathed in deep and slow and let it out ever so slowly. She did this a few times and he calmed down and matched her breathing pattern. She asked him once again, "What's the matter, talk to me?"

"I just verbally assaulted a sixteen-year-old in a driving school car," he started. "She was just learning to drive and screamed the F Word at her with everyone watching in traffic. I even got out of the truck to yell at her."

This was not a behavior she was used to seeing in her husband. The last time he lost it like this, was when their dog Molly was killed by the car in front of their house. She soothed him and said, "Why did you do that?"

He wanted to tell her how scared he was. He wanted to tell her that he had to leave in the morning to join the Army. He wanted to tell her how sorry he was for not paying attention while driving the other day and throwing their life into a tumult. The best he could get out. "I gotta go tomorrow."

She wasn't sure what that meant but was pretty sure she could tell from the context clues that it was about the Army. She said, "Let's go inside."

"No," he said looking up from her shoulder and releasing his grip from her waist, "let's go to dinner."

She liked the idea and said, "Ok where do you want to go? I just have to stop inside real quick and freshen up- I did have a guy drool in my hair today."

"Let's go to the Green and get a pizza and a whole carafe of wine," Simon said, "Then let's get dessert and espresso and sambuca and go to bed drunk, make love, and never wake up."

Sarah realized that there was a time when she needed to tell him how upset she was, that he was doing this, but that this was not one of those times. They went inside. She changed her clothes and brushed her hair and teeth. He swished some mouthwash and had a small glass of gin. Sarah drove to the restaurant and they ate, enjoyed the ambiance, and left with full bellies and broken hearts.

They talked about the fact that he would be gone for three weeks. She wanted to cry at times and the drunker he got, the more his eyes filled with tears. Sarah joked with the waitress saying "We're not drunk, we're just joining the Army tomorrow."

The hostess made a point of thanking him for his service and gave them their coffee and sambuca for free. Sarah paid the bill. Simon staggered to the car where he got in on the passenger side and allowed Sarah to drive home. They got home, brushed their teeth, made love, and fell asleep.

The alarm went off at 4:30 AM Simon opened his eyes to discover that his head was throbbing. He went to shower and did his best to wash away the gin, the wine, and the sambuca. When he got out, he went down to the kitchen and pulled a warm Dr. Pepper from the pantry.

He downed the warm soda in the middle of the kitchen, naked, and ran back upstairs to vomit.

He slunk down onto the floor and rested his chest on the edge of the bowl, while drool slipped from his mouth. The cool porcelain felt good on his bare chest and he realized his ass was getting quite cold. He grabbed a towel and wrapped it around himself.

The noise of him getting sick woke his wife. She rose and went downstairs to brew a pot of coffee and come to life. Simon wandered down a few minutes later in clean sweat pants and a tee-shirt. He sat down next to her at the table and held his head saying "I draaank too much last night."

His wife rose from the table and picked up the coffee pot and a cup and brought it to the table. The night still clung to the early morning and their voices were kept low to honor the silence of the hour.

Simon thanked her without looking up and reached to pour a cup of coffee. He missed the cup and the steaming coffee landed on the table and spilled on the leg of his clean sweat pants and the floor.

"Jesus Simon," his wife half yelled and half-whispered, "watch what you're doing!"

She raced to the sink to get a towel and a sponge to wipe the mess up. Lovingly, she cleaned the mess on the floor and did her best to clean his stained pant leg. She poured him a new cup of coffee and said, "I think that is gonna stain. If you take those off, I will make sure I get them clean for you."

Simon waved his arm and said, "It's okay honey, thanks anyway."

When he had taken his first sip, and she was sure he wasn't going to do any further damage, she left him to go upstairs and put on some clothes to drive him to the station.

She came back down in a few minutes and he was now sitting there with a bag packed and half his cup of coffee gone.

"Do you have everything you need? Did he tell you what you were supposed to bring?" Sarah asked.

Simon mumbled, "Yes. He sent me a list and I had Amy run to the store for me yesterday. I don't have to bring much, I guess they will give me everything I need. They asked me to bring four-inch masking tape for some reason. I got two-inch tape. I hope that is good enough."

By now, it was 5:32 and he knew he had to be at the station at 6. He said, "Sarah, I think we need to get going if we are going to get there on time."

Sarah already had the keys in her hand and turned off the kitchen light, "Ready when you are, soldier."

Simon cringed at the word "soldier," but got up, dragging his brown duffle bag to the door. He turned and looked at the dark kitchen for just a moment and knew this place would look very different when he came back. It was only three weeks he thought, but it felt like it was on the other side of the world.

Sarah walked out the door and he followed pulling the door closed behind him.

## Chapter 10

Jamal walked into the motel and asked Michelle, "Do you know where Tristan is?"

Michelle shrugged her shoulders and said, "I dunno why?"

"Because today is my last day and I need to tell him," said Jamal.

"What? Your *quitting*?" Michelle said with much dramatic emphasis.

"Yup," said Jamal, "Just got a $1000 signing bonus to start tomorrow and I'm moving to Florida."

"Who are you working for?" asked Michelle, still awestruck.

Jamal didn't know how to answer honestly so he said, " Umm... a new start-up that found my resume online and wants me bad. Didn't even know I was still posted on that website, but they saw it and called while I was on my way to work. They said they wired me $1000 to get a bus and get down there tomorrow and I just got the confirmation text. So I'm done here. Now I gotta tell Tristan. When did you see him last?"

"I think he is in the laundry room. One of the cleaning girls got busted with drugs and he had to go down to fire her," said Michelle.

"Great, he'll be in an awesome mood then, right?" said Jamal.

"You know it," said Michelle.

Jamal took the service stairs down to the basement and walked the long gray hallway lined with carts of towels and linens and cleaning buckets. He saw a light and heard voices coming from the laundry.

He peeked his head, cautiously, around the corner and saw Tristan yelling at three of the Mexican girls who were supposed to be upstairs cleaning rooms. "What do you mean you found it in a room? Don't you realize this stuff can kill you?" he yelled.

Jamal cleared his throat and Tristan turned to him and said, "Oh Jamal, it's you. I'll be done here in a minute. Can you wait for me down the hall?"

Jamal nodded and walked six feet down the hall and stood against the wall.

He couldn't hear the rest of the conversation, but could tell Tristan was not a happy man. The girls came out first, crying. They walked past Jamal down the hallway. Tristan came out after, visibly upset.

"What do you need Jamal?" asked Tristan, "this day has been total shit."

"I am afraid it's not gonna get much better," said Jamal, "I need to quit."

"What are you talking about, you can't quit?" Tristan argued, "Who is going to watch the lobby at night?"

"Yeah man, I am sorry, but I got a better job and I need to take it to feed my kids," said Jamal, "They gave me a signing bonus and everything to leave for Florida tomorrow and I have to do it."

Tristan got even more upset and kicked over a cart of towels. "Damn it, Jamal, you can't do this to me? I will have to work all night if you leave?"

"I hate to do this to you," apologized the former night desk clerk, "but they are paying me three times what I make here in a week and..."

"You know, Fuck you, man! I thought we were friends," said Tristan.

"A real friend wouldn't have just said that to me," said Jamal, who turned around and walked away, while the manager picked up towels and the spilled cart.

Jamal spoke to no one as he walked back into the lobby. He unpinned his gold name tag and threw it at the empty front desk and flung open the front door. An older couple with a poodle who were unloading their car were startled by the sudden motion.

The dog barked when Jamal walked out. For a moment, he felt embarrassed that they were watching him but remembered the $1000 in his pocket and the new life he was about to begin. He raised his chin and pushed out his chest. Looking the old man dead in the eye, he walked up to the couple, stood right in their face, and said, "woof,... woof."

He turned and walked down the driveway.

It took him an hour and a half to walk home. He thought all along the way. He wondered what it would be like in Florida and wondered what his mother would say. He wondered what his new job would look like and where Mr. Soros or Gus or The Hawk, or whatever his real name was, would be like for a boss? He wondered if he was making a major mistake because he wasn't even sure if this guy's name was real?

With all the thoughts flooding his brain, he walked most of the way home before he even knew it. As he walked up to the house, he saw things he hadn't noticed before. The brown patches on the yellowing lawn. The peeling paint on the eves of the house. The cracks in the driveway where the dandelions were coming up a month too early.

For the first time in his life, he felt shame about where he lived and wanted something more. He imagined that something more was coming, he just couldn't figure out what that something was.

As he walked in the front door. His two children were playing behind the coffee table and his mother was sitting in her chair with her feet raised. The television was on too loud, as always, and the smell of dinner cooking in the kitchen filled the room.

"Hey Ma," he said, taking off his coat and hanging it on the hooks behind the door. "Shhh," she said, "I'm watching my show. Now you kids hush up now."

He walked into the kitchen and peered in the oven. He saw a pile of chicken she spent the morning frying, keeping warm. A pot of green beans simmered with a massive ham hock on the stove and a tray of macaroni and cheese was cooling on a rack beside the stove. He called into the living room, "Ma this looks great, when are we eating?"

She called back, "When my program is done, now hush up so I can hear him talk."

He snuck a bite of the beans and went back to his bedroom. He changed into his street clothes. And tossed his uniform shirt in the trash. He took a moment to recognize the weight of that action.

Next, he pulled a brown duffel bag that he bought at the military surplus store, out of the closet. He stuffed his clothes and sneakers in it without ceremony. He grabbed his toothbrush from the bathroom and an unopened box of toothpaste from the medicine cabinet. He thought to himself, "I need to tell Ma that I took the last toothpaste."

With his clothes and toothbrush packed, he placed the bag in the middle of the bed and walked back down the hall to see if his mother was done watching her show. She was now in the kitchen and the children sat quietly on the couch watching cartoons.

He walked into the kitchen and his mother said before he could speak, "What are you doing home so early? Did you get fired?"

He said, "Naw Ma, I didn't get fired. I quit. I'm done at the hotel and I need to talk to you about that. Something really good has happened."

"It better be good," she said with annoyance, "because you got two little mouths to feed watching cartoons in the other room and I can't pay for three of you."

"Ma," he said, "I can pay for all three of you now."

"What are you talking about?" she asked.

"I got a new job," he said, pulling the wad of cash from his pocket, "that pays me $1000 a week."

"What do you mean a $1000 a week? Doing *what*?" she questioned, pushing her head forward with her right eyebrow dropped down and fist on her hip.

The position scared him and he stepped back, awaiting a swinging hand.

"I'm joining a new business venture of a client I met at the hotel. He said he will pay me $1000 a week to be his chief of staff and he will give me a car to drive, pay for my meals, and give me a place to stay."

"What do you need that for" she argued, "You have a place to stay, HERE."

"Yeah about that Ma, I am moving to Florida tomorrow at 6 AM."

"You're leaving your babies?" his mother said, softening her tone.

"Ma, I am doing something real, for the first time of my life. I'm gonna take care of all of you and send the money back to you when I get a checking account set up. He said he would help me with that too."

"You're serious?" she asked

"Yes ma'am I am," he replied.

"Alright slow down now, tell me what you're doing?" she asked again.

"I got a job offer to move to Florida with a man that is starting a new business and he will pay me $1000 a week, with a car, food, and shelter."

"How do you know this is real?" she asked, eyeing the money on the table.

"It's as real as that $1000 is sitting there, count it if you like. ten $100 bills, count it," he said.

She said, "I don't question your counting ability, it's your brain waves I question boy. What makes you think this is a good idea?"

"I don't know Ma," he said, "it's better than I am at right now, and even if it doesn't work, I gotta try," he said.

"Tell me about this man," she said.

"His name is uh...Mr. Soros... and he is starting a business down in Florida and he asked me if I would work for him and I said yes," answered Jamal.

"Yeah, but how do you know he is for real," she asked once again.

"I am not supposed to say too much," he explained, "but you know that big crowd of people out at the VFW with all those trailers and such?"

She nodded yes.

"Well one of them stayed with me at the hotel and we started talking late one night. He liked me and invited me down to see him at those trailers and I went there today."

"WHAT? You went there with those white folks carrying guns?" she screamed.

"Yes," he said, "calm down. There were some nice people there and no one said anything bad to me. The man invited me to have a beer and we talked and he offered me a job this time and I said yes"

"Don't tell me to calm down, they had guns, Jamal, every single person I saw had a gun, what do you think they are doing there? To me, it looks like they're planning to fight world war three. I have no idea why the police don't stop them, but with what's happening in this world right now there ain't nothing I can't believe. You are going to work with those people, are you crazy?"

He knew his mother loved him more than anything and he hated to hurt her. She was probably right to be worried, but he just wanted her to understand that he needed this and wasn't going to say no. What he did say though meant he would not be eating any chicken tonight or any time soon.

"Mom," he said while gathering his most forceful tone, "relax. I am a man now and I will make my own way in the world and you're just going to have to like it."

His ears rang immediately as she swung her left fist and knocked him to the ground. He thought for a moment about the phrase, "seeing stars," and realized they did look like stars when someone punched you in the face.

She stood over him and began to yell, but the ringing in his ears made her inaudible.

He tried to get up and she said, "Boy if you want to live one more day, you will stay down."

He pulled himself up by the handle of the stove and steadied himself. She could see she had hurt him and felt horrible for how hard she hit him but refused to give an inch.

"Mom, you can hit me all you like," he said with his voice wavering, "but I am leaving. Please watch my kids and I will send you money back."

He walked to the table, picked up one of the $100 bills, and shoved it in his pocket, leaving the rest of the cash on the table. He then walked out of the kitchen and stabilized himself on the door frame. He could hear his mother crying in the kitchen.

He went into his three-year-old and said, "You be good for Gramma." The child, unsure of what she had done wrong, began to cry. He continued, "and take care of your little brother. I love you, Serena. Don't cry." She said with her bottom lip quivering, "I love you too Daddy." His son, barely 18 months old, looked up quizzically at his father and began to chew on the label of his stuffed bear.

Jamal walked back to his bedroom, grabbed his duffel bag, and walked out the front door without looking back. He heard his mother call his name, just as the door closed behind him, but swore that he would never come back until he made something of himself. He ran up the street and stopped at the bus stop.

A half-hour passed, as he sat on the bench, reading the graffiti on the glass windscreen. At 5:30, the bus arrived and he climbed aboard the bus. He swiped his card and rode the bus to the other side of town. He got off at the mall where he spent $12 on an egg roll and lo mein from Panda Express with a coke. He missed having the chicken that smelled so good at home.

At 8 PM, he got on to the last bus of the day and rode it back to the hotel where he used to work. He held onto his key card when he left and let himself in the back door.

He went up to the fourth floor where he knew they never rented any rooms unless there was some sort of convention in town. He swiped his card and room 436 opened and he went inside.

He put his bag on the far queen bed and pulled the sheet back on the one closest to the door. He knew no one would walk down this hallway until at least 9 AM the next day, and he had the floor to himself.

He took off his shoes and shirt and laid on the cold white sheets feeling the fine cloth on his bare back. It was something he had never done while he worked there, but imagined how good it would feel all the time. He was right. It felt like heaven.

He clicked on the TV and checked the minifridge hoping to find a stray beer or bottle of something someone might have left, but the room was empty. A movie he had never seen was on the television. He watched it for ten minutes before he fell asleep.

At 2 AM, he awoke because he was freezing. The lights were all on and an infomercial was playing on the television. He clicked off the TV and stretched across the bed to pick up his tee-shirt off the floor.

He walked to the bathroom, opened the toothpaste, and brushed his teeth. "Damn It, I forgot to tell Ma," he thought. After spitting out the suds and rinsing out his mouth, he turned off the bathroom light and returned to the bed, this time pulling the comforter up to his chin.

He turned off the light and closed his eyes, but quickly turned it back on. He set an alarm on his phone for 5 AM. He didn't want to be late on his first day. "I have three hours until I have to leave, I better get some sleep," he thought.

He fell back to sleep quickly, and it seemed that he was only asleep for a few moments when the alarm went off. He undressed quickly, despite the chilly early mooring air, walked over to the heater, and cranked it to 90. He then went in, started the shower, and made the water as hot as he could stand it, and showered.

By the time he was done, the room was a pleasant 90 degrees and he dried, got dressed, and packed his things to leave. He turned the heater off as a matter of habit and shut the door behind him as quietly as he could manage. He snuck down the back stairway and out into the cool morning air.

Walking the two miles to the VFW at this hour seemed very foreign to him. It all looked slightly different. When he got to the line of trailers, a guard stopped him and asked, "Who are you and what's your purpose here?" The automatic weapon pointed at Jamal gave him a sense of fear and his mind went blank and his mouth went dry.

"Well..." the guard insisted.

"I..I...I'm Jamal Reese. I'm here to start work for The Hawk."

The guard lowered his weapon and said, "Oh yeah, I heard about you. Do you know where you're going? The Hawk is packing up to leave and is down by the fuel depot."

Jamal said, "I am not sure I know where that is?"

The guard pointed to a row of trailers and said, "Go down that second row, and all the way at the end, you'll see two tanker trucks. He's down there."

Jamal said, "Thank you, sir," and walked briskly toward the trailers.

When he got to the end he could see The Hawk fueling a pickup truck that was attached to a trailer.

"Hawk?" Jamal called out. Gus turned and saw him and said, "Glad you could make it. Right on time."

Jamal checked his phone and it said 5:57.

"So what's the plan?" asked Jamal

"The way I see it," Gus said, "we have about 20 hours of driving with this trailer. I'll take the first three hours and then you can take three and we can alternate and be there by tomorrow morning. Stow your bag in the trailer and I will finish up fueling."

Jamal walked back to the trailer and opened the door. There were several dozen crates on the floor that were painted army green and marked "M-16." He wasn't positive what those were but he figured that he better not ask. He put his bag next to the stack on the floor and went back up to the front.

Gus was putting the cap back in the gas tank and closed the door and said," Y'all set? What did your Mom say?"

Jamal smiled and said, "She made me see stars."

"Well, it's good to know you can take a punch. Climb in let's go," said Gus.

The truck rumbled to life and the morning silence was broken. The unlikely team of men towing a trailer, a load of illegal weapons, and a mission to reclaim America pulled onto the road and headed South.

Gus imagined that this was exactly how General Lee must have felt when he entered Gettysburg more than a hundred and fifty years prior.

## Chapter 11

Simon leaned over to kiss his wife goodbye and she tried to wrap her arms around him. Her hand got caught on the rearview mirror and she couldn't figure out how to get her arm around his back. Simon joked, "Maybe we should do this outside the car."

Neither was dressed for company, but they didn't care, as no one could see them in the darkness. The sun was just beginning to come up behind the trees.

They met at the hood of the car and he grabbed her face with both hands and kissed her.
He could feel her rise up on her toes and the warmth of her body against his made them forget, for a moment, how chilled the early morning hour was through their sweatpants.

When he let her face go, she fell back down again and said, "I'm going to miss you, Simon Gates."

He answered her saying only, "Me too."

She said, "You better get going, it's almost 6."

He looked at his phone. The time said 5:57. The lights were just coming on in the building and when they got there, the place looked abandoned. As the moments clicked by, life began to rise from all directions. An army green tractor-trailer truck lumbered in the parking lot and the wind of the trailer blew Sarah's hair in her face.

Simon pulled her hair back and said, "I need to see your face one more time." She smiled and then grimaced because of the hour and the cold. "Don't do that," he said, "you're beautiful."

She laughed and said, "If you think I'm beautiful now, wait until you come back in three weeks and I have showered."

He shook his head and smiled.

He let her go and went to the trunk to get his bag. He came back and he could tell she was shivering, "You're cold, get in the car. Get warm."

Sarah said, "Just one more kiss," pulling him close to her and kissing him. She pulled away saying, "I will always love you."

He looked up at the bus he heard starting in the back lot and said, "I have always loved you... and always will."

He began walking toward the building and she held his hand a bit longer and let go as she watched his arm fall by his side. She could see the fear in his eyes and the hesitation in his walk. She turned away and got back in the car where the heater was blasting when her hands began to sting.

He watched her pull away before he touched the door handle. When he could no longer see the car, he thumbed the latch and pulled the door open. The smell of a World War II battleship struck him again, as he walked on what looked like a new floor mat.

A coffee pot was gurgling by the wall and a hum of activity seemed to pervade the room. The desks were now all lined in rows and a half dozen people in Army uniforms sat at them typing or talking on the phone. Each desk now had a new laptop and the old Commodore 64 was nowhere to be seen.

He looked over to where he thought he remembered Altieri's office was and a half dozen or so men stood around the opening with no sign of Altieri. He approached the group and one man turned around and made eye contact with Simon.

As Simon neared the group, the man said, "You look like a victim too?"

The group of men laughed quietly and made space for Simon to join the pack. Another man who had a wild beard and weighed at least 300 pounds said, "I haven't been up this early in a while? Most of my clients won't even let me on their property until 10 AM."

The first man said, "What is it that you do?"

The bearded man said, "I am a landscaper. The old ladies in Greenwich need their beauty sleep. I guess it's too late for me."

The men snickered. Simon suggested, "Maybe it would help if we knew each other's names, my name is Simon Gates. I have an insurance agency here in town up by the old Sikorski plant."

The bearded man said his name was Phil Vagnini. The first man who eyed him said his name was Bob Richardson and that he owned a copy place in town. Two other men joined in and said their names were Jos Scizlicki and Matt Taminetti. They told the others that they were partners in a repair shop in Lordship. Simon decided his suggestion was a bad one because he was too hungover to remember any names.

185

A feminine voice spoke up from behind the men. The group turned in surprise to see a woman standing there in jeans and a sweatshirt. She said, "My name is Jessinia Thomas. I have a contracting company in Milford."

Phil stroked his beard and said, "I didn't know this was coed?"

Simon replied, "From what I hear, they'll take anyone. Look at me."

Simon realized he needed to sit down and asked, "When do you think we'll be leaving? Has anyone seen Lieutenant Altieri?"

Bob Richardson said, "He is in his office. He said he had to finish a couple of things before we got started."

The door opened and Altieri stepped out into the hall. The group parted when they saw him.

"Well it looks like this group has made it here," said Altier, "I just spoke to Hartford and they said they are missing two guys, but that they expect they will show up by the time we get there. Are you all ready to go?"

Simon raised his hand and said, "Lieutenant?"

Altieri replied with an official tone, "What's up Gates?"

"I haven't seen any papers or signed anything, shouldn't we be doing some paperwork or something?"

Altieri said, "Good question Gates. You will all be doing your indoc paperwork up in Springfield. You all brought your driver's licenses and birth certificates right?"

Simon said, "No, I don't recall you telling me anything about bringing a birth certificate?"

Bob Richardson said, "Me neither."

Altieri played it off saying, "No worries gentlemen, you can have your folks at home send it to you at Indoc. There's plenty of time for that." he continued, "Well if that's it, let's get on the bus."

They followed Altieri to the back of the building, where they could see a bright sign that read exit. He pushed the door open and shoved a wood wedge under it to hold it. He stood at attention as the people filed out the door.

A bus was running with the interior lights on a few yards from the door. The sky was almost fully lit now, although Simon could not tell if it had risen yet or not.

Bob Richardson got on first, followed by Phil and then Simon. Jessinia went next, followed by Joe and Matt. Everyone sat in their seat and a large man climbed on board to drive the bus. Simon closed his eyes and leaned his head against the window. He was asleep before the bus even left the parking lot.

His next thought came when he opened his eyes. He looked up and saw the big blue onion on the old Colt Armory next to the shuttered I-91. The sound of sirens screamed by the bus as they sat with cars stopped all around them. The road was covered with smoke and no one seemed to be moving.

Simon leaned forward to Bob Richardson who was sitting in the seat in front and asked, "What happened? Are we there yet?"

Bob Richardson turned and his face was ashen, "Did you see what just happened?"

"No, I was sleeping," replied Simon. His head was feeling better, but his stomach was still sore from throwing up. What he was craving now was a big sandwich with bacon. He consoled his hangover with a bottle of water that Amy had packed for him in his bag.

"That school bus over there just exploded," said Bob Richardson.

The driver of the bus yelled back, "Is everyone ok? I don't think we were hit with anything."

Simon peered through the front window of the bus. The shell of a school bus was perpendicular to traffic on top of some jersey barriers with flames shooting from the back and sides. A body lay hanging out of the parting door with blood everywhere. Simon noticed the words of some school system he had never heard of on the side with a huge hole in the roof as the flames and smoke poured from the frames of the blown-out windows that remained.

Simon rose to take a better look. He could see the car in front of the bus had all its windows blown out but wasn't on fire. Beyond that, he could see a giant black crater had been blown around the bus. The cars that had been driving next to the bus just moments before were flipped over and burning.

"Jesus Christ," said Phil as he rose next to Simon, "should we try to help? Hey Driver, what's the plan?"

"I am gonna try and get around the mess and get off on the next road- that is where we are supposed to be anyway." said the driver, "We'll get our orders from there. Everybody have a seat and let me see if I can get through here."

The Army bus had a reinforced frame and bars over the radiator with an oversized steel plate bumper. The driver shifted the bus to a lower gear and nudged the car in front of him. The driver inside the car was unconscious. He used the bus to nudge the car to move far enough forward so that a lane opened between the line of traffic and the jersey barrier. He backed up and pulled the bus into the newly-created breakdown lane.

A line of police, fire, and ambulances were streaming down the highway above and the driver honked as if to thank them. He pushed the bus into a higher gear and began picking up speed and drove past the wreckage. Simon could see people sitting in their burning cars, through the smoke that filled the air.

The driver was able to maneuver the bus onto another road that Simon had been on before but did not know the name. He didn't look at his phone but thought it must be close to 7:30 by now. Simon was surprised at the speed at which this driver weaved through relatively sparse city traffic at this hour.

They moved at an incredible pace that made some of the passengers nervous. Phil joked, "Hey you're scaring some of the people back here? You got a hot date or something?"

The driver paid no attention and pushed on with his speed unaltered. He called back, "I drove convoys through Kabul before I got this job. It's all coming back to me." He took a hard swing around a circle and accelerated as he flew past the State Buildings on Elm street before appearing in front of the state capital. Taking a hard left he drove down a quiet street with the State Capitol on their right and took a quick left onto a wider road that went around the Capitol Building.

Simon stopped watching the driving and pulled out his phone, it was only 7:14. He punched a text into his phone "IM OK. TRUCK EXpLODED in Hartford will Call you when I can." He selected Sarah's name and hit send. She replied immediately and said, "OK I love you."

He wanted to scroll his Facebook feed to see if there was some news about the explosion, but the driver turned hard and he could not focus. His stomach would not let him look at his phone any longer, so he closed it.

The bus came to a hard stop at the State Armory and a military officer came out and got on the bus. "Well, folks I hear you had some fireworks this morning? I got five people to join you and you will be heading right out to Springfield."

Jessinia spoke up and said, "Shouldn't we stop and see if the authorities want to talk to us, we saw it explode?"

"Ma'am you are on a US Army bus," explained the officer, "and on your way to becoming US Army personnel. So as far as I am concerned, you are US Army and someone will talk to the authorities on your behalf. That's the way we do things here, you'll get used to it."

He spoke quietly to the driver who nodded and walked to the front of the bus where he waived to the door. A line of five men walked to the bus and climbed aboard.

The five men walked past the six passengers and each found a seat of their own. Phil quipped as they walked by, "Welcome to the Army gentlemen, you missed the fun part."

All five had wide eyes and Simon had figured they were informed about what happened on their way in. He decided that he would try and fall back asleep and pulled his hood up over his head. He leaned against the window and closed his eyes.

As they pulled onto the base, Simon saw a sign that said Westover Army Air Base. The driver paused at a gate where a helmeted man carrying an M16 waived him in. They drove another few minutes and Simon texted his wife, "We're here at Westover. I'm safe." She replied once again immediately and said, "Good."

The bus finally came to a stop in front of a beige building that had a sign that read "US Military Entrance Processing Command." A man in fatigues came out to the bus and stepped aboard.

"My name is Sergeant Maxwell Saugus. I will be your trainer for the next three weeks and I hope we will become very good friends. I realize you are volunteers and that this is the first class under a new program where we will train people from civilian life to become soldiers in a few short weeks. You are coming here at a time when your Nation needs you and I want to thank you now for your service. I may become quite agitated or I may even yell at you in the next few weeks. I do this because I want you to survive if you ever get in the shit. I have been told you have already experienced some of the antics of the opposition this morning and were a bit uneasy about that. You may as well get over that now because you will experience more like that and much worse I imagine before we are all done. Welcome to the Army, now get off my bus and make a line in front of this building ."

He didn't yell but spoke very loudly, thought Simon. He grabbed his bag and joined the line as they walked off the bus and formed a line in front of the building.

The sun was fully up now and a frost covered the grassy areas of the lawn around the sign. Three other trainers joined the sergeant who began talking very quietly, but in uncomfortable proximity to one of the faces of the men from Harford. Simon took his hood down and stood as straight as he could staring forward with his bag at his feet. His phone rang in his pocket and he was deciding if he should check it or not when a large black trainer came over and got an inch from his face.

"Please put your phone on silent at your earliest convenience sir," he said, not quite yelling, but somehow screaming in a whisper. "We will not be playing with phones for the next three weeks. I also will not yell at you when you do stupid shit like let your phone ring when I am talking at you. Instead, I will get in your face and chew on your ass until you are absolutely certain that you have learned to turn your phone off when information is being relayed. Is that clear?"

"Yes sergeant," said Simon as his phone stopped ringing.

"Well, at least you got that right. I work for a living. Nicely done. What's your name, soldier?"

"Simon sir," replied Simon.

"Am I your girlfriend Simon or am I your drill sergeant?" the sergeant began to yell, "I don't care what your first name is, what is your last name, Simon?"

"Oh sorry, Gates, sergeant."

"No need to apologize, Gates," he ramped up his voice as he addressed the entire class, "Do you now all understand that from here on out you will answer to your last name?"

The class answered, "Yes drill sergeant."

"Excellent now, everyone together, Ten Hut."

The class put their arms at their sides and puffed their chest out.

"Welcome to the United States Army. Now fall out and get ready for rack assignments. Disssss-missed."

The class scattered and ran into the building.

The door opened into a common room with a TV and microwave. Off the main room lead a narrow hallway with doors alternating down each side. The eleven volunteers stood looking down the hall with their bags in hand.

Sergeant Saugus stepped in the door removing his cover, saying, "Your barracks assignment is posted on each door. Find your assignment now."

The class quickly filed into the hallway and began eyeing each door as they walked. Jessinia saw her name first in the first room on the right. Phil was across from her with Bob Richardson. Simon found his room next with a man named Anthony Paladino who was one of the group of men they picked up in Hartford.

As they walked in, they saw their names on sticky notes attached to each bunk. Gates was on the lower bunk and Paladino's name was on the note on the upper bunk.

Simon placed his bag next to the bunk and opened the closet on the left-hand side of the room. There were two desks, two bureaus, two sets of shelves above the desks on the far wall with a window, and two closets on each side of the room by the wall with the door. The bunk beds were situated opposite the bureaus, on the left side of the room.

The floor shined with a fresh coat of wax and the room smelled like pine cleaner.

They heard the sergeant's voice bellow down the hallway, "You have five minutes to stow your gear and post up outside your doors. Whenever you hear me yell 'POST', you will drop whatever it is you are doing and join me in the hallway by your door. Do you understand?"

The class' answer echoed down the empty hallway, "YES drill sergeant."

Simon stashed his bag in the closet and checked his phone for the missed call. It was his wife calling to check on him, which he found out from reading her three text messages. He cleared the messages and the call and put his phone on silent and placed it in his bag.

Closing the closet door, he turned and looked up to find Paladino sitting on his bunk. "Hey my name is Simon, but I guess you have to call me Gates," Simon said.

Paladino hopped down and extended his hand, "I'm Tony."

Simon guessed he was about 35 and asked him, "What do you do in real life?"

Paladino said, "I have an auto body shop in New Britain. My wife is running it while I am gone, how about you?"

"I have an Insurance Agency in Stratford. Don't you think it's strange that they chose all small business owners to do this?" asked Simon.

"Yeah, I think they were looking for people they didn't have to pay who could survive without a paycheck," said Paladino.

Simon replied, "You're probably right. Pretty smart, don't you think? We better get ready to move."

A booming voice echoed down the hallway, "POST!"

Eleven bodies poured into the hallway and stood at attention on either side of the door.

"Welcome to your new home," the large black sergeant who yelled at Simon said, "I did not properly introduce myself or my colleagues outside and will now take this time to do so. I am Sergeant Jose Rodriguez. I believe you have met Sergeant Maxwell Saugus and this is Sergeant Justin Cromwell," he said as he motioned to a very tall and skinny man with a red buzz cut.

"I hope you have enjoyed getting acquainted with your barracks," he continued, "You will become very comfortable with your accommodations because you will keep them clean and well ordered. Once a week on Fridays, we will inspect your quarters for cleanliness, order, and adherence to regulations. You will keep them in inspection worthy condition at all times. Do you understand?"

"YES, drill sergeant!"

"Our next item on the agenda item will involve taking you over to the administrative building to complete your indoc paperwork. When we are done, please lay into your quarters and grab your wallets and birth certificate if you brought them. If you did not bring any of the required paperwork, please let Janice at Admin know so she can arrange to get a copy on your behalf. While I am on the subject of your birth, I realize that most of you are, shall we say,...a bit more mature than our average recruit. We have modified our training schedule to allow for your more advanced age and would like to encourage you to be cognizant of your physical needs at all times. If you get injured, please let us know at your earliest convenience so we may obtain medical treatment for you. You will be afforded 8 hours of sleep per night and three hot meals per day. Meals are served for exactly one-half hour at 0630, 1200, and 1800. If you are late for a meal, you will miss a meal. If you miss a meal, you will go hungry. Please do not be late for meals."

The sergeant continued, "Revelry is at 0530 where we will begin the day with morning calisthenics in the yard out front. Today we will be doing medical evaluations to determine what level of physical conditioning your aging bodies might endure. I will reiterate if you get injured let us know immediately. Taps sounds promptly at 2200. Tattoo is 15 minutes prior to Taps. You will be expected to be in your racks promptly at 2200 and Tattoo will make that possible by giving you fifteen minutes to get yourself in your rack. If you are late getting in your rack, you will owe me one push up for every minute you are late. Please do not be late for taps."

"Sargeant Cromwell," his tone softened, "would you please brief the troops on personal procedures."

Cromwell was enthusiastic, to say the least, "GOOOOOOD MORNING VOLUNTEERS. MY NAME IS JUSTIN CROMWELL. THERE ARE TWO HEADS FOR YOU PERSONAL CARE NEEDS LOCATED IN THIS BARRACKS. ONE IS LOCATED ON THE SOUTH END OF THIS BUILDING AND IS FOR MALE VOLUNTEERS ONLY. ANY FEMALES CAUGHT ENTERING THE MALE HEAD WILL BE DISCIPLINED. THERE IS A SECOND HEAD LOCATED IN THIS BARRACKS ON THE NORTH END OF THIS FACILITY WHERE ALL FEMALE VOLUNTEERS MAY ADDRESS THEIR PERSONAL CARE NEEDS. ANY MALES CAUGHT ENTERING THE NORTH HEAD WILL BE DISCIPLINED. YOU WILL BE EXPECTED TO SHOWER DAILY AND TAKE PARTICULAR CARE OF YOUR TEETH, EXTREMITIES, AND YOUR CREVICES. AS THERE ARE 10 MALES AND ONLY THREE COMMODES, YOU WILL BE REQUIRED TO TAKE TURNS SO FIGURE THAT OUT FOR YOURSELVES. YOU WILL ALSO BE EXPECTED TO MAINTAIN THE CLEANLINESS OF THE HEADS THAT WILL ALSO BE INSPECTED AT FRIDAY INSPECTIONS. THIS SHOULD OFFSET ANY INCONVENIENCE AS THERE ARE TEN MALES TO CARE FOR THE SOUTH HEAD AND ONE FEMALE TO CARE FOR THE NORTH HEAD. PLEASE DO NOT EVER ACCUSE THE US ARMY OF ANY PREFERENTIAL TREATMENT. DO YOU UNDERSTAND?"

"YES, drill sergeant!"

"I believe that concludes my portion of this presentation sergeants," said Cromwell, "they're yours, Sergeant Saugus."

"Thank you, Sergeant Cromwell," said Sergeant Saugus winding up to a holler, "ALRIGHT VOLUNTEERS WE HEAD FOR ADMIN IN TWO MINUTES. LAY IN TO GET YOUR IDS AND FALL IN IN THE YARD FOR ASSEMBLY IN EXACTLY ONE MINUTE AND 45 SECONDS. DIIIIIISSSSS-MISSED."

The hallway erupted with movement as the volunteers popped into their rooms, grabbed their IDs, and ran out front. They lined up shoulder to shoulder as they did before. When the sergeants came out they yelled, "TEN-HUT," and the class came to attention.

Saugus walked out and said, "Now I will teach you to walk. It's not that hard. I believe you have done it before, one foot in front of the other. Your hands should not move more than six inches in front or in back of your leg, as your arms swing to the sides. Please close your hands into a fist with your thumb outside and lined up along the seam of your pants. I will ask you all to walk in cadence and I will call the cadence as we make our way over to Admin. Do you understand?"

"YES, drill sergeant!"

"Left Face."

The class turned left.

"Alright, that sucked, lets try that again."

Everyone chuckled.

"RAAAAAGHT FACE"

The class turned back to the front.

"Eyes," said Saugus. The entire class looked at the sergeant as he said, "I will demonstrate a proper left facing turn."

The sergeant spun on his left heel and stomped his right boot next to his left boot.

"NOW YOU DO IT. LEEEEEEFT FACE!"

The class snapped left in one synchronized movement.

"There is hope for our nation yet," said Saugus, "Forward Mahharchhhhhhh. You're left, you're left, you're left, raught left."

As the platoon marched down the perfectly manicured lane, the sergeant's voice echoed in the budding tree branches.

---

That was the first time Simon had ever heard "Tattoo." He checked his phone and it said 9:45 PM. They were punctual if nothing else, he thought.

His first day in the Army went fine. The sergeants never missed a chance to dig in the fact that they were younger than all the volunteers and that they were getting a "modified," version of training.

He dialed his wife and hoped he could finish the conversation before Paladino got back from the head. The phone rang and went to voicemail. This was the first time in seven years that he had not spoken to his wife before going to bed and it bothered him. He texted her and said, "Good night my sweet I love you." She didn't reply.

He scrolled through Facebook and saw a post from the Connecticut Journal that read, " Terrorist Plot Ends With Premature Explosion in State Capital." He clicked on it with interest.

"What started with a plan to blow up the State Capital, ended in a fiery explosion near the Colt Armory Monday morning during rush hour traffic. Two rebels, who posted a video claiming responsibility for blowing up the State Capitol building, were killed when the school bus they had filled with fertilizer and propane tanks exploded prematurely.

Two alleged assailants, a married couple from Ohio named Jim and Joan Justice, were killed when the bomb they were planning on delivering to the state capital exploded prematurely in traffic killing 12 and injuring scores of others."

"Jesus," thought Simon, "we were right next to them most of the way up and didn't know it."

Paladino walked in and Simon said, "You know that bus that blew up on the highway when we were coming to get you guys?"

Paladino nodded.

"It was a rebel couple who were driving a bomb to Hartford to blow up the State Capital building and it went off on them and killed them," explained Simon.

Paladino said, "My God, that's crazy."

"Christ I know it," said Simon.

"Did you get hold of your wife?" asked Paladino.

"No she was up early with me, she probably fell asleep," said Simon, "I texted her. She'll get back to me when she gets the message."

The sound of Taps started playing and Paladino shut off the desk light and hopped into bed pulling the covers over his white legs. Simon had never slept this close to another man before and wasn't sure he could handle it.

The hallway echoed with Saugus' voice, " Good night volunteers. America thanks you for your service. See you at 0530 for cals."

The hall went dark, except for the red glow of the emergency signs and within minutes Simon was asleep. It seemed exhaustion always had a way of making new sleeping arrangements work.

## Chapter 12

As the miles ticked off, Gus began to think about how he came to be and where he was. Like so many men he knew, he didn't always hate America. He just hated what it had become.

That was one of the reasons why he resigned his commission in the Army and went to work for Dark Pond. At least they had one function and everyone knew it, making money. That life was simple. There were no politics. There were no bad guys. There were no good guys. Just people with guns.

Who knew that 20 years later, he would be driving a trailer full of weapons to Florida and Frank Crawford would be one of the reasons he was doing it.

Frank and Gus joined Dark Pond at the same time. Frank came from a tour in Afghanistan and Gus had just finished his last tour in Iraq. Both were getting sick of Army life and Dark Pond seemed like a good fit.

The two became friends and Gus admired his no-nonsense approach to combat. Frank didn't show weakness or fear, but he also didn't show mercy. When Frank fired on that family in the station wagon in Fallujah, he knew they weren't approaching his principal, but he shot anyway. He killed three kids and a mother with a baby in her arms. Gus didn't like it but always thought Frank would have his back when it came down to it.

When they indicted the four other operatives who shot at the car with Frank, Gus thought Frank would be dragged into it. For some reason, however, they declined to include Frank in the indictments. When Herzog pardoned the four men, Gus thought that would be the end of it forever.

He would have stayed with Dark Pond until his retirement if Frank didn't go political. Gus knew Frank wanted to run for office someday and wouldn't have ever told anyone about what he saw that day on the job, especially after the President pardoned the other guys, but Frank couldn't leave it alone.

Gus remembered his last words with Frank.

"Buddy I trust you, but I need some assurance that you will never come back and tell stories about what we did here?" said Frank with a smile, as he was packing to head back.

"Of course I won't. Why would you even worry about that?" said Gus.

"Because my campaign advisor says I have to. Just know, if I ever hear you have been telling stories, I'm gonna have to kill you?" Frank said with a bigger smile.

"Yeah right, you'd kill me?" said Gus with a chuckle.

"No, your right, *I'd* never kill you," said Frank as the smile went away from his face. "If you were gonna get dead, you'd never know it was me. Now Do the right thing and shut the fuck up."

That was when Gus decided to leave Dark Pond and started his personal security consulting firm. If Frank had just left him alone, he never would have even written *The Plan*, but five years later when the feds showed up that morning and seized his weapons, he knew Frank had something to do with it.

He was providing security for a civil rights attorney when they pulled his license to carry. It was an entirely manufactured weapons charge. When they leaked the story that he was selling black-market weapons, he lost every single client on the same day. They didn't even ask if it was true, they just dropped him.

That was when he started seeing how corrupt the system was and decided that he would fix it.

The pain in his lower back ripped him from his thoughts and back to his driving. He looked at his phone. It was time for Jamal to take a turn.

The truck brakes chattered as he slowed the rig on the off-ramp. The load was heavier than he expected and stopping became more and more of a challenge as they headed south on these back roads.

I-95 would have been much easier, but with it shut down, they had to wind along sideroads. For the most part that meant that they avoided State Police and that was a good thing. The bad thing was the ride was going to take more like 26 hours and they were barely 8 hours in.

The slowing motion woke Jamal, who had been asleep since the Virginia border.

"I need a break and we need gas," said Gus. Gus had been driving since they started, breaking the three-hour agreement, but he knew the kid had a rough day, saying goodbye yesterday and Gus needed the kid rested if things got bad.

Gus felt pretty sure they would be ok as long as they stayed under the speed limit and off the radar, but he needed a restroom break badly and his sciatica was beginning to act up. The kid could take over from here for a while, he thought.

"I imagine you would like to eat something as you haven't had a thing all day and I need a restroom. Let's stop here and recharge. You can drive for the next 100 miles OK?"

Jamal wiped the sleep from his eyes and yawned, saying, " Yes sir."

Gus set the emergency brake and got out of the truck. He walked fast to the restroom and didn't look back to see what Jamal was doing. He figured that they weren't that busy and no one would complain if he took a spot at the pumps while he used the bathroom.

When he got back, Jamal was sitting on the footboard next to the pump. "If you left a card I could have started pumping," Jamal said.

"Yeah we got time," Gus said, handing him a credit card, "Fill it up with premium. We need the good stuff if we are gonna keep this load on the road. What do you want to eat? I hear they got some pretty good chicken here. Would you eat a few pieces if I bought some?"

Jamal said, "Yes sir," lifting the nozzle to insert into the gas tank. He remembered the chicken he missed last night and thought that there was no way this chicken would beat his mothers.

Gus walked into the store and saw a middle-aged Indian man behind the counter, counting packs of cigarettes. Next to him was a woman in a burka, stirring a vat of macaroni and cheese in the case.

"May I get a bucket of 12 pieces and some of that macaroni and cheese please?" asked Gus. He noticed the sign under the security camera in the corner behind the register that read, "Smile and Pray to Allah if you think you're stealing anything!"

The woman asked, "we have crispy and original which would you like?"

Gus said, "Mix it up however you like. I'm going to run back and get some drinks, is that ok?"

The woman had already turned and was reaching into the case to pick out his chicken.

He went to the back of the store and got a dozen Pepsis and some ice. He also pulled a styrofoam cooler down from on top of the soda case and held it up to the man in front saying, "How much is this?"

"$4.99 with a bag of ice or $3.99 without," the man said

Gus put the ice in the cooler and the box of soda on top and walked to the front where he saw his bag of chicken and a container of mac and cheese sitting on the counter. A television chirped from behind the counter. Gus opened an ear to listen when he heard."A husband and wife team from Ohio was killed this morning in the Connecticut State capital when their school bus filled with explosives they were driving exploded in rush hour traffic killing a dozen and wounding dozens more. The couple, Jim and Joan Justice, who were known seditionists and ardent Donald Herzog supporters..."

"Jesus, can you turn that up Mister?" asked Gus of the man behind the counter.

The man complied and turned the volume to max.

The news continued, "The man and wife posted a video to Facebook claiming credit for blowing up the Connecticut State Capitol but inadvertently set their school bus bomb off prematurely while they sat in traffic next to I-91 in Hartford, Connecticut killing a dozen passengers in cars in the traffic that surrounded them. The bomb also killed two pedestrians who were walking along the roadway. Tisha Sauers is at a press conference in Hartford right now where Connecticut State Police who are investigating are speaking, "Thanks Tom, I'm with Connecticut State Police Spokesman...."

"Wow that sounds horrible," said Gus, "What do I owe you?"

"$32.79," said the man behind the counter.

Gus handed him a $50 and waited for change. Jamal walked in and said, "We're all filled up, do you mind if I hit the restroom?"

Gus said, " It's in the back. I will meet you in the truck. Let's get moving, we're in a hurry"

When Jamal got to the truck, he wanted to ask Gus what the hurry was, but he saw that Gus was in the driver seat on the phone. He climbed in on the passenger side and listened. The cab smelled of chicken and Jamal heard him say, "Jim and Joan are dead. They blew themselves up in Connecticut."

Jamal didn't say anything but heard a voice on the other end speaking slow and steady. "John," Gus said, "Do they have any connection to us?" Gus nodded his head and hung up the phone without saying anything.

"What's up?" asked Jamal.

"A couple of friends had some trouble in Connecticut and didn't make it out. Was just calling to check with the brass to see what the plan was. There are no changes on our end," said Gus.

"I thought you wanted me to drive?" asked Jamal

"I changed my mind for now" answered Gus, "The brakes felt funny when we got off the road. I think it would be better if I had the tiller until we got into some more quiet areas."

Jamal looked around and could only see hills and trees and wondered what he classified as quiet. Jamal took a big bite of fried chicken breast and assured himself that this wasn't nearly as good as his mom's chicken, but since he hadn't eaten anything since the Chinese food at the mall the night before, it tasted better than anything he had ever eaten before.

Gus turned on the radio and tuned the station to a news talk station, so Jamal focused on his chicken and took a swig of Pepsi.

## Chapter 13

"They'll be here in 10 mins," shouted Simon down the hall. Today was the first inspection. If it went well, the sergeants promised the class that they could get a few hours of liberty.

Paladino drew the short straw, with Taminetti, and was down in the head cleaning. Simon was just finishing up the last few details of making the room ready for inspection.

He ran a dust cloth along the window ledge and over each mullion. He wiped the walls down on each side of the window and made sure that the window was locked. Phil got two demerits for having an unlocked window on Wednesday and everyone thought Cromwell was going to have an aneurysm when he found it.

Paladino darted in the room. He had a bead of sweat on his brow and his garrison cover was sliding down on his forehead. "Alright I'm done in the head," said Paladino, out of breath. "I cleaned everything from the light covers to that little space behind the valve on the urinal. If they find anything wrong in there, I will lick it clean myself," joked Paladino.

Simon darted to the door and began feverishly taping off Paladino's pant legs saying, "you got toilet paper lint all down your leg, what did you do roll in it?"

Simon found out the hard way that he had brought the wrong tape. During Tuesday's session on uniform standards, Saugus was showing them all how to remove lint. He pulled out a four-inch roll of masking tape and made three stripes of it on the front of his pants, that he wrapped around his hand with the sticky side out. When he checked with each of the volunteers, he almost died laughing when he saw

Simon's two-inch tape. That was Saugus' running joke all week, Gates with the tiny tape. No one dared crack a smile, but he knew everyone had laughed at him on the inside.

His first mission today on liberty was to go get some four-inch masking tape and begin taping off correctly. Paladino had taken pity on the poor soul and allowed Simon to use his tape until Simon could get some proper tape. Simon swore to himself that he'd buy a roll of tape for every damn person in the platoon including the sergeants.

A voice called down the hall, "Five minutes."

Paladino and Gates looked over the room.

There was not a space that a human had not touched or so they thought. They rose at 5 AM and started examining every place that might collect dust in the room. Just then Simon realized that he had not wiped the top of the closet doors.

"Shit," said Simon, "You're taller than me. Can you reach the top of the closet doors? I bet they check their first and I didn't clean up there."

Paladino took the cloth from Simon and reached above the first closet door on his tiptoes and ran the cloth down the length of the door's top edge. The cloth came back black. He spun and did the second door. That one was clean. He did the main door of the room next for good measure and found dust up there as well.

A voice yelled down the hall, "TEN-HUT, Platoon barracks ready for inspection, SIR."

Paladino shoved the dirty rag down the front of his pants and tucked in his shirt, refreshing the reef folds around his lower back. The men came to attention on either side, in front of their desks, facing toward the door.

An officer Simon had never met walked in the room with Sergeant Rodriguez who barked, "Captain Kowalski, Volunteers Gates and Paladino, ready for Inspection SIR."

Simon held his breath and kept his eyes forward.

The officer walked around the room. He opened the top dresser drawer on each bureau and closed it saying, "This looks pretty good Sergeant, you've taught these volunteers well. I wonder if you have taught them attention to detail?"

He reached up with a white-gloved hand and wiped the closet door's top edge on Paladino's side of the room and looked at his fingers. "Very nicely done, Gates and Paladino. Welcome aboard and thank you for your service."

The Captain performed an about-face and walked out of the room. He left faced and turned to inspect the rest of the barracks.

They remained at attention for what felt like an eternity but could hear nothing. Simon imagined the officer and the sergeant, walking into each room, checking each of the closet doors, and then walking out.

Finally, a voice called down the hallway, "DISSSS-missed."

Simon exhaled and his gut unfolded the reef in his shirttails. His uniform felt stiff from all the starch he used. All he wanted to do was sit down and kick off his shoes. He refused to show any weakness though, while Paldino was in the room.

A voice called down the hallway, "POST!"

The two scrambled out the door and stood at attention in the hallway. Saugus was speaking, though Simon could not see him.

"You did well this morning, volunteers. The heads looked impeccable and your barracks received top honors of the company. Congratulations. Liberty has been authorized to begin at 1200 and will expire at 2200 tonight. When taps begins to play, you better be in your racks asleep or it will be the last liberty you get while you are here. Is that clear?"

"YES, drill sergeant."

"DIIIIISSS- Missed."

Simon waited until he saw everyone else move and went into his room with Paldino.

"So what are you doing today," asked Paladino.

"Sarah said she would come up and take me to buy masking tape," said Simon.

Paladino laughed and said, "That sounds like a plan."

Simon asked, " How about you?"

"I dunno," said Paladino, "My wife is at soccer practice with the kids so she couldn't make it up here. I guess I could grab the libo van and go somewhere?"

"Nonsense," said Simon, "You can hitch a ride with us if you want to go buy tape and get some lunch. I think that was our plan and your welcome to join us?"

"That would be great," said Paladino, "I am gonna go to the head and will meet you guys out front in ten minutes if that's OK?"

"Sure," said Simon. He pulled his phone from his desk drawer and swiped it awake. The motion felt oddly unfamiliar to him. He hadn't realized it until this week, but he was addicted to his phone before he left. After a week without it, he noticed that had gotten out of the habit.

He dialed Sarah and heard, "Hello."

"Hey, Sweet It's Me. We are all done here where you at?" said Simon

"I'm at the main gate and there is a line of traffic because some Army guy is pointing a gun at every car that passes," she said, annoyed at the wait.

"I have missed you, my love," he said, "Just follow the signs for MEPS when you get in and we will be waiting in front of the barracks. Oh, by the way, I hope this doesn't get you mad, but I invited Paladino to join us. He had nowhere else to go?"

"No that's fine," she said "the more the merrier. I haven't seen my husband in a week, but bring him and the rest of the platoon along. I don't mind not having any time with my husband at all. Did you invite the sergeant as well?"

The line went silent.

"Simon," she said, "I'm playing with you. Did the Army take your sense of humor?"

"Ha," said Simon, " I'm sorry, I am just really fried after this week. I'll explain when I see you. I love you."

"Be right there, I'm almost at the Guard Station. I love you too," Sarah said as she hung up the phone and rolled down the window to speak to the guard.

Simon put on his jacket and walked down the hall to the front room. It was empty except for Jessinia, who sat on the couch reading.

"What are you doing Thomas?" asked Simon.

"I'm just reading," said Jessinia, "I don't have anywhere to go."

"Wanna come for lunch with us?" asked Simon, "Paladino is joining my wife and me and we're gonna do a little shopping and get something to eat? Plenty of space for one more."

"That sounds lovely," said Jessinia, "Are you leaving now?"

"In a few minutes," said Simon, "Grab what you need and meet us out front, we'll wait for you."

She closed her book, hopped up, and ran back to her room for her coat.

Simon walked outside and saw his wife in the car sitting out front. She popped opened the car door and ran to her husband and gave him a long kiss. He held her in his arms and she pulled his waist close to hers, "I have never seen you in a uniform before," said Sarah, "I think I could get used to this."

Simon laughed and said, "I bet you say that to all the guys. I hope you don't mind, but I invited Jessenia to join us as well. I hope that's OK?"

Sarah said, "Absolutely. Where are we heading?"

"I need to buy masking tape and I was thinking we could grab some lunch. I have until 10 PM tonight, but I don't want you driving home in the dark. Maybe we could hit the mall?" said Simon.

"That sounds good," said Sarah, "But I'm not sure what's open."

"Ah that's right," said Simon, "Maybe we could find an office supply store?"

The feds shut down all the major malls after the last covid-19 spike in 2021. Most of the big stores went out of business after that. Cities like Springfield felt a particular pain when the major sites, like the MGM Casino, went belly up. From what Sarah saw on her way up, there wasn't much open in the city.

Simon googled on his phone and found a shipping supply store the next town over in Chicopee. Next door to it was a Chinese buffet, so he said to her, "Do you feel like Chinese for lunch?"

Jessinia and Paladino walked out of the barracks together. Simon got in the passenger seat and the other two got in the back and they were off.

He briefed them on his plan to buy tape and get Chinese food for lunch.

Paladino said, "As long as I am off base, that sounds amazing."

---

The afternoon grew cloudy and the air smelled like snow. Simon recognized it, but it seemed like he hadn't smelled snow in forever. As they walked to the car with full bellies, Simon said, "I'll be damned, I think it's gonna snow."

Paladino said, "Holy shit that has got to be some kind of record."

In the wake of the global environmental crisis, snow became completely unfamiliar to New Englanders and the idea of it was exciting.

Sarah got in and started the car to warm it up. The three others got in and Simon said to Sarah, "I want to get you on the road as soon as possible. If it is gonna snow I don't want you on those back roads."

With budget cuts, the economic downturn, and the environmental crisis, snow removal budgets were eliminated. The three volunteers were not even issued winter gear, but instead had windbreakers to ward off the cold. The last thing Simon wanted was to hear a story about how his wife wrecked the car in Winstead, because of bad weather. Especially after she drove two hours on side roads to visit him. He looked at his phone. The time said 4:52 and the weather icon had a snowflake with a temperature of 33°F.

"It's almost five," said Simon, "it will be dark soon. Let's go back to base and get you on your way."

Sarah drove them on base and they waited 20 mins in the line at the guard shack. By the time they pulled up to the barracks, it was 5:15 and the sun was almost down.

"Shit," said Simon, "I didn't want you to have to drive back in the dark."

His two platoon mates said thank you and goodbye to Sarah and walked up to the barracks, leaving Simon and Sarah alone in the running car.

"I hate this," said Simon, "I hate to see you go, but I hate it even more than you are driving in the dark."

The first flakes of snow began to fall on the windshield. "Perfect, " he grumbled.

"I'll be fine," said Sarah, "I'll take it slow and will text as soon as I am home safe I promise."

"You better," said Simon, "You're my everything and I couldn't take it if anything happened to you."

"Now you know how I feel," said Sarah.

He leaned over and kissed his wife and she kissed him back.

He said, "I don't know if we will get any more liberty, but I'll keep you posted. Thank you so much for coming up here. You keep me sane. I love you."

"I love you too, Simon Gates. Now go inside and figure out your winter clothes situation," she said with a smile.

He laughed and opened the door to get out of the car.
He looked back over his shoulder and said, "Drive safe and text me the second you get home OK?"

"Yes Simon," she said, "Be safe and I love you."

He got out of the car, closed the door, and turned around. The snow was coming down harder now and was starting to collect on the grassy surfaces. Their eyes met through the wet window and he winked at her and smiled. She revved the car and started to drive forward slowly and he turned to walk inside.

It took her three hours and 40 minutes to get home.

By the time she reached the Connecticut border, the snow was sticking to the paved surfaces. When she got to Hartford, it began mixing with freezing rain. She crossed over onto the Merritt Parkway and it turned over to sleet.

At the end of the ramp in Stratford, Sarah's car fishtailed and she spun 360 degrees around. She came to a stop, just over the line at the stoplight. She didn't hit anything and felt incredibly lucky. When she pulled into the driveway, her nerves were shot and she was shaking all over.

She fumbled to get the keys out for the front door but stopped to check the mail before she walked up the stairs. There were only three pieces of mail. A card from the Crawford Administration urging families to be vigilant against terrorism, a bill from the UI, and an envelope with Simon's name on the front with no return address.

She opened the door and dropped the mail on the desk next to the front door. She turned the lights on. Her coat was wet and she hung it on the hooks next to the door and ran to the bathroom. When she got out, she stopped in the kitchen to send Simon a text that said, " I'm here. No trouble. Have a great week. Call when you can."

He replied immediately saying, "I love you. Thanks."

She poured a glass of wine and slid her shoes off and her slippers on. She brought her glass into the quiet living room and turned the light on in the backyard. Through the french doors, she could see the sleet had turned back over to snow and there was at least an inch collected on the deck that coated the budding branches of the trees. Sarah flipped on the TV and walked back to the front door to get the mail.

She threw the political card in the trash and stashed the electric bill in the bill box by the back door. She then eyed the envelope with Simon's name on it. The handwriting was nothing she had ever seen before and didn't recognize it. A kind of blocky engineering sort of lettering in all caps. She slid her finger down the seam and ripped the flap open. A piece of copy paper was inside folded in thirds. She pulled it out and unfolded it.

It was a copy of Simon's Business card.

She looked inside the envelope and saw nothing else. She laid the paper on the table and thought for a moment that she ought to tell Simon about it, as it seemed weird. She then looked at the envelope once again and saw the postmark was from Pensacola, Florida. Finding that even weirder, she folded the paper and put it back in the envelope, and walked it to the drawer of the desk in the front hallway. It came from Florida after all, so it wasn't something that had to be handled immediately. She placed it inside and went back to the living room to finish her wine. She fell asleep watching the weather on TV.

## Chapter 14

He saw his breath as he stepped out of his trailer and onto the tarmac of the abandoned airfield. The green gulf waters were streaked with white foam and the wind ripped out to sea, bending the palm trees toward the horizon. Broken palm branches and piles of trash were blown up against the fence and the temperatures felt oddly incongruent to the white sands and tropical flora.

A radio played in the hangar that echoed in the huge cavernous space, "Temperatures plunged last night along the east coast, with freezing temps recorded as far south as Miami and a historic snowfall across the Northeast. We'll have that story and more coming up in ten minutes"

Gus walked across the tarmac to see who was in the hangar and checked on the stack of rifles they had moved into the space late last night. He called out, "Jamal is that you?"

A booming voice echoed from the hanger, "Yes sir it's me, I'm making breakfast, do you want some?"

Gus walked around the open hanger door and could see Jamal in a kitchenette area scrambling eggs. He asked, "Where did you get that?"

"There is a small bodega down the road that opens at six. I took the truck down there to get some coffee and saw that they had eggs and bread, so I thought I would try and make breakfast. Hope that's okay?" said Jamal.

"Good thinking," said Gus, "I got some ketchup in the trailer. Do you need anything else?"

"Maybe some salt and pepper and creamer for your coffee, if you take it light?" said Jamal.

Gus walked back to the trailer and stepped inside. The heat felt good on his cold hands and face. He opened the fridge, pulled out a bottle of ketchup, and closed the door. He reached for the salt and pepper in the cupboard as he heard his phone vibrate on the dinette table.

He swiped it open and saw it was a text from John. He punched the text open within his finger and read it out loud. "Tanner and Gayle are leading a convoy of recruits down to you and will arrive on Tuesday. Prepare for the arrival of as many as 100 trailers and recruits."

"It's starting," he said to himself.

He walked back out across the tarmac with the ketchup and the salt and pepper. The wind whipped a piece of corrugated steel across the tarmac, slamming into the fence, and making a thunderous crash. Jamal came running to the hanger door and looked out across the tarmac to Gus. He pointed at the sheet steel pressed against the fence and continued to walk towards the door.

Jamal said, "Damn sir, I thought we were under attack with that bang?"

"No," said Gus, "it's just another thing we have to fix, but let's have breakfast first."

The two men sat at a folding table and ate off Gus'splastic plates. The coffee was good and, when the eggs and black coffee hit his stomach, Gus felt warmed.

When they finished and Jamal was clearing the table, Gus said, "I got news. We're getting company on Tuesday. John texted me. Gayle and Tanner are coming down with a convoy of 100 recruits and trailers. We gotta find a spot to park them and get this place ready for their arrival."

"Yes sir, What do we have to do?" asked Jamal

"Well we need to clear a space along that fence line to park 100 trailers side by side," explained Gus. "We will also need to find a space where at least 150 people can assemble. There was a stack of folding chairs in the back room of the first hangar on the left and I thought I saw a tractor in the back of one of the maintenance sheds as we drove in last night. Maybe what we need to do this morning is assess what assets we have here and begin to assemble them in this hanger, over there," he said motioning to the far side of the hanger.

Jamal said, "Do you mind if I grab a shower first? There is a bathroom up the apartment where you had me stay last night."

"Yeah no worries," said Gus, "you get yourself together and we will convene a scavenging party at 0900. You might as well settle in up there. That will be your housing for the foreseeable future. I'll continue bunking in my trailer and whenever the recruits show up they will be bunking in their trailers. This will work out nicely."

Gus went back to his trailer to get ready to work and Jamal walked up the open wood staircase to the apartment above the kitchenette. The room was small with a single cot someone had brought up with a mini-fridge. He figured they must have stayed here at some point when they were auctioning off the base. The fridge was still plugged in and had two Coors lights inside. The bathroom had a sink and a toilet with a stall shower where someone had washed out a paint bucket and failed to clean the basin afterward.

225

The blue stains surrounding the drain cleaned up quickly with a little bleach and some bathroom cleaner Jamal found under the kitchen sink. He decided that the electric space heater in the apartment was a little too much, with the heat of the steam he created cleaning the bathroom.

He took a hot shower and put on jeans with a hoodie and went down to find Gus.

As he walked out the hanger door, Jamal heard the rumble of a motor come to life. From around the back of the hanger came Gus driving a tractor with the bucket in the air. Jamal laughed and yelled, "Farmer Hawk!"

Gus waived to him and pointed over to the fence line and Jamal jogged over to meet him there. He lowered the bucket of the tractor and yelled over the motor, "Start putting that brush in here and I will take it and dump it."

The two worked along the fence for three hours and when they got to the end, the fence was clear of all the debris and could fit at least 100 trailers. Maybe more thought Jamal.

Gus said, "Hop on, let's get some lunch."

They drove the tractor down to the bodega, where Gus got a corned beef on rye and Jamal got a Cuban sandwich. They both drank cokes and enjoyed the warm sun in a protected corner behind the store. When they were done, Gus said, "Now, let's get those chairs out of the backroom and set them up in the hanger."

He drove the tractor to the back of the hanger and indicated that Jamal should pile the chairs in the bucket. When the bucket was full with fifty chairs, Gus backed it over the corner of the hanger and the two unloaded the chairs, setting them up. They made rows of ten with a space in the middle for a center aisle. By 3 PM, they set up 150 chairs and were both ready for another break.

Jamal ran up to his room and grabbed the two beers in the fridge. He came down with a big smile and handed one to Gus. The two men sat on the hubs of the tractor. They drank the beers enjoying the work they had completed, and the beginnings of a friendship.

When the beers were empty, Gus ordered Jamal to clean up the office and see about getting some computers set up. Gus went back to his trailer to make calls and check his email.

When he got there, Gus saw that he had missed two calls and had 23 emails waiting for him. The two calls came from Tanner, who wanted to touch base with Gus now that they were on the road.

Most of the emails were from John's new assistant, Tammy, who would be taking over all correspondence for the newly appointed leader. One email said, if you wanted to set up a meeting with the President, you needed to now submit it in writing. Gus laughed at the notion of making an appointment with John.

The last email he read, was one from Evan who outlined the protocols for emails and how to access the secure server. In the email, he said, "With the recent developments in Connecticut with the shooting and the most recent failed detonation, we must now increase our security protocols and continue to be ever watchful that our channels are not compromised by outside actors. Accordingly, I have set up your email and phone lines to filter through secure servers that will be monitored on an ongoing basis for cryptic traffic and nonloyal correspondence."

"Please be aware of this security feature when disseminating any information and know that we are working to maintain a secure perimeter, at all times, both on the ground and in the cloud."

Gus closed the email, without finishing it. He thought about deleting it but instead archived the email. He might need it someday but did not want to hear any more about how they were watching him.

He next called Tanner on speakerphone and waited for him to pick up.

"Yeah, this is Tanner."

Gus picked the phone when he answered and turned the speaker off, "Tanner, this is Gus returning your call."

"Hey good to hear from you. Gayle and I are heading up a convoy of about 100 trailers. We are now almost to Virginia and will be down to you by Tuesday or Wednesday."

"Yeah that's what John said in his text this morning," said Gus, "Take it easy. It's a long haul in a trailer. We had to stop every six hours and it took us a full two days longer than we expected with that weight we were carrying."

"Yeah we're not making great time trying to keep all the trailers together, but we'll get there whenever we get there," said Tanner.

"I bet you're some sight," said Gus, "any trouble from the law with all you guys traveling together?"

"Nah, I had a couple of friends of mine escort us out of Maryland and they called ahead to the stateys down the line telling them to keep an eye out for us. We're in good hands," said Tanner, "Hey, by the way, you still have that colored boy working for you?"

"Colored Boy? You mean Jamal," questioned Gus.

"Yeah him, how's he working out?" Tanner asked.

"He's doing real good, do you have a problem with his color?" asked Gus.

"Nah no problem, at all," laughed Tanner, "We all could use a good nigger at times you know?"

Gus felt his stomach turn and wanted to punch him in the face.

Instead, he said, "You know, I don't tolerate that kind of language and if you have a problem with blacks we need to talk about it now."

Tanner laughed again and said, "Naw, I don't have a problem, I'll watch my language when I am around him. I'll see you in a few days, OK Hawk. Be safe. B-Bye." The line went dead.

Gus was sick. The entire reason *The Plan* was going to work, was because they got rid of the white supremacist garbage with The Seditionists. When the Justices were killed, he felt finally they had a chance to build an organization that wasn't about being white. Now Tanner showed his stripes and Gus didn't know how to handle this.

Tanner was head of security and close with John. How did John not know his security guy was a bigot? Why didn't he say anything to Gus about it? He read *The Plan*, he knew that the only way it would work is if we got rid of the hate and worked together.

Gus was very clear about that in the book when he wrote, "The Government does not care if it is a brown face or black face that it starves, beats or murders. A bullet has no racial preference. The only way to reclaim America is if we put our differences behind us and fight shoulder to shoulder as one people, regardless of race."

Did John think he was just gonna give up on that point, and roll over to a bunch of bigots?

He calmed himself and centered his focus.

"I need to build an Army." he thought, "That is the only way we will win this thing. No one said that the only recruits I could use were coming down with Tanner. What if I had a company of my recruits standing at attention when they got here?"

He only had three days at most, but he had 500 rifles sitting in crates. What if he and Jamal could recruit a hundred people of color and have them standing here when the convoy pulled in?

He stuck his head out the door and yelled for Jamal. Then he clicked on the light over the dinette and pulled out an atlas. He thumbed through it until he got to Florida with a blowup of Pensacola. His mind raced between the seditionists trashing the capital and the Black Lives Matter protesters raiding the police barracks. If he could reach the leaders of these groups, they could help him. He needed a power broker in Florida, who was sympathetic to both their causes.

What about the guy who gave them the base? Would he know who they could talk to without making big waves? He texted John and asked for the number of Travis LaPierre. John messaged him back within seconds and asked why. He answered, "Because I need to know a few things about the base and it would be way faster if I talked to him directly?"

"Oh ok," responded John. Gus's phone chimed with a message that read, "John has shared a contact. Travis LaPierre 305-555-6258."

Gus clicked the number and added it to his phone. He then dialed the phone.

It rang twice and picked up, "Travis here." He clicked off the speaker and put the phone to his ear.

"Hi, Travis. This is The Hawk, the new field commander at your base. I believe you spoke to John about us coming down here? I am here in Pensacola," said Gus.

"Oh yeah, hey Hawk, what do you think of it? Will it work for you?" asked Travis.

"Yes sir, it will work great. We moved into the hanger down closest to the water. There was a tractor we found keys to and used it today to clear out a spot where we will receive our first 100 recruits coming in on Tuesday. Jamal and I worked like dogs and are getting a spot ready to start receiving recruits asap," said Gus.

"Oh yeah? Who's Jamal?" asked Travis.

"Oh, he's my new chief of staff. He is an African American kid I met in Gettysburg that impressed me. I brought him along," said Gus, "I wish I had a hundred more recruits just like him."

He waited to hear what Travis would say next before he would broach the subject he wanted to talk about.

"Oh that's great," said Travis, "You know Hawk, one of the things that always bothered me about the militias in the old days, was their white supremacy crap. Do you think we can count on the blacks to support this resistance?"

"As I wrote in *The Plan*," said Gus, "that is the only way we will truly reclaim America."

"You did say that, didn't you. I read that," said Travis, "I'd like to come down and talk a bit further. Do you mind if I come down tomorrow and you show me around the place and tell me about your plans some more?"

"That would be great," said Gus, "I hope to have a few other visitors tomorrow. I'm trying to reach out to the local community to find some sympathetic means of recruitment"

"Oh yeah? Where are you looking? What are you looking for?" asked Travis.

"I need 100 men, preferably with a more ethnic appearance, who would be willing to join our efforts," said Gus, "To balance out the diversity of the force."

"Balance the diversity? You sound like a liberal, but I think I know what you mean. I have a couple of friends around here, that may be of service. I will see if I can get Carlo Martinez to join me. Would that be alright? I also have some friends up in Mississippi as well that I may invite, if that's okay?"

"The more the merrier, sir. We need bodies in a big way and the more stakeholders we can get involved the better," said Gus.

Jamal knocked, opened the door of the trailer, walked in, and stood in silence.

"Alright Travis," said Gus, "I will see you tomorrow noon?"

"See you then Hawk," and Travis hung up the phone.

Gus turned to Jamal and said, "We got work to do."

"Oh yeah, what's that, sir?" said Jamal.

"We need to recruit 100 black men before Tuesday."

"Why's that sir?" asked Jamal.

"Because this Army won't make it if the bigots get a say, and the only way to keep them from talking is if we outflank them. And I need your help," said Gus.

"Yes sir, what do you need?" said Jamal.

"Street cred Jamal, I need street cred," said Gus.

## Chapter 15

They could hear the helicopter long before they could ever see it. The sound echoed across the empty hangers and the wide flat tarmac. It sounded like a rapid-fire gun with the pressure it created in their ears.

A long black helicopter, with a gold stripe down its side, appeared over the buildings. It looked like something from a 1980's television series thought Jamal. He could have sworn he saw the same thing on one of those old A-team episodes or maybe on Airwolf. He loved watching those old shows. To see a real-life relic like the one that was landing in front of him, was a thrill.

The huey touched down on the tarmac and Jamal worried that it would blow all the old palm branches and leaves they had removed yesterday, back into the fence line.

When the rotor stopped, three men got out of the helicopter and walked toward Gus. The first man to speak had on an Atlanta Braves hat and a long handlebar mustache. "So do you like my Navy base?" asked Travis.

Gus nodded and said, "Yes sir, this place has everything we need to recruit an army."

"It better," said Travis, "buying a Naval air station was not easy."

He turned to the dark-skinned man on his right and said, "I still can't believe they put it up for sale. Did you know you can get anything these days through the GSA? That's where I got that helicopter too. Carlo, You wouldn't believe the stuff you can get for cheap at the Government auctions these days. I should offer interductions," said the billionaire, turned government surplus hoarder.

"To my right, may I present Mister Carlo Martinez of The Cuban Florida Independence League out of Miami. To my left," said Travis pointing to the black man with a fistful of rings and a diamond stud in his ear, "please let me introduce Mister Dwight Roosevelt of Pascagoula. He is the former founder of the Mississippi Chapter of Black Voters In Arms."

The three men represented a huge chunk of the Resistance donor base and Gus knew he had to walk softly if he was going to stay on everyone's good side.

"This is your base, Sir, tell me where you would like to start," said Gus.

"Well, why don't we all go inside and have a seat and talk, and get out this cold," said Travis.

The three men and Gus started walking toward the door of the open hanger. Jamal trailed behind. Travis stalled his gait and waited for Jamal to catch up saying, "You must be Jamal."

"Yes sir," said Jamal, "I am."

"I have heard you have been working quite hard to get this base in order. How do you like working with the Hawk?" asked Travis.

"This is great," said Jamal, "I can't wait to get some recruits training and get this place booming."

"I like the way you think," said Travis, "You are unlike most of the people we have gotten into this cause, do you know that?"

"You mean black?" asked Jamal, "Yeah I got that sense when I joined up in Gettysburg. Felt kinda out of place."

"I bet, something like a chocolate chip surgah cookie I imagine?" said Travis

"Yes sir, something like that," Jamal said smiling.

"What if I told you that not every member of this outfit was a white supremacist? What if I told you that many of us are quite fairly minded? How would that strike you?" asked Travis.

"Well sir, I would find that hard to believe, but very welcome news if true," said Jamal, "present company excluded, *I am sure*," Jamal said, tagging on a little drawl for effect.

Travis's eyes got wide and he laughed a boisterous belly laugh that echoed across the tarmac and made the corners of his mustache flutter, "Why I do believe young man you are mocking me? But I love your southern accent!"

"No sir, not mocking, just appreciating," said Jamal with a big grin on his face

They walked into the hanger and over to the table where Jamal and Gus had breakfast. The four older men sat at the four corners of the table, while Jamal sat in a chair against the wall.

Travis started by saying, "Gentlemen, it has come to my attention that The Hawk, our man with the plan here, would like to see some more

237

faces of color within his ranks of recruits. Would that be fair to say, Hawk?"

"I have never heard it put so eloquently, Sir," answered Gus.

"Tell me, Hawk," said Carlo, "Why do you think we cannot win the battles with the current, shall we say, complexion of the organization?"

"Sir, as I see it," Gus began, " there are a great many people in this nation who have a decidedly darker complexion than our current recruitment efforts are fulfilling. For this cause to have legs we must have a force that represents all the faces of our Nation, not just the white ones."

"Well said, Mr. Hawk," replied Carlo, "Well said, indeed."

"How do you envision our support aiding in your cause Hawk?" asked Mr. Roosevelt.

"To be honest sir, I was hoping we might enlist the support of each of your organizations to fill out a 100 man unit. Our first field of recruits will be coming down from Gettysburg on Tuesday and I was hoping we might balance the scales so to speak, say if we had a hundred men of color waiting when they got here?"

"Am I to understand, that this group of inbound recruits has a decidedly paler complexion?" asked Roosevelt.

"Yes sir, they are part of the trailer fleet that collected at Gettysburg and they are coming down as a convoy under the command of Tanner Martin of Maine."

"I see. I haven't met Mr. Martin yet, but I understand he is part of our legal relations efforts," said Roosevelt.

"Yes sir, that is correct," answered Gus.

"What is your feeling about Mr. Martin, Hawk," asked Mr. Roosevelt.

"Sir, he is a devoted and integral member of the senior staff and I very much look forward to working with him," said Hawk.

"Yes, but what do you *think* of him Hawk?" pressed Mr. Roosevelt

"Sir, I am very impressed by his work thus far. I feel we are well served by his legal relations efforts within the law enforcement community," said Hawk, "However, I am a bit dismayed by certain comments he has made to me recently about our efforts to create a force that is more representative of the demographic of our community at large."

"In other words, he's a bigot?" asked Travis directly.

"Yes sir, I think he is. But may I say, while I don't think that precludes him from service, it does not bode well for a successful campaign," said Hawk laying it all out there.

"Thank you for your direct answer Hawk, and thank you for your insight," said Travis, "When we bankrolled this effort, it was made quite clear that we were not in favor of supporting some of the more fringe beliefs that were espoused by our predecessors. While I do not believe we will ever completely tamp out those beliefs, particularly within the ranks of the Resistance, I hope that we will rise above them and show them the error of their ways."

"Yes sir," said Gus, "I could not agree more."

"Well gentleman," said Travis, "Can we raise 100 men for this field commander by Tuesday?"

Gus swallowed hard and worried that he had overplayed his hand.

"Where will they live and how will they eat?" asked Roosevelt, "This place doesn't seem ready to support the needs of 100 men by Tuesday."

"I have a budget to work within, Sir, to develop accommodations and provisions for 100 men, but that was with the understanding that they would all bring their trailers when they came here and could be self-contained," said Gus, " With an additional 100 men, who don't have trailers, we would need barracks for them as well as a dining and sanitary facilities with supplies. The facilities on base here are in rough shape from what I can tell and we ought to keep our footprint small to ensure security. Perhaps tents set up on the tarmac here would be best. While we're at it, we should also probably be working on uniforms as well. I do have enough weapons for 500 men though."

"Gentlemen, I think we could pool our resources and provide the Provisional Field commander with what he needs, do you agree?" said Travis. The other two men nodded.

"I have a warehouse in Argentina that has enough field supplies for 1000 people that I could have here on a flight tomorrow," said Carlo.

"I am sure I can get several of our families to volunteer to cook for y'all if you need it. It won't be anything special but our families make some outstanding rice and beans that will keep your belly full if that suits your taste," said Roosevelt, "I'll see about getting the church fundraising committee to donate their cooking tents. The bazaar isn't until August so you can have that for at least a few months I would think."

"I am told there is an old Navy athletic building on the base with bathrooms and hot showers on this property somewhere. Hawk, can you hunt that down and tell me what it needs to be serviceable?" asked Travis.

"Certainly sir, I'll have a report for you by 1800 this evening," answered Hawk.

"I think that is everything needed gentlemen? I thank you," said Travis, "We are fighting for America and America will help those who are doing the fighting for it. Am I right? Of course, Hawk if you need anything else you will let me know?"

"Well sir about those uniforms, I think it's time we look like an Army if we are going to become one. It is something that will bring us all together?" asked Hawk.

"Why don't you get me a list of items you will need to compose a proper uniform for 500 men and I will have my people get them delivered to you by Wednesday, along with whatever upgrades the locker room might need for use. Will that work Hawk?" asked Travis.

"Yes sir, I will have that list and a report on the condition of the locker room sent over to you by 1800 this evening," said Hawk.

"Excellent Provisional Field Commander Hawk," said Travis, "The next thing we need to do is get you a title that will fit inside this hanger."

"Yes sir," said Hawk.

"Now Gentlemen, would you like a tour?" asked Travis.

The four men stood and walked toward the hangar door. Jamal came following after.

Travis walked them around the hangers and the field. He walked them down the runway to the waterfront. He told them about how the Navy used to train and run air missions across the Gulf from here.

He told them how he bought it to store his helicopters and have a place to land his jet. He finished by telling them how this was such a better use of the property now that the Resistance was going to be basing their recruitment efforts out of this facility. They walked to board the helicopter to leave and Travis pulled Gus and Jamal aside while the pilot strapped the two other gentlemen into the aircraft.

"Gus," said Travis, "Thank you for trusting me and bringing this to my attention. We are fighting for the good of our nation and while I may not be the one who pulls the trigger when the time comes, I want you to know that I will do all I can to give you the support you need to make it happen. Jamal, you have a hell of a commander here and you two are going to do some great things I can feel it. Take this, if you need anything, this should cover it."

He handed Gus a suitcase and walked toward the helicopter.

The thunderous concussion of the rotors deafened the two men as they watched the aircraft lift off into the sunset. When it was out of sight, and they could hear again Gus said, "You did that."

Jamal with his ears still ringing, said, "what do you mean, sir?"

"Travis sized you up when he was talking to you and took a shine to you," said Gus, "he's a very generous man and when he likes you, he lets you know it."

"Yeah but he gave you the suitcase sir?" said Jamal laughing.

"Yes, he did, didn't he," Gus said as he smiled, "Why don't you run down to the pizza place and get us a large with whatever you want on it. And grab a case of beer, whatever they have cold and domestic. Here take the truck," he said handing Jamal the keys.

As Jamal drove off, Gus started to think about Uniforms. He wanted to make an impression but they needed to be functional and above all. They needed to be rugged. In these early days, these guys would only get a few of them, to last them for months.

He went into his trailer, clicked on the light over the dinette, and began writing a list.

Gray Tactical pants
Black Tee shirts
Gray Button-down Tactical long sleeve shirts with epaulets
8" steel toe tactical boot
Black canvas web belt with brass buckle
Athletic socks/grey
Garrison cover black

## Chapter 16

He turned the shower knob on and a spray of rusty water shot out. The water ran across the dirty tiles in a stream through the dust, towards the drain in the center of the shower room. Within a few seconds, a clean stream of water shot out and he could feel the steam begin to build.

Jamal yelled, "It's on in here," and turned the knob off.

He walked out of the shower and saw Gus patting the workman who was climbing out from the water heater room on the shoulder. "We have showers and toilets now," he said smiling as he saw Jamal walking towards him.

The three men walked out the door to see six more semi-trailers driving down the road towards the main hanger. Gus told the workman to check all the faucets and heads one more time before he left, and motioned to Jamal to get in the truck. They caught up and followed the tractor-trailers down toward the waterfront.

When the six trucks stopped, he pulled around the front and opened the truck door before shutting off the engine. Gus waived to the driver of the first truck and walked over to speak to him.

"Are there any tents from Mr. Martinez?" Gus asked the driver.

"That is the last three. Mine and this one are boxes of clothes and dry goods. Where do you want them?" the truck driver asked.

"Do you need a forklift or do you guys have a way to unload them?" said Gus, "There is a loading dock around back?"

"Naw sir, we all got a pallet jack and ramps. That should work just fine and they ain't that heavy. Just tell me where you want everything," said the lead driver.

"Put the boxes in the hanger. The supplies from Mr. Martinez should go over by the fence. I'll send Jamal over to show you where we want those and once the first tent is up,.... you are going to set the tents up, correct? You can put the dry goods under the first tent, once you have it set up."

The driver said, "Aye Sir," and went back to direct the other drivers.

Within minutes, the field was buzzing with swinging hammers and shuffling boxes. Gus told Jamal to keep an eye on things and went back to his trailer to check on the progress of the trailer convoy, he expected it any minute.

He swiped his phone open and dialed Tanner. When he heard "Tanner here," he picked it up and turned off the speaker.

"Hey Tanner, Hawk here. What's your ETA?"

"Yeah, we are still in Georgia and the GPS says we are about 10 hours out," said Tanner, " We likely won't make it until tomorrow at this pace."

"Do you still have 100 trailers behind you?" asked Gus.

"Nah we lost six of them through the Carolinas due to mechanical failure," explained Tanner, "They'll fix their rigs and rejoin us when they get back on the road."

"Very good," said Hawk, "We cleared enough space for 150 rigs on the edge of the runway. That's ready for you when you get here. We also have enough tents for a bunch more people and got dining facilities, shower facilities, and bathrooms on line. Travis LaPierre and a few of his friends stopped in and offered us everything we need for at least one hundred more recruits that they say should show up later today."

"Wow the big wigs were there," said Tanner, "and you got another hundred guys on the way? That's incredible. What else have you been doing down there on the beach?"

"We got uniforms today for the men, and we will assemble two companies in uniform when you get here. We're making progress, Tanner, I tell you, it's happening," said Gus.

"That's awesome Hawk, we'll put the pedal to the metal and get there as soon as we can. I'll call you when we are an hour out. Talk to you later," said Tanner as he hung up.

Gus thought to himself, "that went well."

He went in to shower and changed. He poured himself a second cup of coffee, while he looked at the news. CNN was still talking about Jim and Joan Justice and their failed attempt to blow up the state capital in Connecticut. He knew exactly where they were killed and drove that section of I-91 all the time when he was working for Pratt and Whitney. His team flew out of the Air National Guard Station at Brainard, while they were providing security for that new airplane engine in Iraq.

That seemed like a lifetime ago. Working as a private contractor. Flying missions to Iraq. Those were good times, he thought. He missed his team. It was lonely without his friends and... her.

His mind drifted to his ex-wife, Melissa. He met her in Connecticut at a wedding for his best friend at the time. What was his name? Tom, Tim, Todd...shit I can't remember, he thought. She wore a pink flowered sundress, he remembered. They were at that castle overlooking the river down in, where was that, Haddam. He saw the setting sun as it filtered through her auburn hair against the green leaves that covered the banks of the river. He thought there was nothing more beautiful than that image of the woman he loved more than anything in the world on that day. His mind then went to the argument they had when he was shipping out, yet again, to fly to some war zone in the middle east.

"You love your work more than me," she yelled as she smashed the glass of wine against the wall. He laughed and thought they probably still haven't gotten that stain out yet.

"Yes I do," he said, "at least my job isn't drunk on box wine by 10 AM every day."

He threw his bag down the flight of stairs and remembered that that was the last time he would ever look out the window over the river in their house in Fairhaven. He remembered seeing the oyster boats, dragging the river, stirring up the smell of low tide, as it crept up the banks to his balcony overlooking the tree lines. He remembered the sound of the horn of the bridge on Grand Avenue, opening in the late afternoon to let the boats back in from a day of fishing.

He remembered the sound of her crying when he walked down the stairs and left her in her puddle of self-doubt and sorrow on the bed. The sound of the door slamming made him cringe, as he remembered walking down the walk to the waiting cab and looking back one last time, to see if she was watching him leave in the window. She wasn't there.

He was on duty at the consulate, when he got the call telling him that she was found dead from an overdose of pills on Christmas night. That was when he remembered sending a copy of that guy's card to him in the mail.

"Why did I do that?" he asked himself, "What made me send that? It was dangerous to keep up contact, they might trace it to me."

He decided he would give anything to get that copy back and destroy it. He next called Travis, who picked up on the third ring. "Yes sir, how's things on base?" Travis started.

Clearing his throat he answered, "The uniforms arrived this morning and the tents are being set up right now as we speak. The convoy is ten hours out and we got the bathrooms online. Any word on the recruits and the cooking crews?"

"I just spoke to Roosevelt. He says that they are loading buses now with recruits and a cooking crew from the church. He says they will arrive around noon," said Travis.

"How did Martinez make out with his recruitment goals?" asked Gus

"He was doing well, the last time I spoke to him. He said that they had a sign-up list going at the community center where they had seventy-four names signed up as of last evening," said Travis, "They should be coming in later today, I think. I was gonna fly down and meet them all when they arrived if that was OK?" asked Travis.

"Yes sir that would be great. Maybe by that time, we will have the dining tent up and running. You could stay for dinner? Would you like that?" suggested Gus.

"If it is no imposition, I would love to join you folks for dinner," said Travis, "See you around 4 PM."

Gus hung up the phone and decided to go check on the progress of the tents. He opened the door and saw blue lights flashing on the runway. He walked quickly to see what was going on.

Jamal was speaking to a sheriff and looked nervous.

As Gus approached, he could hear Jamal saying, "we're just setting up some tents for an event. Here is my boss, you can ask him."

"May I help you, sheriff?" asked Gus.

"Sir, do you have some identification?" asked the Sheriff, "Your young friend here seems to have misplaced his."

"Yes I do, but may I ask why you felt the need to trespass on private property?" asked Gus.

"I saw the trucks come in here," the officer said, "and to the best of my knowledge this place is abandoned."

"Well as you can see, it is quite the opposite of abandoned and you may verify that with the owner, Travis LaPierre. Would you like to speak to him? I just got off the phone with him and can call him right back?" Gus said, with a sarcastic tone as he offered his phone to the sheriff.

"You know Travis LaPierre?" asked the sheriff.

"Yes I do, and he will be here later today around four if you would like to meet him as well?" said Gus.

The sheriff tipped his hat and said, "My mistake gentlemen. Please excuse me."

He backed up to his car and climbed in. Gus saw him pick up the mic for his radio and say something into the radio. He then took off his cover and waived to Gus and drove away.

"What was that all about?" Gus said as he turned to Jamal when the officer rounded the corner out of sight.

"He drove up and started saying 'what the hell are you doing boy'? I didn't like his tone," said Jamal.

"Yeah, we gotta watch out for that. Until we get some sort of agreement from the local police, we need to keep things quiet. Tanner will be here tomorrow and can start working on that, but if anybody shows up today, asking any questions, tell them we're hosting a fundraiser for Mr. LaPierre," explained Gus, "How are we coming along?"

He saw the first tent had been set up with at least a dozen stacks of boxes and bags piled under it. The crew was now working on the second tent, piling the stakes through the pavement.

"It's going good sir. They loaded the boxes of uniforms into the hanger and emptied the dry goods trailer under the tent, now they are working on the rest of the tents," said Jamal.

"How many tents do they have to set up?" asked Gus

"They said they have 30 of them that Martinez sent over. I told them to go ahead and just set them up in a line along the runway," answered Jamal.

"Jesus, this is going to be a small city when we're done," said Gus, " I'm going to go look at the uniforms. Keep this moving along will you?"

Jamal nodded and Gus strode over towards the open hanger door. Inside he saw a hundred or so boxes stacked neatly in the corner. He walked over and grabbed one of the ones he could reach and opened it.

Inside were 500 garrison covers wrapped in plastic. He untwisted the tie that held the bag closed and opened the bag to pull one out. The smell of polyester mixed with plastic made him want to vomit, but he held his breath and reached in to grab one. He slid it from a wax sleeve that covered each one and fingered the label that had the size, saying, "7 ⅛. Perfect."

He slid the cover over his head and measured two fingers from his brow. It felt naked without the insignia but reminded him of his days in basic when he first put his green army garrison on his head. It felt right, it felt like home. It felt like he had a mission once again.

He then dug through the boxes and found a pair of pants, a tee-shirt, a button-down, and a pair of boots. The last box on the bottom, in the back corner, had the belts and he unstacked 65 boxes to find it. He took the stack of clothes, with the garrison on his head, and walked back to his trailer.

He stopped at Jamal and said, "I found my uniform. When you get a minute go dig one out for yourself and put it on. You will feel like a new man."

He walked the rest of the way to his trailer and went inside and changed.

The boots felt stiff and the belt needed to be trimmed. He rifled through his closet and pulled out his iron and safety deposit box.

Opening the safety deposit box, he found his ribbon holder with his ribbons still in place. He laid his shirt on the dinette table and spread a towel on the tabletop. He then plugged in the iron and waited for it to get hot.

The smell of the heating iron brought him back to his days in the Army and he remembered how much pleasure he got out of ironing.

When he got the folds in the shirt flattened, he began decorating it by pinning his ribbon holder to the left breast panel. He then rifled through his safety deposit box and pulled out his epaulets. He rubbed the oak leaf and remembered his rank, Major. He then slid the cloth strap through the straps on each shoulder of the shirt and buttoned them on.

Next, he opened a small jewelry box, where he kept his wedding ring and lifted the felt holder with the ring to expose his oak leaf insignia that he pinned to the front of his garrison cover.

He stood in the mirror and looked at himself. It didn't look right, with a gray uniform on instead of his Army green one, but it was a uniform, just the same. Simple, understated, but authoritative. It was perfect.

He bloused the pants into his boots and gave the entire thing a dusting with a lint brush. And faced right as he turned to walk out the door. He still had the snap he thought. He was still a soldier.

---

The afternoon sun was stronger than it was when he was in Connecticut. He looked at his phone and the time said 3:42. Travis would be landing any minute and he still hadn't heard from Martinez or Roosevelt with their recruits.

He eyed the tents lined up on the left side of the runway and imagined what it would look like when 96 trailers (both his and Tanner's would be part of the line) were on the other side.

He walked over to the hanger and looked inside. Jamal was in the back corner at the table trying to figure out how his belt was supposed to work. He walked to the back of the hanger and listened to the sound of his boots echoing on the concrete and remembered how much he loved that sound.

"You need a hand?" asked Gus.

"Yes sir, I've never done this before," said Jamal.

The younger man had the pants and shirt on, but he had yet to remove his cover from the wax sleeve and was fumbling with the belt trying to figure out how to get the brass buckle to go on the right way. He sat there in his black socks, afraid to put the boots on.

"Well first, we have to size this belt for you. See this raw end? Slide it through this clamp on the back of the buckle and clamp it down. Now slide it through your belt loops."

Jamal wove the belt around his astoundingly skinny waste. Gus joked, "Jesus son, we have to fatten you up a bit."

He laid the finished end through the buckle and pulled it tight. Gus took out his pocket knife and cut the extra webbing off and clamped the brass finishing clasp on the end. He then showed the young man how to tuck his shirt in and create a 'reef' on his back, to keep the front of his shirt from billowing out too much.

He then had Jamal put the boots on. He showed him how to tuck them in and blouse his pant legs. The next step was to teach the young man how to fold his sleeves up with the two-inch cuffs up above his elbows. And finally, Gus slid the garrison cover from the wax paper sleeve and placed it on the young man's head, showing him how to measure its peak, two fingers from his brow.

The young soldier, newly transformed from a civilian, stood at attention and saluted the senior officer. Gus gently took his hand down from his forehead, folded his thumb into his palm pressing his four fingers together. He then demonstrated a salute, showing him how to snap his hand up to his brow and then down again. Jamal tried once more and this time received a return salute from Major Spiros.

When the lesson was finished, and both soldiers looked in order, they heard the unmistakable sound of an inbound helicopter. They walked to the door and saw the black helo with the gold stripe, descending on the runway. They waited for Travis to get out.

When the rotor stopped and the door opened, Travis's face appeared in the door beaming beneath a long brown mustache from ear to ear. He called out, "Gentleman, I do believe we have the beginning of an Army in our midst."

Travis walked over and shook the hands of both men and said, "We saw the busses coming in. There are six of them and I think you will be pleased with the class of recruits... Major."

Gus was surprised at first that the man, with the hobby of collecting Government surplus, knew what the gold oak leaf meant on his cap without asking, but he said nothing.

The three men walked over to the hanger and talked about the 30 tents and the new uniforms. When the conversation grew sparse, they heard the first rumbles of the bus convoy and saw the cloud of dust they created coming down the drive before they ever eyed the busses.

Six busses loaded with men and women of all ages, cruised down the runway past the tent city and stopped in front of the hangar. Mr. Roosevelt got off first and walked toward the three men saying, "Carlo wanted to be here but was called away on business. He sent his regards and sixty-seven recruits from Cuban-American League. The rest of these men and women come from the Black Soldiers for Equal Justice of Mississippi. I believe they are ready to kick some ass if you don't mind my use of the vernacular."

Gus saw the females on the buses and asked Roosevelt, "Are those females I see on those buses, Mr. Roosevelt?"

"Yes Hawk, they are. When we put the call out, several of our ladies asked if they might volunteer as well and I could not find it in my heart to tell them no. We aim to enlist the support of our entire Nation and at last check, over fifty-one percent of this nation was women right?"

The thought of including women in the Army did not occur to Gus, but as Roosevelt so aptly explained, they were a viable and sizable force that should not be ignored. His mind raced on how he would integrate women into *The Plan* but remembered that Gayle was on the way and thought she might have some insight as well.

When he finished talking, Roosevelt walked to the side of the line of buses and whistled loudly. Three hundred black, Hispanic, Asian, white, and Native recruits stepped off the buses and formed ranks in front of Major Hawk. Hawk was about to speak when another 8 vans with the signs for the First AME Church of Pascagoula on the side pulled in behind the buses.

Gus turned to Jamal and said, "Would you please go show the AME vans where to park and help them get started on dinner, while I address the troops?"

Jamal popped to attention and saluted and said, "Yes Sir."

Gus spoke loudly, "Recruits, my name is Major Gus Spiros. You may call me Major or Sir. When I indicate that I would like an answer to my question you will answer, 'YES Sir,' for the affirmative and, 'No Sir,' to the negative. Is that clear?"

"YES SIR," the newly formed regiment of men and women replied.

The sound of three hundred recruits speaking in unison gave Hawk goosebumps.

He explained to them that they would be taking part in a force to reclaim America and that from now on they were sworn to absolute secrecy

257

about all matters that occurred while in this service upon pain of death. He informed them that they would be required to make up their barracks tonight and that they would be eating late this evening. He said they would be given full details after breakfast in the morning, and that for tonight they were to remain in the ranks in which they were now formed, but would be assigned to platoons and companies when the full company of troops was present.

He concluded by saying, "Ladies and Gentlemen, welcome to the Resistance. Disssssss-Missed."

The recruits scattered and went to explore the base and the tent city. Gus turned and saw Travis watching him with a grin across his face.

"Forgive me sir, but I must ask, what's with this shit-eating grin?" he asked

"I believe you are in your element, Major, it is a pleasure to watch," Travis began, "We have a fine officer in charge of our field command and I am proud to say I have helped put you in that command. God bless us all Major and may God bless our Army."

The two men walked toward the tents to inspect the dining facilities and see what the newly arrived recruits were up to. The sun was beginning to set and pelicans flew in formation across the waves. A pale moon appeared on the horizon and the green waves of the gulf were calming to a gentle roll. If one listened close enough, they could hear the drums of war beginning to beat.

## Chapter 17

Simon counted the white tee-shirts and boxer shorts, as he pulled them from his bureau, "1,2,3,4,5,6,7,8,9...1,2,3,4,5,6,7,8,9."

He placed them neatly in his duffel and began pulling the balls of black socks out and counting them as well. He stopped halfway through counting and looked at the word printed on the toes. He hadn't noticed the printing before and wondered how many levels of bureaucracy had to be satisfied for the Army to allow the word, "Powersox," to be printed on government-issued footwear.

He finished stashing the socks in the corner of his duffel, walked to his closet where he removed his fatigues and rolled them before stashing them in the bag. When he got here, there was a lot more room in the bag, but with all the issued gear, he wasn't sure he was going to fit it all in.

When he got to basic, he envisioned getting a big green army bag, like the ones he saw in all the movies. The sergeant said, however, that due to budget cuts and the fact they were short-timers, the Army decided they didn't need an issued army duffel and cut that from their list of issued gear.

Instead, they made available a box of garbage bags, if the volunteers needed additional space to carry their issued gear. He stuffed his boots and work out gear into a big clear plastic bag and tied a knot around the mouth of the bag to keep it shut. The sergeant told them that they would be issued combination covers when they got back to their home bases because the Army also failed to allocate those, along with greatcoats for the volunteers.

He froze his ass off in the freak snowfall in the issued windbreaker they gave him and he was very happy when the thermometer got back up to 70. None of their issued gear was winter-grade, again because of budget cuts, so the sergeants had them PT in the barracks for the three days when the temps got below freezing.

Simon heard the bus pull up out front and decided he was pretty much packed. He pulled all the drawers out of the dresser and opened the closet one last time, wondering if he would ever miss this place. He decided there that it was a great experience, but he never wanted to do it again.

He shouldered his duffel and put the plastic bag under his arm and walked into the hall. It was empty and he wondered where everyone was. When he got on the bus, he realized he was the last one out of the building. He sat down across from Jessinia and said, "I didn't say goodbye to the sergeants."

She snorted and said, "Do you think they'll miss you?"

Simon leaned back and closed his eyes. He thought of the explosion they drove through on the way up.

---

The piles of snow were stained with brown bits and dirt from the asphalt in the unity station parking lot. Streams of water slid down the driveway from the bottom of the piles and made her think of those videos she saw of the melting glaciers in Alaska.

The bus was running late. Simon said they would be in by noon, but the time was now quarter past and still, there was no sign. There were at least a half dozen other cars in the parking lot with waiting families inside. She assumed they were getting as hot as she was, in the warm afternoon sun with the windows closed.

She cracked the window and turned the thermostat to 68. The cool breeze shooting from the dashboard felt good on Sarah's warm face but also felt oddly strange parked next to a 16-foot pile of snow.

She was about to unzip her coat when the bus rumbled into the parking lot. When the driver hit the air brakes, it startled her. Sarah could see the six soldiers sitting in the steamed windows of the bus but could not make out Simon's face.

The bus stopped at the back door of the building and the folded doors opened. The waiting family's heads pooped out of the cars and ran to wait for their soldier to get off the bus. Sarah joined them, but felt oddly alone, without a child or parent in tow, the way all the other families seemed to be assembled.

She waited in the back of the group, craning her neck to see Simon. He was the fourth person off the bus and walked around the front of the bus, also craning his neck to find her. Their eyes met and Sarah pushed through the group and ran to Simon where he wrapped his arms around her and kissed her neck.

She felt his body and it seemed thinner and a bit more toned. He smelled like spray starch and soap and she began to cry thinking about how much she missed him and his smell. He never smelled like spray starch before, but this was Simon just the same. She could always recognize him.

He pulled her head off his shoulder and looked her in the eye and said, "You're crying."

"Yes," she said, "I'll be fine. I just missed you."

She wiped her cheeks and nose with the back of her hand and said, "Alright you're home now, what do you want to do first? Are you hungry?"

Simon said, "Yeah, I am, let's go get a hot dog at Dan's Drive-In."

The afternoon was perfect for eating in the car and they always loved watching the river down the hill while fighting the seagulls for french fries. He ordered two-foot-long hotdogs with chili and cheese and she got a grilled chicken sandwich with fries. They shared a coke. The restaurant went silent when he walked in to order and began clapping. He almost forgot he was in uniform and raised his hand to waive in embarrassment.

One by one, the patrons walked by him with their food and thanked him for his service. He didn't ask for it, but the girl behind the counter gave them 10% off their order. For the first time, he noticed that the walls were covered with memorabilia pointing to the fact that the original owner, who he assumed was long since gone, served in the Marines during World War II.

When their food was ready, they walked back to their car and ate it, taking care not to spill chili on his uniform. He threw two french fries out the car window and a scene out the Hitchock's The Birds ensued with what seemed like a hundred gulls dive-bombing the car. They screamed and pecked at each other, as they fought over the two fries on the pavement. The scene he caused embarrassed him when the people in the other cars began to stare. He asked Sarah to start the car and leave before they had a chance to throw out their trash.

When they got home, he walked into the house and immediately went upstairs to change. He threw his bag of clothes in the corner and remembered the coffee stain on his sweat pants that seemed like it happened a lifetime ago. He pulled the sweat pants out and laid them on the bed for Sarah to see, so she could do her magic to get the stain out.

He slid a pair of shorts on and his bare white legs felt chilled in the cool empty room. He grabbed a sweatshirt from the closet and slid on slippers. He walked downstairs to find Sarah, stretched out of the couch with her eyes closed. Tiptoeing in the room, he picked up a throw from the back of the chair and put it on his napping wife.

She stirred and her eyes opened slowly and said, "I'm sorry honey I must have fallen asleep."

"Stay sleeping, I want to check on the yard," he whispered.

She rolled over and pulled the blanket up over her shoulder. He stopped at the fridge to grab a beer and stepped out from the french doors onto the deck. The last traces of snow lay in stripes from the shadows of the pickets below the railings where the sun never got a chance to shine. The plants were all brown and dead in the pots on the deck. The grass looked burned, crusty, and pressed down from the recent snowmelt.

Up until he left, the grass had never gone into dormancy and he remembered cutting the lawn in early February. Now it was March and just when it was supposed to start coming up, it was frozen and dead looking. He was going to have to fertilize a lot, he thought, to compensate for the unexpected snowstorm.

He twisted the top off the beer, placed it on the table, and sat down on the patio chair. The pad was wet and he felt the cold water soak through the seat of his shorts. "Shit," he said.

The warm sun mixed with patches of winter air that still hung beneath the bare oak branches and hid in the needles of the hemlock bushes. A gentle breeze moved the still air and he went from being warm to cold back to warm as the currents moved over his bare legs. He thought, "I should go in and get a dry pair of shorts or I will get sick."

His wife was napping and the cold beer tasted good after three weeks of Army life mixed with the Spring afternoon. The dry shorts could wait.

The last three weeks changed him, he thought. He noticed things he had never noticed before. The buds on the trees and the robin picking at the ground in the garden. He heard the breeze blowing through the bare tree branches and the sound of a motorcycle three blocks away accelerating. He wondered why he had never noticed these things before, as he knew they must have always been there. But today, they seemed new and undiscovered.

The door slid open and Sarah stuck her head out and asked, "Want some company?"

"Yeah, that would be great, but grab a towel and another beer for me if you would pleeeeeease?" plead Simon.

She ducked back in and reappeared a few moments later with a beach towel and two lite beers.

She placed the beers on the table and Simon grabbed them both and opened each of them with a twist of his wrist. She asked, "What's the towel for?"

"I soaked my shorts. The pads are wet from the snow. Sit on the towel if you want to keep your underwear dry," said Simon.

"Really after three weeks, that's what you want?" she asked dryly.

He laughed and said, "We'll get to that, but I don't want you to get pneumonia before we do."

She doubled the towel over and laid it in the chair and sat down next to her husband.

"So how does the yard look?" she asked.

"As if it suffered through a blizzard," Simon answered, "The grass is dead, I'll have to fertilize the hell out of it to get it to come back."

"Yeah, when I got back from visiting you that night, it started snowing just as I was getting in," explained Sarah, "It snowed the entire next day non-stop. We had three feet. Thank God for Tom next door, or I never would have gotten the car out of the driveway."

"Why, did he shovel the whole driveway out?" asked Simon.

"No, he had an old snowblower in his garage that he got running and did the whole neighborhood. I think he just liked using it because he blew snow for three days straight. They never sent any plows around, so he cleared the whole street," Sarah continued, "I'm glad you mentioned that. Stay right here, I have to show you something."

She ran inside and reappeared at the door with a white envelope.

She handed it to him and sat down and he said, "What is that?"

He looked at the postmark and read, "Pensacola, Florida," out loud and asked, "who do we know there?"

Sarah said, "Look inside."

He opened the envelope and unfolded the piece of copy paper and saw a copy of his business card, "What the hell is this?" he asked.

"That's exactly what I want to know," said Sarah, "I thought you might have some sort of idea."

"This isn't...You don't think he...You know what this is, .... This is a copy of the card I gave to that guy," Simon said.

"The guy who was in here?" she asked, raising her eyebrow.

"Yeah, remember how he left that card in the door?" Simon explained, "He must have made a copy of it and sent this to me. But why?"

"Why did he come here and break-in? He's creepy and a killer Simon," Sarah's voice cracked when she said the word 'killer'.

Simon had almost forgotten about the car accident and the killing while he was gone. Seeing this copy pulled him right back into reality and the reason why he chose to go up to Springfield in the first place.

"I gotta find this guy," said Simon.

Those spoken words caused both of them to miss a beat. Simon heard his own words and wondered where they came from. Sarah heard his words and wondered "who is this man sitting before me saying such things?" Both of them knew this was not how the old Simon would have responded to the alarming letter.

The old Simon would have burned the letter and buried the fear of it with the ashes. He would have ignored the risk and stuffed his head in the sand like some ostrich in the face of danger. He was not a man to face reality and challenges, but one who ran from them to the safety of a woman's arms and the drudgery of insurance sales. This man, saying he wanted to find danger, was an entirely new species that neither of them knew.

Sarah broke the silence saying, 'You want to find him? And do what, take away his copier?"

The dismissal angered Simon. The fear angered Simon. The fact that this guy intimidated him during the accident, angered Simon. The fact that this guy took away his sense of safety and his sense of normalcy angered Simon. He looked at Sarah in a way she had never seen before. His eyes had a fire in them and his jaw was set in a way that she had never noticed before. She became afraid for a moment, thinking she had said the wrong thing.

Simon finally replied saying, "He'll be missing a lot more than a copier if I do find him."

Sarah wondered what this man had been through in the last three weeks to give him the rage that she now saw in his eyes. She asked, "Simon, what's going on? You're different."

Simon shook his head and came back to the table. "I don't know Sarah. I'm mad. I'm tired of waiting for the next shoe to drop and I don't want to be afraid anymore. Something happened this week when I was shooting that M16. The noise, the flash, the power. It scared me to fire that weapon, but I envisioned firing it at every bastard that ever made me look away in fear. I wanted to kill every fucker who ever intimidated me and now that you brought that guy back to me, I want to put him at the top of the list. I'm just so tired of being afraid in this world and they brought something out of me where I'm still afraid, but I no longer feel powerless to fight it. Does that make any sense?"

She had tears in her eyes and was biting her bottom lip. She cleared her throat and said, "Simon, That's the first time I ever saw real anger in your eyes. I never knew how afraid you were. I always thought you were just a stable kinda guy that didn't take too many chances, but I didn't know you were doing that because you were afraid. I'm afraid too and it's scarier every second of every day. I thought you were killed in that crash on your way up and when you left I thought I would never see you again. That scares the hell out of me, to think I might lose you. If these last few weeks have given you some sense of freedom from that fear, then I think you are doing exactly what should be doing. And I am proud to call you my husband."

He leaned over and kissed his wife hard. He took her hand and led her inside where he undressed her in the kitchen and laid her on the table and made love to her.

When they had finished, they wandered up the stairs and climbed into bed. He fell hard asleep in an instant and slept through until the next morning when he was supposed to report to the station to get his assignment. But as he slept, he dreamt of the weapon and the accident.

He dreamed he was climbing a staircase and the stairs were melting beneath his feet like warm butter and the faster he climbed, the harder it got to pull his legs out and reach the next stair. Just before he was consumed by the melting staircase, he awoke and realized that it was a new day.

He showered and put on the uniform he had become so accustomed to wearing and walked out to his truck which was all fixed and sitting in his driveway. He beeped the door and the lock opened and he climbed inside. The air was warm, so he did not have to scrape the windshield but started the truck and backed out of the driveway without hesitation.

He arrived at the station and it felt familiar like he belonged here now. He went inside and saw his platoon mates, all standing at attention outside Altieri's office. He joined the line and came to attention.

Altieri walked out of his office and said, "Good morning volunteers. Welcome back. We have a lot to do and you could not have come back at a more needed time. Let's all head into the conference room and I will brief you on our current status and what your roles will be in the coming days."

The line filed into the empty conference room and Altieri followed them in, closing the door behind himself.

## Chapter 18

Gus stood in the new watchtower that oversaw the entire camp and could barely believe what he was taking in. In two weeks, four hundred men and women from all walks of life had turned into a single-purpose unit of freedom.

The First and Third companies were head to head in a war game in the backfield designed to teach them the value of a silent approach. A kind of capture the flag with weapons and prisoners. The team that won managed to capture the other team's leader and make it back to safe territory without being detected.

The second company was on watch duty, with two-person teams roving the perimeter every half hour. They now had a full watch schedule, where no one came or went through any of the gates without approval from the command center. Every single person was accounted for at all times.

The Fourth company, where Jamal was attached, was serving administrative functions and coordinating the supply lines, the duty rosters, and most importantly, managing the dining tent.

The churches fed them well for the first week but had to return to their normal lives, They spent the time they were there, training a kitchen staff of soldiers to keep the food flowing which was the real challenge, with four hundred trainees burning 5,000 calories a day.

He marveled at how well the machinery moved with each cog knowing its purpose and fulfilling its mission, without complaint or comment.

Jamal poked his head up through the trap door and said, "Major, Captain Tanner requests your presence in the main hangar at your earliest convenience."

"Thanks, Jamal, tell him I'll be right down," answered Gus.

Jamal was now a Corporal having been bumped up above the ranks of Private and Private first class, by virtue of his duty station at the outset. It made sense due to the fact that he was an assistant to the highest-ranking officer in the battalion, but Gus still referred to him by his Christian name as was his privilege.

Gus hated heights but loved a good view and this was the best seat in the house. He had no problem coming up, but getting down, the ladder gave him nightmares. He propped the door and gingerly put one foot on the top rung with white knuckles hanging onto the railing for dear life. He put the other foot on the rung and squared himself in the hole. He gently lowered his foot down to the next rung and exhaled deeply.

Ten minutes later his foot finally hit the dirt and he wanted to get down and kiss the ground. He thought better of it with the whole fourth company watching him from across the way.

He settled himself, squared his corner, and walked briskly to the hanger where Tanner awaited his presence. Jamal fell in behind him and followed his Major to his appointment, staring down a pair of privates who were snickering at the Major's dismount from the tower.

Gus rounded the corner and saw Tanner sitting in the back corner at the table where he and Jamal shared their first breakfast on base, thumbing through a magazine. Boots clapping on the concrete announced the Major's presence and Tanner stood at the table, not quite at attention, but also not quite slouching.

When Tanner arrived two weeks earlier, he pulled in with ninety-six trailers and the song Dixie blasting on his trailer PA system. Gus was not polite when Tanner stopped the convoy and got out. He shook his hand and pulled him close and whispered into his ear, "Turn that Goddamn song off now, we are not at a Klan rally."

Thankfully Travis and Roosevelt weren't there because Gus wasn't sure how they would have handled the display of poor judgment by the head of law enforcement relations.

Since his arrival, Tanner did prove more than useful to the cause. He had a sit-down with the sheriff's office who was headed by a good old boy named Carver Worthington. He was elected sheriff in every election since the second Obama term. His platform slogan made national news the first time he used it, "White lives don't just matter, they are the reason we have a Nation," and he has used it in every run since.

Tanner got him to agree to a policy of mutual distant admiration: as long as they admired from a distance, so would the Resistance. That put an end to unexpected visitors like the one Gus dealt with early on.

As Gus approached the table, Tanner took the liberty of having a seat without his superior officer giving him leave to do so. Gus chalked it up to the fact that Tanner was hauling lobster pots in Downeast Maine when Gus was doing marching tours in full tactical gear in the rain and 90-degree heat in basic.

Gus pulled out a chair and joined Tanner at the table. Jamal stood ten feet behind his Major, awaiting orders.

"Maybe you would like to have this conversation private Major, perhaps without your boy here?" asked Tanner.

Gus knew what he meant but hoped that Jamal hadn't taken notice. He was getting sick of apologizing for Tanner's bigotry.

"Why don't we go into the back office where we can speak frankly," suggested Gus.

Since they had moved in, they set up an office for the senior officers to use as needed. It wasn't great, but it had a couple of chairs, a desk with a computer, and a big cherry wood conference table, they found stashed in a building on the other side of the base during a scavenging mission.

The two men walked side by side to the back office and shut the door. Jamal stood guard outside the door.

Jamal took a seat and waited next to the door. He heard voices proceed to get louder and louder. He couldn't make out most of the words, but there were a few he recognized without trouble. The terms, "nigger," and "mother fucker," seemed to punctuate the conversation liberally at the start and were unmistakably heard through the heavy oak door.

As the conversation wore on, the voices got softer and began to sound more agreeable and he could barely hear them, let alone hear what they were saying. He decided that if the door opened, he didn't want them to think he was listening. He got up and stood at ease, twenty yards from the office door in the empty hanger.

When the door opened, the stench of foul language seemed to emanate from the room, like a cloud of rancid air. The two men walked out, this time the Captain followed the Major. Gus turned around and looked Tanner in the eye and Tanner snapped to attention.

"Captain, I thank you for bringing your concerns to my attention," said the Major, "I trust that our understanding will see our dealings through without further issue?"

The Captain saluted and said, "Yes Major. Thank you for your time."

The Major returned the salute and said, "dismissed."

Tanner walked briskly to the hanger door and walked out, without looking back.

"Major," said Jamal, "Your schedule is clear for the balance of the afternoon. Would you like me to clear your six so you can go get a bit of time to recover from that conversation?"

"That is very considerate of you corporal. That as you probably heard, was mostly about you," said Gus.

"Major, I was not listening, but I did hear a few terms related to race. I hope I didn't make the captain too mad?" asked Jamal.

"Jamal, your race irritates the Captain. It's a sad fact that while most of this country is starving, without a job, health care, a proper education, or a future, men like him want to spend their energy dividing us up based on our skin color. He was on food stamps back in Maine but hates black people for being on welfare. It makes no sense," explained Gus.

"Will he be a problem Major?" asked Jamal

"Not anymore Jamal," answered Gus, "I used something I learned back in Kuwait on managerial tactics. You see most Tunisian decision-makers are autocratic, meaning they don't welcome a variety of opinions at the table. I simply reminded the captain, that this was MY plan and that for it to work we needed all colors of the rainbow. And I suggested that if he didn't like it, I knew about 300 ways to separate his head from his body, and was willing to do so. I convinced him when I pressed my sidearm into his crotch and pulled the trigger. It wasn't loaded but he got the point."

Jamal smiled and said, "Major, you are an inspiration in modern persuasion tactics. May I be dismissed ...sir?"

"Get out of here, and make sure the dinner crew is going to serve on time tonight," said Gus.

He pulled his 45 from his holster and the clip from his pocket. He pulled back on the slide and put the clip back in. The slide closed and he switched the safety on. He then returned the weapon to its holster. Sitting back in the chair, he marveled at how far they had come in such a short time.

## Chapter 19

Simon felt stupid, asking strangers about their politics. As Altieri explained, however, it was a way the volunteers could use their community connections best. They had been sitting outside the Stop and Save since 0800 and only had three sign-ups.

The Army clearly didn't understand the local traffic flow at the supermarket. Before ten o'clock on a weekend, everyone knew that senior citizens and parents rushing to baseball practice were the only one's shopping. He hoped that by noon, a more sympathetic crowd would start showing up and he could stop begging people to talk to him.

Jessinia was speaking to an older woman with salt and pepper hair tied on top of her head in a pink scarf. Simon listened in.

"Yes ma'am. We are part of that new Patriotic Unity Station up on Nichols Ave," Jessinia explained.

"Do you all have guns up there? Are you expecting to go to war?" asked the old lady, "My son served in the Navy during Vietnam. He was on a hospital ship, so he didn't see any real combat. He's now a bartender up at the country club on weekends. Such a disappointment. I bet your mother is so proud of you."

Simon did not know what to expect with this new adventure he was on but was pretty sure at some point the hostilities would start in some fashion. The question was whether they would be part of it, or whether they would be sitting in shopping mall parking lots doing community relations. Jessinia took the duty in stride, handling the old woman as only a woman could.

"You may know my Mother, Margaret Thomas. She lives in those condos down by the Boatramp? She used to go to the Baldwin Center all the time for bingo. But you're too young for the senior center aren't you?" Jessinia turned and winked at Simon.

"Oh you dear, I used to go there all the time before they closed it. God Damn pandemic. Remember those God Damn masks and all that crap about the vaccinations. I got one and it made me sick as hell. I was on the toilet for a month and damn near died from that shot. I never even went back for the second one..."

Jessinia interrupted, "Wow, that's horrible. Glad you're feeling better. Tell you what, I have to talk to a bunch of people here today. I'll tell my Mom and ran into you, what's your name?"

"My name is Judy Stoffan. She may not remember me but" answered the old lady.

"I'll be sure to tell her. Have a great day Mrs. Stoffan. It was very nice speaking with you."

Jessinia squeezed her arm and directed the woman towards the parking lot.

When she came back to the folding table, she restacked the pamphlets and arranged the pens saying, "I'm not sure this is a target-rich environment."

Simon said, "It's still early, around noon things will pick up."

Simon looked up and saw a man walking towards the table with a dog he thought he recognized on a leash. As the man came closer, he called out, "Simon Gates. What the hell are you doing in that uniform?"

"Pete McCauley, what's going on brother?" answered Simon as he rose to his feet and extended his hand, "I haven't seen you in ten years, since the 15-year reunion right?"

"Yeah, I think that was it. How's life? Are you married and what are you doing in a military uniform?" asked his friend.

"Yeah I married my second wife Sarah and we live up by Paradise Green. As far as the uniform goes, I am part of an Army volunteer force stationed at the old reserve center in the north end of town, one of those new Patriotic Unity Stations. I just got back from a three-week training up at Westover in Springfield, where they trained us to shoot, hand to hand combat, use hand grenades, and stuff like that. You'd like it. It's like a gym membership, with explosives," explained Simon.

"Wow really? Simon Gates gets his gun. Who would have thought it was in you. Do they pay you or give you any kind of perks?" asked his friend.

"Well I have that insurance agency over on River Road still, so I don't get paid," said Simon, "but I have to put ten hours of volunteer time in each week to stay current. They give you all sorts of perks like being able to shop at military bases, go to military doctors for free, and things like that. But the fun part is the exercise and the training. I lost 10 pounds during my basic and now run 5 miles a week on training missions. I'm getting in really good shape and serving my country at the same time."

Simon was gilding the lily a bit, he hadn't done any training runs yet, and had only been doing those community service outings. He did lose weight though and wanted to get at least one sign up today from someone that would show up.

"Pete, you were a boy scout. Don't you have some settlement that you live off of so you don't have to work a 9-5 anymore? You would be a perfect candidate for this," said Simon.

Jessinia stepped in to suggest an introduction.

"Oh yeah, this is my platoon mate, Jessinia Thomas. She's a volunteer as well. Do you want to take a swing at convincing this guy, Thomas? I went to school with him and he would be a great asset to our command," Simon suggested.

"Sure," said Jessinia, "Peter tell me about yourself?"

"Well, I have a house over in Lordship on Russain Beach that I bought when a town garbage truck crashed into my first house. The driver was drunk and the town had to pay me a $12 million settlement. So I upgraded. I now have a small picture framing shop in the center of town and enjoy walking Bailey here on the beach most days," he said lifting the leash. The German shorthaired pointer looked up at him when he heard his name.

"You see what I'm saying, Thomas, is he not perfect for the Unity Station? I can't believe I didn't think of you before now. Come up for a tour at least and I'll show you around?" interrupted Simon.

"Well, I'd be more convinced Simon if Ms. Thomas here gave me the tour? Did you say your name was Jessinia? What a beautiful name," said Peter.

This wasn't the first time Jessinia had been hit on. She was attractive with long dark hair and a well-formed figure. Her skin was the color of light coffee and she knew how to use it to her advantage.

"Peter, I'd love to show you around, what's your schedule look like? I am at the station on Tuesdays, Thursdays, and Saturdays?" she said through grinning teeth.

"How does lunch on Tuesday sound?" asked Peter, "I'll bring sandwiches. Do you like Italian subs? I know a great place in town that serves amazing sandwiches, just like ones you get in the city on Arthur Ave."

Peter had never eaten a sandwich on Arthur ave. He rarely, if ever, even went to the city, except of course to see the Rockefeller Plaza at Christmas. The place he went to for lunch every Tuesday, however, had a sign posted that said they were as good as Arthur Avenue and he wanted to sound worldly to the attractive soldier.

"The Army feeds me pretty well," said Jessinia, "But I never turn down a good sandwich. You bring lunch and I'll do the talking. See you at Noon on Tuesday Peter."

Simon smiled to himself and felt good about what he did for both the Army and Jessinia. Peter forgot that he was going shopping and started walking back to his car.

"Wait can I get some contact info from you for my sign-ups, I'm on duty today you know?" Jessenia called after Peter.

Peter turned abruptly and tripped on the dog. He looked up embarrassed and yanked the dog to his side. The dog sunk to the ground and put his ears back, tucking the stump its tail between its legs. Peter walked back to the table with a silly grin on his face and filled out the contact sheet.

"This time I'll walk away without looking like an ass. How does that sound?" he said with a wide smarmy grin.

Jessinia smiled and said, "Absolutely."

When Peter had driven away and the coast was clear. Simon turned to Jessina, like they were two teens at a slumber party, and said, "well what did you think?"

"Just doing my duty Gates, just doing my duty," laughed Jessinia.

They stayed at the supermarket for another four hours and got seventeen phone numbers and set up three tours including the one with Peter. They collected the pamphlets and pens and folded up the table.

Simon said, "Not a bad day for community action, you think?"

Jessinia said, "I'm exhausted and tired of talking. I'll give you half my sandwich on Tuesday if you take this stuff back to the station and let me go home. If I stop in there, I'll be there until 8 o'clock tonight talking to horney soldiers."

"Ha, no worries get out of here," said Simon.

He loaded the table and chairs and supplies into his truck bed and pulled the bed cover back down. He fired up the truck and took an hour driving back to the station in the Saturday afternoon traffic.

When he got to the station, it was 5 PM and the sun was low in the sky. He could see from the cars in the parking lot, the station duty chief, a sergeant named Ed Wilcox, was on. When he got out of the truck he could hear a team of soldiers running drills in the backwoods.

When he got inside, the empty coffee pot was scorching on the hot burner. The offices were all dark and the duty chief was at the station desk with a sidearm on his hip, a white belt, and gloves. His combination cover sat back on his head while he scrolled through a page on a website on the computer.

"Gates, welcome back," he said as he frantically closed windows on the computer. Wilcox was from Ohio and had a wide ruddy face with a rosy nose that indicated his affinity for beer.

"Hey, Sarge," said Gates, "I have the set up from the community event today at the supermarket. Where do you want me to put it?"

"You can stick that stuff in the closet at the end of the hall. Just make sure the pens don't spill all over the place again. The last guy let them spill. One broke and got all over the flags back there," Wilcox said complaining.

Simon was putting the last chair in the closet when the door to the back opened and six men in full tactical gear came walking in out of breath. Each man had a drill rifle strapped to his shoulder and the commotion seemed to bring the room to life, in direct contrast to the calm silence that existed when it was just he and the sergeant in the room.

They walked by Simon without saying a word and when they reached the end of the dimly lit hall, a large man at the end of the line yelled, "OOH-RAH Sergeant."

The sergeant smiled and said, "how'd you guys make out?"

"We ran the whole course in forty-five minutes and logged fifteen kills," said a red-faced man who couldn't have been more than twenty-one. The six-man team made Gates feel old and out of place. Simon walked into the main room and saw the seven men jovial and laughing in a group.

Three of the men had taken their helmets off and sat in chairs around the sergeant. Three of the other men were standing behind the seated soldiers, with their helmets still on, but with the chin straps undone. The stack of drill rifles was piled up against the copier.

Simon interrupted the group by asking the sergeant if there was anything else he needed. The group went silent and turned to look at Simon. The sergeant said, "Naw Gates that's all, you can sign out now."

Simon snapped to attention and the sergeant dismissed him with a salute. He turned and walked to the signout sheet that was posted next to the coffee pot.

He switched off the coffee pot, signed his name on the sheet, and began walking out. The seven men talked quietly together. Simon heard one of them say, "What do we need these fucking volunteers for? They are so fucking old."

He didn't turn back to look who said it and didn't stick around to hear anything else.

He got in his truck, took off his Garrison cap, and started the ignition. He was tired from standing in the parking lot all day. He felt embarrassed to be the oldest man in the room. And he was fuming when he replayed what he heard in his mind.

He decided that he was still new there and he was part of a program that was sure to rile up a few full-timer feathers. He told himself that a 21-year-old enlisted kid was not worth getting upset over. He filed the comment in the back of his mind and turned on the radio.

A Rage Against The Machine Song was playing and he turned it up to full volume. He started to drive out of the parking lot while he sang along, "FUCK YOU, I WON'T DO WHAT YOU TELL ME. FUCK YOU, I WON'T DO WHAT YOU TELL ME. FUCK YOU, I WON'T DO WHAT YOU TELL ME....MOTHER FUCKER!"

## Chapter 20

"Dinner was good," he thought to himself. Roasted chicken quarters with parsley potatoes and a garden salad. Gus liked simple meals now, without a bunch of deep-fried coating or cream sauces. The last three dinners were either fried to a crisp or served in a bath of greasy white gravy. His stomach couldn't take much more of it.

His body told him each morning that he wasn't a young man anymore. When he was 20, he could down a 12-pack of beer and a pile of chicken wings in hot sauce that would gag a horse and still run ten miles the next day. Now, if he missed his morning fiber, he paid the price for it with six weeks of hemorrhoids. It just wasn't fair, he thought.

Now that he was in charge of a real fighting force, that could do some real good in the world, he had to get enough sleep, watch his water intake and eat lots of high fiber food. Fiber sucked, he told himself and he wanted none of it.

The mess tent was empty, except for him and a few of the cadre who lingered over a cup of coffee. He listened to the men talk and said nothing for fear that they might brace up and rob him of his intel.

"When I was back home, we all had a piece. You didn't go down the block with being strapped," said a young Hispanic man from the Third company. Gus didn't know their names but had seen them and was impressed by their military bearing. How so many people from questionable upbringing could become disciplined buttoned-down soldiers in a month astounded him.

The young man continued talking to the three other cadres, "That was why I got in with Martinez, he wanted a place where our families could walk the streets safely and not worry about being braced up by the cops or the turds."

'Turd' was a term Gus had heard but only knew what it meant out of context until he asked Jamal a few days prior.

The occupying soldiers that moved in a few years back had a habit of rousting up the young Latinos in the neighborhoods of Miami. They called them 'Turds' because of their olive-green uniforms. The young kids of Miami thought they looked like baby-shit green.

Gus chuckled and the cadre heard him. They came to attention and stopped talking.

"As you were gentlemen," said Gus, "I was just eavesdropping a bit. I hope you don't mind?"

"Not at all Major," barked the young man who was speaking to the other three.

"Would you mind if I joined your conversation?" asked Gus.

"The Major is welcome in all our conversations, sir. Please take my seat," barked the young man again.

"Now stop that," said Gus, "As you were."

The four men sat back down and Gus picked up his coffee and walked over to sit down next to them.

"Ok now, sit and be normal people for a few minutes. I'm off duty and so are you, so let's talk like men," said Gus.

The four men looked uncomfortable but took their seats next to their commander.

"You were talking about the 'turds'?" asked Gus. The four men snickered. "My chief of staff tells me that is what you all called the Army forces who moved into your neighborhoods in Miami?"

A young black soldier answered, "That's what they called them in Miami, I'm from Baton Rouge and we just called them shit heads."

The table erupted in laughter.

"Why did you hate them so much?" asked Gus

"When they first got there it was OK. It felt like it was safer after they blew up Tampa," answered the young black soldier, "but they started acting like they were better than everyone. They stopped paying for their meals and started messing with our girls. One Army guy even raped a girl in my neighborhood and no one did nothing about it."

"Yeah down in Miami," interrupted the Hispanic man, "they came in and started calling the shots. They made you get off the streets at like 6 PM and if you got caught out they beat you up. My brother got four teeth knocked out one night when he was going to get pampers for his kids."

"Sounds rough," said Gus, "Is that why you guys joined up?"

A third man spoke who had pale black skin and blue eyes. "That's not why I joined up," he said with a thick Texas accent.

Gus said, "Tell me more?"

"I was working on a farm out near Austin," the young man started, "We had a few guns on the property and my boss was a Herzog supporter. The police stormed the place and took him in saying he was a rebel when Crawford started rounding up people. They took his land and fired me and said I was done. I left with no job, I didn't even get to grab my clothes. They just kicked me off the property and said my boss shouldn't have voted the way he did. I went to Pascagoula and met up with Mr. Roosevelt and he told me to join up here."

"How about you?" asked Gus of the one man who had said nothing. He was a white kid and had a cleft palate.

"I-I-I came in with the trailers. My dad told us we had to move into our trailer when our farm was repossessed by the bank. He got covid and died in 2021 and I started driving for my family. We met up with John, I mean President Eustace, out in Kingman and when he told us to go to Gettysburg we went. I followed the convoy down with Tanner,... oh...I mean Captain Martin."

Gus smiled and said, "I know who you mean son. So, what do you guys think of the camp?"

The man with the blue eyes said, "This is awesome. I love what we're doing, When do you think we will see some action, Major?"

The three other men nodded in agreement.

"Well I don't know right now," said Gus, "we need to first make sure you are all ready to fight, and then we need to get orders. That is something

I have been waiting to hear as much as you guys. As soon as I know what our orders are, I will let y'all know. But the harder you work now and the faster we get ready, the sooner we can deploy."

The four men nodded.

"Now I think we all got something we ought to be doing right now? Is your coffee done?" asked Gus.

The four men smiled and looked ashamed.

"Let's hit it, gentleman," said the major and all four men got up with Gus and went different directions.

Gus sat back down and enjoyed the quiet of the empty mess tent. He sipped his coffee and went to pour another cup when Gayle walked in.

After their "conversation," Tanner headed up to Montana, but Gayle decided to stick around and help with training. Gus liked Gayle, even if she had a racist for a husband. She had become the de facto liaison between the trailerites and the tent soldiers.

The trailerites also contributed to the 85 females who arrived on the bus with Roosevelt and they now had 141 women serving in the brigade. At first, he worried about their showering and sleeping arrangements, but the women who lived in trailers were self-contained and they had more than enough tents to set aside three additional tents for the females. The showers had already been separated when the Navy operated this base and Travis was only too happy to assist in getting these facilities operational for the newly arrived women.

"I just had a very enlightening conversation with a few of the cadre, LT," said Gus.

"Oh yeah, Major?" said Gayle.

"These young people have endured quite a bit before coming here. They have as much a gripe against the Government as we do," said Gus.

"We all have our reasons to be here Hawk," said Gayle, "the fact that we all can work together is the miracle."

"How are you holding up?" He asked, "Have you talked to Tanner?"

"Yeah he called last night," she said, "He says he got up to the site in Montana, and Jay and Jeff have been busy. He says they are gonna have a few weeks of work just organizing all the stuff they have brought in."

"That's good. We will build the soldiers and they will arm them," said Gus.

"Do you think the women will ever be allowed to fight too? I mean, I know we are training the gurls, but are they gonna fight?" asked Gayle.

"I would think we need all hands who want to fight at the ready when the time comes, men and women. We all have something to fight for you know?" said Gus.

"That's good," Gayle said changing the subject and getting serious, "Hey Gus, I need to tell you how sorry I am about what my husband said."

"You didn't say it and I don't hold you responsible for him at all. I rather think the fact that you are working so hard training these men and women, regardless of race, is a testament to your character. You don't need to apologize," said Gus.

She covered her face with her hands and started to cry. Gus put his arm around her shoulders and said, "Hey now, what's this all about?"

"I miss him, Major, but I hate the fact that I don't miss how much of an asshole he can be," she said.

"My ex-wife was a tough one to love too," said Gus, "She drank too much and that made it hard sometimes. No one ever said that marriage was easy right?"

"You know it, Major," replied Gayle.

Gus took his arm off her back and stood up and said, "If you need an ear Gayle, I'm always here."

"Yes sir," she said.

"I'm gonna take a walk and enjoy this Florida evening, care to join me?" he asked Gayle.

"No sir, I'm gonna grab a cup of coffee and go read, thanks anyway," she replied.

Gus left the mess tent and walked down the dark runway to his trailer.

The blackness and the quiet of the base made him think that this must have been what it was like when the first settlers came ashore here. The moon had not yet risen and every light was extinguished for security.

He saw a kid light a cigarette in a guard tower on the perimeter. It reminded him that he would have to issue a security briefing about that and explain to the troops how the Germans would watch for matches lighting a cigarette as a target in World War One in the trenches.

He walked to his trailer and pulled the shades closed before he turned on the light above the dinette. His cell phone was blinking and swiped it open. He had a voice message from John. He dialed in to listen.

"Hey Hawk, this is John. I got a mission for you if you think your men are ready. Give me a call so we can discuss it."

He noted the time and saw that the call came in a half-hour prior and thought that John would still be up so he called him.

"John, this is Hawk. Got your message what's up?" said Gus

"Yeah hey, Hawk, I'm gonna have Evan send you over the details on a thing we want to do in New Orleans. Do you have guys ready to fight?"

"Yes sir, we are ready. Tell me what you got," said Hawk.

"Check your email when you get a chance and call me back with any questions, okay?" said the President.

"Copy that. I'll keep an eye out sir. Bye for now," said Hawk, silencing the phone.

He waited for ten minutes and checked his email on his computer. It was a five-page dossier on a person in New Orleans he had never heard of. The orders were to find the man, execute him, and fire the building. He hit print on the document and sent it to his printer. The sheets slowly punched out from the machine.

The title on the page was Operation: Big Easy and his target was the national democratic chair who lived in a mansion in the French Quarter. His name was Cecil Mortimer and he was a heavy donor to the Crawford campaign. One of the best ways to demoralize the enemy was to lop off its head and this guy headed up all the fundraising efforts for the Democrats nationwide. He was the wind beneath Crawford's wings.

The orders were to assault the building and execute Mortimer and anyone else in the building, then burn the place to the ground. It wasn't a full-on military assault, but any action would build morale among the men.

His mind started buzzing with ideas and he quickly decided that they would approach by land and get out by the sea. He would need a boat waiting on the waterfront and that would require a little piracy. They would need two men waiting on a fast boat that they would appropriate from somewhere where no one would miss it and a four-man assault team. He would ensure that the men would not have any identifying marks on their person, just in case things went bad. He wanted full deniability if anyone didn't make it out.

When the team was extracted, the boat would be driven out to the middle of the gulf and scuttled. They would need to find a way to get the team back onshore. Maybe Travis could help with his helo?

He called Jamal in.

"Jamal, we got a job. I need six men from the best platoon we have. Who do you have?" asked Gus.

"Third platoon is kicking ass on the courses, sir, do you want them?" replied Jamal.

"Yes, have them assemble at 0500 in front of my trailer and I will brief them and we'll begin preparations," ordered the Major.

Jamal said, "Yes Major," and left his trailer.

Gus turned off the lights and opened the shades. He opened the window and felt the cool gulf breeze blowing in his otherwise stuffy trailer. The fresh air made him fall asleep quickly.

---

Gus woke early to shower and got dressed. He was ready for assembly by 0445. He didn't dare go outside before the team assembled out front, because that would remove the whole sense of anticipation. He kept quiet and sipped a cup of coffee in the dark at his dinette.

At 0457, the first four men of the platoon showed up and by the time the clock struck 5, thirty soldiers were assembled in front of the trailer with Jamal at the head. When Gus stepped out the door, Jamal yelled "Ten-HUT!" and all came to attention under the moonlight.

Gus could barely make out their faces but saw that they were evenly spaced, dressed in their uniforms, and at attention. That was a good start.

He began with, "Good Morning Ladies and Gentlemen. Late last night, I received orders from our President. It's called Operation Big Easy and it will involve an attack on a target inside the city of New Orleans. Our mission is to insert a team into the target's home, neutralize the target, and then fire the domicile without detection.

'

"There will be no prisoners taken and ancillary casualties around the target are acceptable. You're going to be killing a leader of the Democratic party who is responsible for a great many of the atrocities that have been committed against the American people. Not least of which, include funding those who were instrumental in the occupation of our Nation by a military force, the corruption of our political system through bribery, chicanery, and fraud. He is also guilty of dereliction of duty to serve the people of this Nation in a manner that is befitting the spirit and letter set out by the Constitution of these United States.

"This act will be the first in a series of acts that will engage our force in an armed conflict against the United States Government and will be the birth cry of an organization we have termed to this point simply as "The Resistance". Going forward, however, while you will bear no identifying marks or flags and will not identify your affiliation to anyone outside this organization, you will be known as The Independent Army Of The Resistance.

"We have two days to prepare ourselves for this purpose. Six of you will participate in the action, while the remainder of this platoon will help facilitate the success of this mission. If there are any who wish to be excused from this and subsequent missions, you are free to depart at this time. You may collect your belongings and leave this facility at once without retribution or fear of reprisals. Transportation will be provided to you at no charge to your desired location. Please fall out now if you wish to be excused."

He could not see any faces in the dark but did not detect any motion. He counted to thirty before he said another word.

He continued, "May I take that silence as your unspoken agreement to go to war?"

The platoon woke the entire camp with their answer, "YES SIR!"

"Very good platoon. Let us begin with a run over to our training grounds where we will discuss the intricacies of entry and extraction of a target. Corporal, the platoon is yours.

Jamal stepped in and said, "Platoon, Right....face. Quick time,...March."

The platoon trotted off into the darkness and the Major watched them go.

Within a few steps, Gus heard someone calling cadence in the last minutes of darkness before a new day would begin and smiled.

"A little bird, A LITTLE BIRD,
with a little bill, A LITTLE BILL,
was sitting on, WAS SITTING ON,
my window sill, MY WINDOW SILL,
I lured him in, I LURED HIM IN,
with a piece of bread, A PIECE OF BREAD
and then I smashed, AND THEN I SMASHED,
his fucking head, HIS FUCKING HEAD
I SMASHED HIS FUCKING HEAD, OOH-RAH."

## Chapter 21

Gus had a hard time sleeping that night and tossed and turned as visions of failure danced in his head. These recruits were still quite green. He worried about what would happen if they lost their nerve and decided to abandon the cause.

He worried that they would climb in the house and get cold feet or maybe not even get out of the van when they drove up to the place. What would they do to each other? What would they do to themselves? What would they do to the cause?

He wanted to go with them, to guide them, encourage them. Keep the weapons pointing in the right direction. But he knew, he had to stay back and watch from afar.

The Army had satellites and drones to watch their teams sneak up on targets when he was in the Middle East. Now, all he had was Jamal and a cell phone to give him the play by play. If Jamal went down, the mission went blind.

When he decided to get out of bed, the sky was still dark and the birds were not even chirping yet. He washed and dressed and climbed the watchtower to watch the sunrise, but still had an hour to wait before that happened.

He surveyed the dark base and looked for any kind of movement. The guard shacks were all lit up and moving and that gave him hope. If they could be trusted to do their job at 4 AM, maybe he could trust his six-person team to fulfill their mission.

He ran over his selection of soldiers in his mind a thousand times. The decision on which team had the best shots, the best instincts, and the best speed was not an easy thing to determine.

Of the thirty soldiers, only half of them were young enough to climb the stairs in under ten seconds in silence, and of those fifteen, only three could shoot with laser accuracy. Those three, McCormack, Gonzalez, and Littleton were obvious choices for the insertion team. Of the seven recruits who were physically able to do the task, however, which three were smart and disciplined enough to be trusted to steal a boat?

They would have to drive it into the rally point and get the team out of the city, then run the boat out to the middle of the Gulf and scuttle it. He settled on Jones, Ramirez, and Jenkins as the recovery crew who would save the day.

Now all he had left to do was tell them his decision when they rose. He decided he would assemble the platoon one more time, and tell those who he wanted for the mission and send the rest of the platoon out onto the field to continue training. When the time came for action, he would invite the platoon leaders to listen in on the call from Jamal.

He sat down on the floor of the tower and closed his eyes. The next thing he knew was the trap door opening and Jamal poking his head up, "Major the troops are assembled in front of your trailer."

Gus wiped the sleep from his eyes and said, "Oh Ok. Yeah, I'll be right down."

He took a deep breath and began his long descent.

When his boots touched the ground, the platoon yelled, "OOH Rah!!"

He waved his hand and laughed, as he walked in front of the platoon. The men stood at attention and he could only guess what the hour was. Maybe 0600, maybe later.

He started saying, "Sorry folks, I slept late."

The soldiers snickered but did their best to keep their military bearing.

"Recruits, we have some very important work to do. Six of you will leave this place and might not be coming back. The rest of you will be asked to pray for their safety. You have all demonstrated a commitment to military excellence that I must admit, surprised me."

"When you arrived here three weeks ago," Gus continued, "you came from everywhere. Some served in the U.S. military, some served in other countries. Some never served a day in their lives and some never thought they would ever serve. But you all have stepped up and offered your lives for a cause that will ensure our Nation is returned to its rightful owner."

He paused and looked at their faces. A woman directly in front of him looked to be roughly his age and he looked beyond her and saw a boy not more than 18. He saw brown faces, tan faces, pale faces, and dark faces. He wanted to cry but refused to allow the emotion to enter.

"I have a tough job this morning and a tougher job tonight. I have to pick six of the best of the best to go into harm's way and tell twenty-four of you that you must stand down and watch."

A voice called from the back of the platoon, "We got em Major."

"I know you do sir, I know you do. But if we send 30 of you into the target bedroom, I don't think they will be happy with what happens to the carpets. I don't think we will have time for you to wipe your feet," replied Hawk.

The platoon erupted in laughter. Jamal yelled, "Ten HUT!" and the platoon stopped laughing.

"Sorry corporal," Gus said.

"Alright, so here's the plan. Six of you will fall out and come with me. 24 of you will head out on training today. If you're not one of the selected six team members joining us, please know, your time will come and this is just the start of our offensive. Please wish your platoon mates well."

"Now, If you hear your name, fall out, and please form a line to my right," ordered the Major.

"Corporal please join me up here as you will be leading this mission. Would the following soldiers, join me up here:

"McCormack
Gonzalez
Littleton
Jones
Ramirez
Jenkins."

The four men and two women walked forward and stood at attention next to the Corporal."

"Alright platoon, you are dismissed, Platoon Commander, see that these recruits get double deserts at today's lunch, okay?" said Gus.

The platoon erupted in cheers. The four platoon commanders ordered their platoon to remain at attention. One commander said, "Platoon, hand ….salute."

Twenty-four soldiers snapped to salute their commanding officer and their platoon mates. Gus's lip began to quiver. He returned the salute. Almost as if on automatic pilot, the platoon was ordered to right-face and quick-timed down the runway.

Gus squared his corner and walked in front of the team.

"Alright soldiers, we have eighteen hours until you have a date with a New Orleans Democrat," explained the Major, "You will spend that time briefing on the layout of the building, the street layout, and your exit to the water. We will also find a boat that you will need to commandeer without detection and use that boat to extract the team from the city waterfront and out to sea. Is that clear?"

"Yes sir," said the team.

"Okay then, let's lay into the hanger where we will do the research and get you ready to roll. Right... face. …..Forward ……March. Quick time….. March," Gus and the seven younger soldiers jogged to the hanger to get ready.

---

The two vans pulled up in front of the hanger at 1300. One would head directly to the French Quarter with 200 pounds of fertilizer, 10 gallons of diesel fuel, and enough ammunition to kill a small village. The other was heading to South Shore Marina, where they were told the Pegasus III was moored.

The boat was an integral part of the whole plan. They thought that when the house was set ablaze, the quarter would erupt in panic and there was no way the van would get them out of there without detection. By picking them up in the river and running through the Lake Borgne surge barrier and out the Bayou Bienvenue, they hoped they could slip out to open water undetected.

That would put them in Lake Borgne, for a very long time and that was a busy waterway. If they cut back and went out of the abandoned Gulf canal, they were sure to be in empty water the whole way with a much more direct route to open water. The only problem with that plan was the barrier that the feds put in the canal after it flooded the city during Katrina.

Budget cuts decimated the levy maintenance system since Crawford took office, but a report from 2021, that they found on Google from the Army Corp of Engineers, suggested that the barrier had been breached by a tropical storm that same year. There were no updated reports that they could find and it seemed no one had been out there since to do any assessment. Even if the barrier was breached, the channel was littered with sunken vessels and storm debris that might kill the propeller and potentially sink the boat.

The fact that it was abandoned was invaluable though. Running to the gulf unseen was preferred. If however, the barrier was not sufficiently failed or they caught any hazards on the way out, they would be stuck. The extraction team would have to make that decision when they saw what the traffic looked like.

The plan was to send them to get the boat early and have them scout the canals in daylight to map a path out as an escape route on GPS. Once they had their route planned, the team could hang out in the marsh until it was time. They carried 10 pounds of C4 and half a dozen shovels if they decided to improvise.

Jamal was going to drive the New Orleans bound van. The van would drop the team off at the St Peter's mansion. The front windows of the house meant that they could have eyes inside with Jamal waiting in the van. Thankfully it was a single floor home with a set of french doors on the side, that they could use a glass cutter to open

Once inside, Gonzalez would set up the fertilizer bomb in the kitchen, and McCormack and Littleton would neutralize the home's occupants in the four bedrooms. They were told that the prime target and his partner were presumably going to be sleeping in the master bedroom and the daughter from the prime target's first marriage was there with her husband and her two kids. All occupants were to be neutralized and it bothered Gus that he was giving orders to kill children.

When they were done, the team would run down St. Peters Street and find their boat waiting for them at the Mississippi River Pier. With all six soldiers aboard, they would run full throttle down and out the gulf canal and head out to the gulf where they would scuttle the ship with the remaining C4 and get picked up by a fishing boat they had charted earlier that week.

If all went well, they would be back on base by midday.

Gus sat at the table with the seven and said, "It's time."

The soldiers rose and began picking up their gear and loading it into their respective vans. The boat team was lucky to find out that Ramirez had been a boat mechanic for a bunch of years and Jones came from a family of longliners. Jenkins had no idea how to drive a boat but seemed to pick up the finer point of setting a C4 explosive in training particularly well. On the shore side of the equation, all three had been trained in small arms handling and were taught to build fertilizer bombs.

If anyone went down inside, the two others could pick up the slack, but it was likely if that happened that all three would never make it out alive.

Jamal hopped in the driver's seat and put an earpiece in his ear. He called Gus and when he picked up on the first ring, Jamal laughed and said, "Just checking Major." When the gear was loaded and the four soldiers were inside, the van heading for New Orleans departed. When they reached the gate they turned left out of the entry and headed for Route 90.

When the all-clear was given, the other three soldiers got into their van. Jenkins had loaded the shovels and explosives and Ramierez jumped into drive. Gus had talked with Ramirez about hot wiring a boat and Ramirez seemed like he had done that more than a few times before.

"We had a workboat at my last job that had a bad ignition, I used to start that all the time without a key," said Ramirez, "this shouldn't be too hard."

"Good," said the Major, "call me when you get there and let me know when you have found the boat."

"Yes sir," said Ramirez as he started the van. The three men drove out and turned right to ensure they did not come anywhere near the first van as they headed to Route 90.

---

Gus's phone rang. He looked at the time, 17:42, and figured it had to be the boat team checking in.

"GO," answered Gus.

"Major this is the boat team," said Ramirez, "We have located the vessel and are waiting for the last marina employees to leave. I was looking at the chart, Major, and analyzing Bayou Bienvenu. The traffic there could be pretty bad with the fishing tournament this weekend. I think I would prefer to take my chances with the barrier in the Gulf Canal, with your permission sir?"

"You're the boating expert, Ramirez," said Gus, "You do what you think, is right."

"Copy that sir, we'll be shoving off at 1830 and should be scouting the barrier by sunset."

"Very good Ramirez, be safe," Gus said as he hung up the phone.

Twenty minutes later his phone rang again and this time it was Jamal. "Go Corporal, answered Gus."

"Major, we have arrived in New Orleans. Proceeding to scout the location and sequester until 0200."

"Copy that Corporal. The mission is a go."

Gus went to his trailer to close his eyes and decompress until it was time. He would go to the command center at 1200 and check in with the teams at that time.

---

He walked into the hangar and strode back to the command center. Everything was quiet and dark on base. The only light and noise came from the tiny room in the back of the hanger. He eyed his phone and the time said 23:54.

Opening the door, he saw two privates scanning google maps on the computer.

"Ten-hut," was announced and the two privates rose from their seats. The Major said, "as you were."

"Private, any news?" asked the Major.

"No, sir. All is quiet. We got a text at 2200 that said the boat team had opened the barrier and that an escape route had been established," answered the Private.

"Very good," Gus answered nodding his head.

His phone rang at exactly midnight and it was Ramirez.

"Major we are inbound and just entering the river. We are about forty minutes from the pier."

"Very good Ramirez. Maintain communication as long as possible," said Gus.

An hour passed and the room was silent. Gus poured a cup of coffee and wondered what the two private's stories were. "Private, where are you from?" asked Gus

"I'm from Biloxi," said a young dark-skinned man named Kennedy. "I'm from Tampa Bay," said a lighter-skinned man named Garcia.

"How do you like the service?" asked Gus

The men didn't have a chance to answer and Gus' phone rang again from the Boat Team.
Ramirez was whispering this time, "Major we have arrived on station. All is quiet on the waterfront."

Gus lowered his voice and said, "Very well. Remain hidden and available. I'll check in with the shore unit."

He texted Jamal, "Status Check?"

Jamal texted back writing, "Team is ready to deploy. Waiting in Walmart parking lot for 30 mins more."

Gus texted back, "Copy."

He watched his phone count the minutes to 0200. At 0159, he told the privates, "It's time."

He received a text from Jamal at 0200. "Team is away, will wait for engagement then exit location."

At 0201, his phone rang and it was Ramirez, "We are standing by. See you in the morning."

"Very well," said Gus, "text me if you have any issues."

The phone went silent.

At 0203, Jamal texted, "TWO MUZZLE FLASHES. EXITING LOCATION."

Gus wondered what happened to the other three kills. Maybe they were in the back bedrooms and Jamal couldn't see them? Maybe they weren't there? His mind raced with different scenarios and his heart pounded as he waited for the next text message.

At 0209, Ramirez texted, "Loud explosion in town. Expect arrival shortly"
At 0212, Ramirez texted, "Making way at full throttle"
At 0227 Ramirez texted, "Two shore team on board. Entering ICW."
At 0312 Ramirez texted, "Entering Gulf Canal"
At 0520 Ramirez texted, "Current position 29.61 N, 89.32 W. ETA 0910 29.48N, 87.73W"

Gus ordered, "Private, dispatch the charter boat to 29.48N, 87.73W for 0900"

---

The van pulled in and Jamal got out looking very dejected.

"Corporal, why the long face?" asked Gus.

"Major, I regret to inform you that Private McCormack did not make it out of the residence alive," answered the Corporal.

Gus grew cold and angry and said, "What happened?"

"I am told that McCormack went into the bedroom to neutralize the kids and the mother and she saw them crying in a corner," explained Jamal, "She paused and the husband came out and fired two rounds into her back. Jenkins went back to try and get her, but the trigger had already been set on the bomb. He and Gonzalez exited the building leaving McCormack behind."

"Did they know what happened to the husband and wife and the kids after?" asked Gus.

"No sir, they ran down to the boat and I heard the building go when they were halfway there," answered Jamal.

"Who told you this, Corporal?" asked Gus.

"When I picked them up from the boat dock, Gonzalez told me," The Corporal finished.

"Alright, get everybody fed and washed, and let's meet for a debrief at 1500 in the conference room. Get me the President on the phone, Corporal," said Gus storming back to his trailer.

When he got there, as he was walking in, his phone rang. A voice said, "Please hold for President Eustace."

Gus paused with the phone to his ear and waited to hear John come on the line, "Hawk, you there?" asked the President

"Yes sir, Hawk here," answered Gus, " I have some unfortunate news, Mr. President. I have yet to fully debrief the teams, but it has come to my attention that one of the team was lost in the incursion and her body was left behind. Furthermore, I have no confirmation on the neutralization of the family, but I can confirm that the primary target was neutralized."

"Well that's not all bad news, Major, At least we achieved our primary objective," said the President. "We saw a story on CNN that the DNC Chair was killed and his house was detonated. They have not released any details on who is responsible yet so I don't know what they got from the scene. There was no word of the family on any of the videos from the scene either."

"Mr. President, Once I have had a chance to formally debrief the team, I will send you over a written report," said Gus.

"That'd be fine," said President Eustace, "Talk soon," and the line went dead.

## Chapter 22

Simon parked the truck, got out, and slammed the door. He ripped the garrison cover from his head and stomped to the front door, muttering under his breath.

When he walked in the door, his wife was sitting on the couch reading. She looked up and saw the anger in her husband's eyes. "What's wrong?" she asked.

"Those enlisted assholes won't let up. They treat me like I am a senior fucking citizen and Altieri won't do a God Damn thing about it?"

"What happened?" Asked Sarah.

"Today we were supposed to train with live fire in the back range," started Simon. "Jessinia, Phil, and I were all told that we would be doing three-man training drills today with live weapons. So I wore my fatigues and was ready to go when I got there this morning. Jessinia and Phil did too. We waited for two hours for someone to show up to train us and when no one came by 10 AM, I called Aliteiri and asked where everyone was."

"He said that the trainer was out running drills with enlisted folks and that we were to go do community canvassing again at the supermarket," Simon continued, "So we did. Let's just forget the fact for a moment, that we have been out of basic for three weeks and have spent every second of every day we have been here, handing out flyers at the supermarket and cleaning toilets. But when we got back this evening, I overheard the enlisted guys joking that the 'senior citizen volunteers' thought that they would be getting real training today. The desk sergeant yelled at me for going in public in my fatigues. It was all a setup and they did it deliberately."

"How do you know it was deliberate, Altieri said the trainer was called away on other duties, didn't he?" asked Sarah.

"Don't defend them, Your MY wife and you didn't even want me to do this, remember," said Simon.

"I'm not defending them, but maybe you're being a little dramatic about this?" she answered her husband.

"Dramatic? They told me to come dressed one way and then yelled at me for it. Then they told me that we were gonna do something related to being in the Army and then screwed us over there too. How am I being dramatic?" asked Simon waving his arms above his head and screaming.

Trying to diffuse the situation and calm her husband, she said, "When you see Altieri next, ask him what's going on. There's probably a good reason. Can I get you a beer?"

"You and your good reasons," said Simon, "Why do you have to be so flipping reasonable?"

He asked with a smile coming over his face. He didn't know how she did it, but she almost always could reel him in when he went high and to the right. She handed him the beer. He unzipped his windbreaker and unbuttoned his shirt.

"I gotta be there tomorrow at 0800," Simon said with a frown.

"What for?" she asked.

"They are having inspection Friday and need someone to get the facilities ready," said Simon, "The volunteers pulled cleaning duty *once again*."

She wondered why her husband would work so hard for these people who treated him like the cleaning crew but decided it was better to keep her mouth shut. She told herself that Altieri knew what was going on and had a plan, but knew deep down inside that he wasn't to be trusted.

Simon and Sarah made dinner, shared a bottle of wine, and then went to bed. Simon woke the next morning and put on his fatigues and reported back to the station ready to clean and get ready for inspection.

He walked in and saw the light on in Altieri's office. Simon went to ask him about the conversation he overheard the day before. Altieri was on the phone and motioned for Simon to take a seat.

Simon was seated and waited for the lieutenant to get off the phone. Altieri wasn't talking and it didn't appear to Simon that he was listening all that intently either. Eventually, Altieri said, "Great call guys, thanks for keeping me in the loop. Talk next week," and hung up.

"That was a conference call on the volunteer program. We had 100 station commanders from all over the country on that call, I doubt they knew who I was," said Altieri.

"How's it going everywhere else?" asked Simon.

"Well, they are having a tough time getting volunteers. Our state had one of the best turnouts of them all nationwide. You were the first,

Gates. They are all excited about you," said Altieri with a smile, "Sorry, you stopped in with a question and I kept you waiting. What's up?"

"Well…" Simon began, "I overheard something yesterday that made me a little concerned. You see I showed up for training with Jessinia and Phil and our trainer was supposedly out training enlisted soldiers. When I got back, I got the impression that the misinformation was set up deliberately and that we are not very welcome among some of the men here. I worry that all we are ever gonna do is clean and do supermarket events."

"What do you want to do?" asked Altieri, "we are not actively engaged in combat and we do have an inspection tomorrow."

"Yes sir, I get that," stammered Simon, "but it seems there is some resentment about our presence from the men and that is why our training schedule is so light. I get the feeling that no one wants to train us?"

"I'm sorry you feel that way Gates, but I'm sure your training is right on schedule. Give it a couple more weeks will ya? This is a changing time for the Army and people take time to get used to new things. Be patient please," the lieutenant explained

"Of course, sir, thanks for hearing me out," Simon replied.

"No worries Gates dismissed," he said.

Simon rose to leave the office.

"By the way Gates, there is a bulb out in the men's head, would you see that gets replaced?" added Altieri.

Simon said, "Yes sir," and walked out.

He felt unheard, dismissed, and undervalued. He wanted to quit, but his attention was quickly diverted from his woes when he heard a special report come on the TV in the corner of the main room.

"The Nation mourns this morning on news that the Democratic party chairperson and his partner were killed last night in their New Orleans French Quarter home. Assailants broke in and shot the senior political party head and then detonated a bomb inside his home. His family was spared, getting out seconds before the bomb exploded and police are combing through the debris to find clues as to who may be responsible. We now go live in New Orleans where Mimi Benson is on the scene at a briefing by police. Mimi?"

The field reporter began "Thanks Tom, I'm here with police officials who are about to make a public statement about an explosion that occurred just down the street from here last evening. Let's listen in."

A police officer with lots of gold braiding on his cover came on saying, "Overnight, at approximately 2 AM, Cecil Mortimer, of the Democratic National Party, was killed when we believe as many as four men entered his residence, shot him and his life partner Lionel Beauregard, as they slept. When units arrived on the scene, the residence was fully engulfed in flames and Moritmier's daughter, husband, and their two children were found taking shelter behind a parked car across the street."

The officer continued, "New Orleans Fire Department suppressed the flames and by 8 AM, we were able to enter the residence to discover three bodies, two of which belonged to the victim and his partner and a third which we believe to be one of the assailants. We have yet to identify the third body, but our investigation has found out that the deceased was dead before being consumed by the flames when the victim's son-in-law shot and killed the perpetrator. This is an ongoing investigation and we will have more as the day progresses. Thank you."

"Well Tom, here's what we know right now..." the field reporter continued. Simon looked around him and a group had collected. Jessinia said, "Jesus, I met him once at a fundraising event in Harford for Senator Bloomfield."

Phil said, "Looks like some Bible beater decided to take things a little too literal."

Several men in the group laughed.

Jessinia said, "Shut up, assholes," and walked away.

Simon followed close behind.

They went into the supply room to collect the supplies they would need for the duty today: A mop, Brasso, lemon cleaner, and rags.

Jessinia said, "Why are there so many assholes here? I don't know if I can stand one more shit head comment from Phil."

Simon answered, "Is this what you expected when you signed up? Cleaning, polishing, and handing out supermarket flyers?"

"Not really, but I also didn't expect the chauvinism either, so I stopped expecting much. It's the Army, that's what you do until someone starts shooting right?" she said, raising her eyebrow.

"I guess," said Simon, "I just thought we would be doing more stuff outside like drilling and weapons training. They said this would be like a gym membership, but I have already gained four pounds."

"I know right?" said Jessinia, "It's those God damned donuts everybody brings in."

The two laughed and filled a bucket with hot water. They started on the heads. Jessinia in the lady's head and Simon in the men's.

By 2 PM, they had cleaned the main hallway and the locker rooms and were moving into the bunk room, when a general alarm sounded and a message came across the PA system, "All hands are ordered to assemble in the courtyard at this time, All Hands, All Hands."

Simon hadn't been out there yet. He and Jessinia followed the crowd to a concrete area that was surrounded by the U-shaped building. It had a World War One cannon parked in front of it, next to a flagpole, and in front of that, stood an officer Simon had never seen before.

The entire unit was assembled and there were at least forty people, Simon thought, standing at attention. The officer had many more ribbons than Altieri and the Lieutenant saluted him and said, "3rd Battalion present and accounted for, Sir." Altieri squared his corner and walked over to the side of the unit and stood at attention.

"Ladies and Gentlemen," the senior officer started, "My name is Colonel Richard Pullman. I have just come in from Washington where the word has gotten out about the success of your Unit's volunteer program. The way you have adapted to the addition of volunteer forces to your ranks and the success you have demonstrated integrating as a unit should be an example to the more than one hundred units that have been established nationwide.

"And I think I speak for many of our officers when I say that your success could not have come at a more opportune time. If you saw the news this morning, the DNC chair was killed last night in a terrorist assault of his residence. Not only are you the first group of volunteers, but you were also witness to the failed bombing of the State Capitol while on your way to basic as well. You have a true understanding of what our Nation is up against.

"Our nation is under attack and rebel forces are growing. Your unit was created to help combat the growth of those rebel forces. While we are not confirmed that this attack this morning was part of a larger force, our intel indicates that it will happen sooner rather than later.

"As such, this unit is now ordered to THREATCON CHARLIE. As of 1800 today, all hands will maintain a 24-hour watch at this unit. Liberty has been canceled for all enlisted personnel and volunteer personnel are granted until 1800 today to settle their affairs at home and report for watch duty. Ladies and Gentlemen, our Nation thanks you for your service."

The Colonel came to attention and raised his hand for a salute. Altieri saluted in return and the Colonel walked back toward the building.

Altieri walked to the front of the unit and said, "I know this is new for you volunteers and even some of you enlisted folks have never served under a THREATCON CHARLIE. This unit has never been under that kind of order as long as I have been part of it. But we are in new times now and things are changing. Uniforms of the day will be full tactical gear. For you vols, that means your fatigues and we will issue you helmets and body armor later tonight. There's gonna be a lot of questions, I am sure, but we will get through it and figure it all out together. All right, I will see you all here tonight at 1800, DISSSSS-missed."


The unit scattered. Simon turned to Jessenia and said, "I guess this means we are staying here?" Altieri overheard the comment and said, "Yup Gates, pack your toothbrush, you're getting the real Army experience, just like you wanted."


Simon's heart sunk. He wanted to train like a soldier, but he never thought he would have to fight. Was this a prelude to war? Or was this just cautionary prep? What the hell was happening and how was he going to tell his wife that he wasn't coming home tonight?"


He joined the crowd, running to their cars. When he got to the end of the parking lot, he saw a pile of empty sandbags and a truck dumping a pile of sand. The guard was in full tactical gear with a rifle and waving his hand to stop traffic to allow the line of cars to leave the unit parking lot.


Simon drove home with his mind blazing with thoughts and fears. Mostly he wondered how Sarah would handle the news.


He pulled in the driveway and Sarah wasn't home yet. He looked at his phone and the time said 4:30. She wouldn't be leaving work for another half hour and he only had an hour and a half until he had to be back at the unit. He called her phone. She picked up on the second ring.


"Sarah, it's me," Simon said, "I'm at home and have been ordered to stay at the unit for the next few days. We are at THREATCON CHARLIE or something like that and some officers from Washington told us that we need to get ready to fight a war with some rebels, so they said I have to stay there and do watch duty."

"Wait a sec, wait a sec, Simon, What are you saying? What about a war?" asked Sarah.

"I don't know what I am saying," said Simon, "but I gotta be there by six and I was worried I was gonna miss you because they said I had to bring my toothbrush."

"Don't go anywhere, I'll be home in 10 minutes," she said and hung up the phone.

Just as she promised, her car screamed in the driveway in 10 minutes. He met her at the front door.

"What do you mean you have to stay there?" she yelled.

He had packed his bag and stood in front of her in fatigues and combat boots. In those clothes, he used to feel powerful. At that moment, however, he was afraid of his wife. He also feared the next few hours, the next few days but most of all, he feared the outside world.

"An officer from Washington showed up while I was cleaning today and we assembled. He told us we were a great unit and that we were at THREATCON CHARLIE now. I don't know what that means. But everyone got real serious and they started putting sandbags at the entrance to the parking lot. I think it has something to do with that bombing in New Orleans and the DNC chairperson's death. Did you hear about that?" Simon talked fast, making very little sense.

"Yeah I heard on the radio that some big Democrat was killed and that they think it was some kind of terrorist thing," she answered.

"Well, they think that some rebel forces were behind it and that they might be organizing and now they want to put us on alert. That's all I know," said Simon, "So I have to go stay at the station and do watch duty until they decide what's next."

"But you were just supposed to do ten hours a week? Where did this come from?" asked Sarah.

"I had to put a minimum of ten hours a week in, they never told me what the max was. So I guess I gotta go?" said Simon.

His wife started to cry.

"Why are you crying?" he asked, taking her in his arms.

"This is scary," she said, "I don't want to lose you."

"You're not gonna lose me, I'm just going to the Unit. Remember how I was pissed that they would only let me clean? Well this is better, don't you think?" he explained.

"Can I call you? Can I see you?" asked Sarah.

"I think so, yeah. Well, you can call me at least, I gotta find out how they handle visitors, but as soon as I know that, I will let you know. Now stop crying," he said, stroking her hair.

She wiped her face and he unwrapped his arms.

"Did you get everything you need," she asked.

"Yeah, I'm packing the same as I packed for basic," he said.

"Did you remember four-inch tape, toothpaste, shampoo, and soap?" she asked

"Damn, I forgot the soap. I need a towel too. Very funny about the tape by the way," he said.

"I'll get it, stay here," she said, running up the stairs. She came down with an unopened box of toothpaste and a white bath towel. He shoved them in his new army duffle, that he bought from the Army surplus store the day before.

"Where'd you get that bag?" she asked.

"I bought it yesterday, at that place over on Barnum Ave. They never issued us one at basic," he said, "Never thought I would need it so soon though."

"Do you have time to eat?" she asked. He looked at his phone and it said 5:02.

"I've got an hour, you want to split a can of soup before I go?" he said.

"As long as I can have a glass of wine," she joked.

"Can I have one too?" he asked.

"You get the glasses, I'll start the soup. Chowder okay?" she asked

They ate the soup, finished their glasses of wine and he picked up his bag to walk out the door. She grabbed his arm and said, "You're not leaving without a kiss."

He grabbed her waist with one hand and the back of her head with the other. He kissed her mouth with a passion that he did not even muster on their wedding day. When he released, she was flushed and her eyes fluttered.

"I love you, wife," he said, picking up the bag once again.

"I love you husband" she replied, steadying herself on the hall table. "Make sure you come back to me," she said as she smiled.

"I will, I promise," he said, looking her in the eye as he donned his garrison and opened the front door.

She watched him walk to his truck. He threw the big army bag in the passenger seat and climbed in the truck and started it. She knew this man intimately but didn't recognize the look in his eye. It was a new man she had just said goodbye to and she wondered if she would ever get to know him. They had just met and he was going to war.

When he got to the station, a crew of enlisted were filling the sandbags and a mounted gun was set up facing toward the road. Everyone wore full tactical gear and a humvee was parked blocking the entrance.

A man he recognized as one of the enlisted, came to the truck and asked him for ID. He showed his ID to the soldier. The soldier waved to the humvee and it backed up, allowing Simon to drive in.

Simon pulled into a parking spot and saw the Colonel speaking to a young woman with red hair. Simon got out of his truck and began walking in. The woman grabbed the colonel's arm and said, "Is he one of the volunteers?"

The colonel said, "Yes I believe he is. Soldier, would you come here for a moment?" Simon looked up and saw that the colonel was speaking to him. He turned and lowered his bag to his hip and walked over to the talking couple.

"Christy, is that your name?" the Colonel asked, looking at the red-haired reporter, "This is... ?"

"I'm Simon Gates, sir." finishing the Colonel's sentence.

"Gates is one of our volunteers who went up to Springfield last month, I believe", the Colonel continued, "he has been assigned to the third battalion and is a local from here in town, is that right, Gates?"

"Yes Sir", replied Simon. "Gates, Christy here, is from the New York Hour and is doing a story on our elevated condition and the usage of volunteer forces to protect our hometowns. She'd like to speak to you if that is alright" asked the Colonel.

"Yes sir that would be fine", said Gates. "Great, well Christy, I will leave you with Gates for now. When you're done, you can meet me in my office inside. You remember how to get there?" the Colonel asked.

She nodded yes. "Gates, you are representing our volunteer force and we want to share with the world how appreciative we are for your service," continued the Colonel, "you treat this lady nice now, you understand?"

"Yes sir," said Gates.

Christy and Gates walked over to a series of rocks that marked the edge of the parking lot and had a seat. Her photographer joined them, as they walked over.

"Did I hear your first name is Simon," asked Christy?

"Yes ma'am. Simon Gates, ma'am," answered Simon.

"If you don't mind me asking, Simon Gates, how old are you? You don't look like a fresh recruit out of high school," Christy began. Her red hair glistened in the fading spring sunlight.

"Yes, I'm 45," explained Simon, "I have an insurance agency here in town and a wife and home and a mortgage. I'm quite far from my eighteenth birthday, but I am a recruit, just the same."

"And I am told you serve without pay, that you're a volunteer?" asked the reporter.
The photographer snapped a dozen photos in succession.

"Yes, I serve as a volunteer. The idea is that we are part of this community, so we are more apt to protect it," he added.

"What made you want to do this?" asked the young woman.

"I am afraid of where we are headed as a nation and I wanted to do my part to protect it. My wife wasn't thrilled about the idea, but she understands that it's something I feel I must do," he explained.

"Your wife, what is her name?" she asked

"Sarah Gates, why?" he answered.

"Do you mind if I get her perspective on your service, by asking her a few questions?" she said beneath batting red eyelashes.

"You would have to ask her. Let me text her and ask," he said, pulling his phone from his pocket.

"Sure that would be great," she said, as her face lit up when she heard how cooperative

Simon texted Sarah and said, "I'm getting interviewed by the NY Hour. They want to talk to you. Can I give them your number?"

Sarah replied immediately, "Yes."

He gave the reporter Sarahs' phone number and she wrote it down while the photographer took a few dozen more photos. They finished the interview and the reporter said, "Well Simon I think that's all I need. Thank you for your service? Is that what we're supposed to say?"

"You're very welcome, and please, thank my wife for letting me serve," he said with a small laugh.

The reporter went inside and Simon sat for a few more minutes on the stone, watching the light fade from the day. He wondered who the men were, stacking the sandbags at the entrance as they didn't look familiar. He then heard a general alarm and the PA system announced another assembly in the main courtyard. He got up, threw his bag on his shoulder, and jogged to assembly.

## Chapter 23

"Why didn't she take the shot?" asked the Major. Gonzalez and Littleton fidgeted in their seats. They were uncomfortable with the tone the officer was using.

It was clear now, that Gonzalez was in the kitchen with the bomb, and Littleton and McCormack had gone into the bedrooms. What Gus did not understand at this point, however, was why McCormack had frozen, resulting in her own death.

Littleton sounded raspy and needed to clear his throat, "Major, I killed the two men and McCormack went in to kill the rest. I heard her say 'stop crying' and that's when I heard the shots. I ran down the hall and thought she was behind me, but when I got to the kitchen she wasn't there. Gonzalez yelled that the trigger was set and he grabbed me and we ran out the door and down to the boat. I never saw the family."

The reports that the family had escaped meant two things. One, there were witnesses. And two, they had a body. Eventually, they would look at dental records and figure out who McCormack was, even if no one knew her. No one in camp knew her on the outside or who might care enough to tell that she was dead?

McCormack was one of Tanner's trailer people. She had a small single axle that she dragged behind a 1990 F150, alone with no family. No one knew where she was born or if she even had any relatives. They thought she was twenty-seven, but no one knew her birthday or anything else about her other than her first name, Kelly.

331

There were at least a hundred others like her in their ranks, with no apparent family, no connection to the world, and no one to miss them. But they all came from somewhere.

The bigger problem was the witnesses. The husband and wife and the two kids saw McCormack and her uniform. They may have even seen the direction the two other men ran away and could perhaps describe each of the team members in detail. Gus was certain that the police were going to push them until they had something resembling an answer.

He thought Tanner's connections could run a little interference with the local cops, but the feds and FBI would be all over this given the man's position as party chair. He needed to circle the wagons and make some space between his Army and the killings. They weren't ready for head to head conflict yet.

He dismissed the men and looked at Jamal saying, "This is bad Jamal. We needed to get out of there without being seen."

Jamal said, "Do you want to go after the family?"

Gus shook his head and said, "No, that won't work. Those folks are so deep inside Federal protection now, that we may never hear from them ever again. Our best bet is to go deep and wait for the smoke to clear."

He knew moving would be a tough mission to tackle. Transporting four hundred soldiers across the country with one hundred trailers and a full encampment would take a fleet of trucks or maybe even a train. The encampment could be moved if he explained his concerns to Travis. The beauty of a hundred trailers was they all had wheels and could travel at a moment's notice. He began to strategize his next objective.

332

If they moved all the gear into the trailers and filled every seat with a soldier, maybe they could get the regiment moving. They had that Fort Peck facility where the surplus military gear was being trucked. If they put all the men and the gear in the middle of nowhere for a couple of months, they might be ready for a major offensive, when it was all said and done.

It could work, he thought.

Jamal was standing at parade rest and Gus thought he saw him falling asleep.

"Jamal- you awake?" asked Gus.

"Yes Sir," said Jamal, snapping to attention.

"Good. I need every recruit assembled in the hanger at 1800. Right now, I need you to get the President on the line and I need you to start packing up my trailer. We're moving," said Gus.

---

Jamal handed the phone to Gus and said, "The President for you, sir."

"Mr. President. Major Sipros here," Gus began.

"Yeah Hawk, what's up?" asked the President.

"Mr. President our position here has been compromised and we are unable to hold this position if attacked. Our best option is to consolidate forces and get this camp moved to Fort Peck ASAP," said Hawk.

"What's going on Major?" asked The President.

"Well sir, the soldier who was left behind will be identified and there was a family of witnesses that may have seen at least one or more of the men and the direction they exited the area. Odds are, eventually our location will be detected and we will be required to defend ourselves," the Major explained.

"Given our weaponry and our vulnerability," the Major continued, "without air or sea support, I feel that this location is indefensible and we would be better served in a more defensible area with equipment. In short, rather than move the mountain to Mohamed, let's move Mohamed to the mountain. Four-hundred personnel and a pile of military equipment in one spot is way more defensible than an army with no weapons or a warehouse with weapons and no Army."

"I like the way you think Hawk. What's the plan?" asked the President.

"I will load every trailer full of equipment and personnel and I'll have this place broken down by 0800 tomorrow morning. We will drive convoy-style to Fort Peck and we'll be there in three days with your permission, Mr. President," said Hawk.

"You have that Major. What else do you need?" said the President.

"Well sir, we will need some cash to keep the tanks full and feed the troops on the road. We will also need a little safe passage from any law enforcement. Can you have Tanner clear our path for us?" asked the Major.

"I hear you two had some fireworks, a couple of weeks ago?" asked the President.

"Yes sir, I convinced the Captain that diversity was a better bet than white supremacy. A sentiment I do hope you share?" Gus knew the answer to this question would determine the future for this President and this cause and he hoped that John Eustace understood that as well.

"Major, your leadership and vision will win the day, I'm sure of it," answered the President, "Your cash will be in your hand by morning and your path will be clear for takeoff."

"Many thanks, Mr. President," Gus tried to get the phrase out, but the line went dead.

He handed the phone back to Jamal and said, "Call assembly, now."

---

Jamal went into the command center and pulled the cd case out that had all the bugle calls. He knew <u>Taps</u> was track number 2 and <u>Revelry</u> was track number 15. But he didn't know what the bugle call was for formation. He ran his finger down the list and saw track number 7 was labeled <u>Assembly</u>. He popped in the cd, cued it to number 7, and hit play.

He knew it sounded familiar, but figured no one else in the camp would know what it meant either, so he got on the microphone when it finished playing and said, "All Hands All Hands All Hands, General Assembly in the main hangar at this time. All Hands All Hands All Hands."

"When he walked out of the office, three hundred eighty soldiers stood at attention with the twenty soldiers standing guard at their stations. He

335

walked to the front and yelled at the top of his lungs, "TEN HUT." His voice echoed through the hanger.

He remained at attention until the Major came and dismissed him. Jamal then took his position at the side of the first platoon.

Gus stood in front, looking out over the battalion. He began to speak.

"Ladies and Gentlemen, it's time to take a road trip. We will be heading to Fort Peck, Montana where the remainder of our munitions is being stored for safekeeping. We need to be on the road by 0800 and need every tent, every stake, every rifle, and every pot accounted for packed and stored in every trailer that is on this base. We will also require some assistance from those soldiers who have trailers to make space for their fellow soldiers who may not have use of vehicles at this time for this mobilization. This convoy will transport the entire contents of this base to a new facility, two thousand miles away. Other armies have tried this with varying degrees of success with the full support of Nations and Kings. We will be doing this with no support from the Nation that currently rules this land and make every effort to do so undetected by that Nation. Do I make myself clear? The mess tent will be open all night with coffee and snacks and will not close until you take it down at 0600 tomorrow morning. Let's get to work. Dismissed."

Jamal yelled, "DISSSSS-MISSED," and 380 bodies scattered to begin their work.

By midnight, the entire tent city had been taken down and packed except for the mess tent. The trailers were all hooked up and parked in a line down the center of the runway. To save weight, and ensure security, weapons were distributed to each soldier with one case of ammunition per trailer.

When the sun began to rise, the entire encampment was ready to roll. Jamal handed the Major a cup of coffee and informed him that they were ready to roll at 0715. Gus said, "You drive the first three hours, will you?"

Jamal said, "Yes sir," started the truck, and led the hundred trailer convoy out the unmanned gates and on towards Montana.

**Chapter 24**

## THE NEW YORK HOUR

### U.S. ARMY TURNS TO VOLS TO FIGHT REBEL WAR
By Christy Hellman

(March 17, 2024, Stratford, Connecticut) - The last time the military asked soldiers to serve without a paycheck was in 1777, when Congress decided that the Continental Army wasn't worth it. The Crawford Administration has dusted that concept off this year, with a new class of recruits who serve as volunteers in a fight to win back the hearts and minds of America and to avert a civil war.

Like the now-defunct National Guard, which was disbanded due to budget cuts in 2022, these citizen soldiers sell insurance, run landscaping businesses or run hair salons in their civilian lives. When their Nation calls, however, they put on fatigues and helmets and stand a post to defend their hometowns. They do it away from their families, away from their businesses, and without any more in return than a thank you.

Simon Gates, an insurance salesman serving in the Stratford, Connecticut-based Third Mechanized Battalion, finished up a modified version of boot camp in February. On Thursday, when his battalion went to threat condition Charlie, the second-highest level of security alert the U.S. Army uses in war readiness, both he and his wife learned just how close our Nation is to Civil War.

"I joined to feel safe and get in shape," Gates said in an interview Thursday, just before his unit went on lockdown. "But today, I had to say goodbye to my home and my wife and get ready to fight if they need me."

Earlier this year, the former reserve base was selected as one of 100 facilities around the lower 48, Alaska and Hawaii, that would be repurposed as Patriotic Unity Stations. The Stations would be staffed by a mixture of full-time Army, enlisted and officers, as well as a unit of volunteer small business owners who have the financial independence to serve without the need for payment.

Mr. Gates found out about the opportunity to volunteer by email and was the first recruit to sign up as part of the first 11-person class to train at the Military Entrance Processing Station located in Chicopee, Massachusetts. The conflict they were volunteering for however came to them before they ever started training, when a school bus loaded with fertilizer and diesel fuel and destined for the State Capital in Hartford, accidentally exploded in front of them as they traveled on their bus up to the training facility.

"It was surreal, cars were on fire all around us and our transport bus just piled through it all and got us to safety," said Gates. The transport stopped in Hartford, to pick up the balance of recruits who were stationed at the other Connecticut Patriotic Unity Station located inside the State Armory in Hartford.

Other regional unity stations that went into lockdown Thursday include bases in Cranston, Rhode Island, Westfield, Massachusetts, Concord, New Hampshire, Brooklyn, New York, East Farmingdale, New York, and Newark, New Jersey.

While there are no confirmations from the White House that the Army is ramping up its posture on US Soil, in response to increased activity from the rebel forces, anonymous Pentagon sources have said that the lockdown was ordered in response to the killing of DNC chair and longtime Crawford affiliate, Cecil Mortimer, in his French Quarter home early Thursday morning

At 6 PM Thursday, all the 100 stations nationwide, as well as all active-duty military installations on US soil, went into full lockdown. The Stratford station, located in a suburban neighborhood in the north end of the small Connecticut town, installed machine gun nests at the entrance and recalled over 50 personnel, including all the recruit volunteers, to serve watch duty in preparation for pending military activity.

Gates' wife, Sarah, says she doesn't remember a time when the military had such a presence in the streets of suburban America and worries that her husband has signed on for more than he asked for, "Simon wanted to serve and I supported him in that, but I had no idea they would take him from me and make him live on base like some kind of active duty warrior. He's going to be 45 after all."

The Army recruited Simon and more than 300 other volunteers nationwide, telling them that they were required to volunteer at least 10 hours per week at the Unity Stations. Colonel Richard Pullman, commanding officer for Simon's unit, says that recent events have caused them to reevaluate the need for the volunteers, "They agreed when they signed up, to serve as needed subject to the requirements of the service. We need them now and we expect them to fulfill their service agreements."

Gates who has been unreachable, since the unit went into full lockdown on Thursday, says that while he is concerned that this will require a heavy burden on his part, he is willing to serve as an American and a soldier, "I hate leaving my wife and business, but when my country calls on me, I am prepared to do what is needed when it's needed."

That doesn't make his wife feel any better, "I'm going to miss him and I worry that I may never see him again. I don't want him to get killed fighting a battle that no one can win."

White House officials have come under fire recently, from civil liberties groups for the stationing of military forces on US Soil. Critics say the US is using its military in violation of the Posse Comitatus Act.

White House officials defend their use of the Military as a policing force to combat the rebellion saying they have authority under the 1981 Military Cooperation with Civilian Law Enforcement Agencies Act. They say that authority was extended by the Supreme Court ruling in 2022 that allowed the Crawford administration's use of the Insurrection Act to move Naval and Army assets back to the United States from positions abroad in response to the Tampa City bombings.

Prior to the 6-5 ruling, by the court in September of 2022, it was considered unconstitutional to use military personnel to enforce local laws. In 2008, President Bush attempted to use the act to force military forces into Louisiana in response to Hurricane Katrina but was rebuffed when the 50 governors of the states condemned his efforts. The Herzog administration tried again in the summer of 2020 to use the act when he called for every state to employ their National Guard to restore order during the Black Lives Matter protests.

Crawford was the first president in modern history, in March of 2022, to employ the act, when he ordered the Navy to return all fleets to the United States and the Army to abandon all international positions and return to US soil for homeland security duty. He further solidified his military reconfiguration, when he disbanded the National Guard, Coast Guard, Air Force, and the Marines in an effort to streamline Military functions saying at the time, "the redundancy of five different air, land and sea forces was bankrupting the US economy."

FBI sources familiar with the actions of rebel actors say that there has been a surge in activity related to the former Herzog loyalists. Federal Agent John Cummings of the homeland security division in Quantico, Virginia, says, "Herzog escaped prosecution in Argentina, but the ideology he started and the idea that he was supposed to be president, never really went away. It just morphed into a new philosophy that believes that the US government has abandoned its adherence to the US Constitution and aims to reclaim an America they believe has been lost."

Pentagon and White House sources declined to comment on the resurgence of rebel forces, but sources close to the administration say that Crawford is taking a special interest in rooting out rebel sympathizers and organizers in an attempt to shore up his political positioning.

Crawford's favorability ratings have flagged since the first days of his administration in response to his decision to disband several branches of the Military and repurpose US Military forces on US Soil.

*Editor's Note: This article was printed unfinished upon the disappearance of its author, Christy Hellman. The owners of the New York Hour Company have offered a $1 million reward for any information relating to her disappearance. The Crawford Administration challenged the right of The New York Hour to publish this article in its partial form in District Court, and a case is pending in the US Supreme Court concerning the right of NYH to publish this article, and others like it.*

.

## Chapter 25

The windshield wipers began to mesmerize Jamal as the snow came down. Back and forth at full speed and still, they could not keep up. Gus was snoring and the heat in the cab made Jamal want to vomit.

"Major,... Major,... Hawk, wake up, I need a break," said Jamal. Gus stirred and rubbed his hands over his nose and eyes.

"What time is it?" asked Gus, "How many hours have I been asleep?"

"Two," said Jamal, "it's 1500 sir."

The snow falling and the dark clouds made it look like night time and Gus felt very disoriented.

"Sir, I need to stop," said Jamal, "we need to stop. The snow is coming down too hard now and we're gonna wreck. I am only going ten miles an hour and losing my mind sir."

Gus came to life and said, "Where are we now?"

"Henderson, Tennessee, sir," said Jamal, "It's snowing harder now."

A freak snowstorm had moved in across the south and it had been snowing since they crossed the Mississippi line. What should have taken them no more than an hour, had taken three.

"Alright let's pull over at the next exit and regroup," he said, picking up the CB microphone, "All Stations, All Stations, All Stations, This is Hawk One, Ordering a stop at the next exit, follow my lead to our stop."

A hundred clicks came through the microphone.

They saw an exit with signs that read, "Pinson Mound State Park just ahead."

Gus said, "That's our stop."

He checked the GPS on his phone and looked for somewhere where 100 trailers would not look out of place. They were in luck. There was a Walmart, seven miles up ahead. He got back on the CB.

"All Stations, All Stations, All Stations. We will proceed to Walmart, seven miles up ahead on the left. Repeat Walmart, seven miles ahead on the left."

They responded again with 100 clicks.
When they pulled in, the parking lot was empty. The Walmart was closed due to the weather. Just as well, thought Gus, no sense in testing the security guard's attention span.

The convoy lined up side by side on the far side of the parking lot and was covered with snow within minutes. Gus radioed the platoon commanders to meet him in his trailer in ten minutes.
He then swiped his cell phone and googled train depots. There was a CSX depot another seven miles up the road. He called Travis.

The phone rang three times and Travis picked up, "Hey Hawk, how's it going? What's happening on base?"

"Sir, we had a change of plans and we are now located in Jackson, Tennessee," Gus replied.

'What are you doing there? Shouldn't you be on base with the troops?" asked Travis.

"No sir, I am with the troops in Jackson. All 400 of them," said Gus.

"What? Who's on base then?" asked Travis.

"Sir, we had to abandon our position on the base due to security concerns. Details you probably don't want to know about. All you need to know is we have abandoned the base and are heading north. It had something to do with the DNC chief in New Orleans," explained Gus.

"Yeah, I thought that looked like you," said Travis, "well then, how can I help?"

"Sir, do you know anyone with a train?" asked Gus.

"A train? Like choo choo?" asked Travis.

"Yes sir, we need to move 100 trailers and 400 soldiers to Montana in March and we are sitting in a blizzard right now at a Walmart in Jackson, Tennessee. Do you know anybody that can do that by rail?" asked Gus.

"Well," said Travis, "that's gonna take some doing, but I think I can help. I'll call you back," said Travis. The phone went dead.

Gus got out of the truck and covered his head with his hands. His blood had become used to the tropical weather in Pensacola and now he was in an arctic blast in Tennessee. He walked back to the trailer. Jamal came out around the other side, also looking chilled to the bone.

He dropped the step and unlocked the door and stepped inside. It was cold and felt hollow without any lights or heat.

"Jamal, would you pull out the generator and plug us in?" Gus asked.

Jamal went back out in the snow to dig out the generator. Within a few moments, he heard the familiar hum of the Honda and flipped the switch for the power. The trailer came to life. He clicked the heater on and checked the fridge for lights. It all worked.

A knock came at the door and Jamal came in with two of the platoon leaders and Gayle. The other eleven leaders showed up within minutes. The fifteen soldiers, frozen to the bone, piled into the trailer elbow to elbow. The heavy breathing and melting snow on everyone's shoulders made it feel humid and claustrophobic inside the small space.

"This weather is something, isn't it?" asked Gus.

The troops nodded in agreement.

"Wel, I think it's gonna be like this up to Montanna and I don't think this is very much fun do you?" asked the Major.

A man named Franz yelled from the back of the pack, "Ooh-Rah Major." "I'm working on getting us a ride," explained the Major, "Tell your people to hunker down as best they can for the night, and come morning, we will head out with a way to get to Montana in one piece. How's everyone running?"

The soldiers looked at each other and back at the Major, "No worries on our end," said a woman named Murray, "We're gonna make it, Major."

"That's what I wanted to hear. Very good. Platoon Commanders, Dis--missed," said Gus.

The soldiers and Gayle filed out of the trailer into the winter night to settle in with their platoons. The storm raged all night.

By morning, there was a foot and half of wet snow piled on the convoy.

Gus woke shortly after 5 AM and surveyed the fleet. It looked like a glacier with a hundred cracks in it. He figured that Walmart would open up soon and he wanted to get the news to the platoon commanders. In the middle of the night, Travis texted him and told him to have the fleet at the CSX up the road by 0700.

Gus knew that they would be hungry and cold and ready to sleep in a warm bed soon enough and he needed to get the brigade moving to get in a better spot.

Jamal walked up and looked pretty rough.
"How'd you sleep Corporal?" asked Gus.

"I got a few hours of sleep sir," Jamal said rubbing his neck, "but I kept having to turn the heater back on in the compartment. The propane kept shutting off."

Jamal slept in one of the trailers that was owned by a platoon commander as Gus only had one bed in his trailer.

"Well, we will be there before you know it. I got us a ride on the railroad and we gotta get there by 0700. It's gonna take some time with this snow to get there, can we have everyone ready to move by 0615?"

"Yes sir, I'll pass the word. 0615 lined up and ready to roll," said Jamal.

When the clock struck six, the snow was all cleared from the trailers and the trucks were all warming. Jamal climbed in the cab with Gus and said, "We're ready to roll Major."

"Very well," said Gus, and he keyed the mic on the CB and said, "All hands... Forward... march."

Gus pulled forward with his trailer in tow. One by one, the convoy assembled, as it pulled onto the roadway.

It took them 30 minutes, but when they entered the gates of the railyard, a grizzled old man in a stocking cap with a cigar sticking from his snow-crusted beard stopped the first truck. He looked at the row behind him, spewing exhaust with wipers flinging wet snow left and right.

Gus rolled down the window and the man asked, "You the Major?"

"Yes sir, I'm Major Gus Spiros. Friend of Travis LaPierre."

"Yeah, I was told to expect you at seven, you're twenty minutes early. Nicely done Major," said the old man, "We have a hundred flatcars here and they are ready to be loaded. Can you have your men drive them down to the loading yard and our guys will help you get them on?"

Gus headed the convoy down and the trucks and trailers were loaded one at a time onto the train cars. The loading took six hours and the snow never stopped falling.

By 1500, the convoy was all loaded and the train was ready to depart. Gus closed his eyes and laid his head back on the driver's seat headrest of his truck and felt the massive train edge forward. Before long, the steady sound of rails clapping under his rig settled him into a deep hibernative sleep.

The first day, they slowed only once when they went through a yard just outside of St. Louis. They picked up speed after that and made great time all the way out to Kansas City. The next run-up to Fargo lasted eighteen hours and then it was on to Bismark before their final stop, Glendive, Montana.

The three days were spent sleeping and snacking before they woke to unload in Glendive. It took a half-day to get them all unloaded and there was another hour and a half up to the warehouse outside of Wolf Point.

When they pulled in, Tanner was waiting at the corner of a dirt road. Gus stopped and said, "Hello Captain, Gayle is a few trailers back. Mighty nice day out here. How much further?"

"Just up over that hill," said Tanner, "there's a warehouse at the end of the dirt road. You can set up camp behind that."

"Thanks, Captain. It's been a long run and will be happy to set down some stakes," said Gus.

Gus led the convoy up the dirt road that was frozen solid but blessedly free of snow. It was tiny on the horizon at first, but as he approached, he could see the rows and rows of artillery, humvees, and every other machine of war ever bought by the US Military. Jason and Jeff had been busy, although he had no idea where they were right now. He saw the warehouse and the road that led behind it.

"Christ," he said to Jamal, who was wide-eyed with all the equipment surrounding him, "we could see a truck coming from ten miles off here."

They lead the convoy behind the warehouse, where a field that seemed to spread out forever hosted a few hundred cows that were grazing.

"I guess this is it," Gus said. He backed the trailer into a flat with setting sun on the driver's side, and got on the radio, saying, "Back your trailers down from me. We will set the tent city up on the opposite side."

One by one, the trailers backed in, until all one-hundred were in a line side by side. Gus walked out in front of the line and about halfway down the row he yelled, "FALL IN!"

The men rushed from their rigs to assemble in front of Gus between him and the trailers.

The vast emptiness made the four hundred soldiers look tiny. Gus yelled as loud as he could but was sure some in the back could not hear him due to the wide expanse and the incessant wind. It was cold and felt like it blew straight down from the arctic, across this flat and harsh landscape.

"Ladies and Gentlemen, welcome to sunny Montana," he began, "we have a couple of hours of daylight left and when the sun goes down we can use the headlights of the trucks to see. We need a base, right here, right now. Get to work."

The brigade erupted with cheers and scattered in every direction to unload the trailers and rebuild what they had dismantled in Pensacola, four long days ago.

By sunset, a mess tent was up and the smell of meat cooking and smoke rising billowed from the flaps. By midnight, the bones of a tent city were evident and humming generators were keeping the lights on. They worked clear into the morning when the first watches were set and a security tower was being constructed with lumber they scavenged from an old collapsed barn they found on the edge of the property.

Gus offered liberty to anyone who wanted it at noon the next day. A few soldiers drove the three hours to the nearest Walmart for supplies, but the vast majority kept working.

By sunset on the second day, the base looked just like Pensacola, although there was no runway and certainly no palm trees swaying in the breezes coming across the gulf waters.

It was cold and bleak here. The young soldiers who had lived their entire lives in the humidity of Biloxi and Pascagoula were cold shocked. Their teeth chattered and their eyes were wide with fear that they might never get warm again.

It would be an adjustment for most of them, thought Gus. This was a hard place with hard people. It would make the troops stronger while they lived and trained here. They would learn to work, not just as the team they were, but as a force for fighting that they would become. They would learn to use the weapons they saw here and learn to deploy those weapons with skill and bravery. They left Florida as a team of recruits, but they would become the Army that would reclaim America, here on the plains of Montana.

## Chapter 26

Gus flipped through an old New York Hour from St. Patrick's day, he found sitting on a coffee-stained table inside the warehouse. The racks inside the cavernous steel building were laden with crates of ammunition and rifles. As he looked around, he saw crates of grenades and rockets. He saw boxes and boxes of MREs, water, and everything else a soldier might need to win a war. He thought he could fit out 10,000 men, with all these supplies, as he thumbed through the pages of the newspaper.

He wasn't reading, just looking at the pictures, when he saw the article about Stratford.

He loved being there and regretted his quick exit after the accident. If it was up to him, he would have bought a house in Lordship and walked on Russian beach every night with a girlfriend and a pair of Great Danes. But things didn't work out that way.

It surprised him, to see the name of the tiny town that hid in the shadow of Fairfield County's gold coast, so prominently displayed in the Sunday edition of the New York Hour. He read it with interest because it also mentioned the volunteer program the Army was starting that he told John about back in Gettysburg.

When he reached Simon's name in the article, his blood ran cold. That was the bastard who shot out in front of him causing the accident. All of sudden, he remembered walking around the man's house and sending the photocopy to him in the mail.

He read that he was now in the Army as a volunteer and that they had locked down all the military installations after the botched mission in New Orleans. It was all coming together and the fact that he was reading this article in the middle of the plains of Montana was just too much to comprehend.

Gus was familiar with the installation identified in the article. He had been inside it more than once when he was working at Sikorski for Dark Pond. Those were days when he could remember Crawford fondly. Gus was quite certain the President-gone-rogue was kicking puppies right about now, over what happened in New Orleans.

He was quite proud that the mission in New Orleans set the entire US military on edge. It had the effect he wanted. But the article made no mention of the Resistance soldier lost in the mission.

He thought about the machine gun nests, they mentioned in the article, and he eyed the crates and crates of rifles. He thought about how many men it would take to destroy that unit in Stratford and wondered how he could transport them there without getting caught.

The trailers once again popped into his head. That was it. He could take fifteen people in three trailers with enough gear to blow that place sky-high...with Simon Gates in it. Getting out, they could make their way down to the beach and catch a speed boat out into Long Island Sound.

His mouth watered with the idea that he could kill two birds with one stone. He could go get the guy who messed up his plan and at the same time, get the chance to show the world that he could confront the Army head-on.

"Corporal," his voice echoed in the massive warehouse, "Get me the President!"

He folded the paper in half and in half again, making sure that the article with all its corners was visible. Jamal came over with the phone and Gus threw the paper at him, "Read that," he said, taking the phone into his hand.

"Mr. President," he barked. The line was still dead and the President had yet to pick up the phone. Gus tapped his foot waiting for the leader to come on the line.

"Hawk! How's Montana?" started the President.

"It's good. We're all moved in and the camp is fully operational. We start artillery training in the morning," answered the Major.

"Great. You guys amaze me with how fast you can get to business. What can I do for you, Major?" said Eustace.

Gus started slowly, "Sir, I wonder if you have seen a story in the New York Hour about the new volunteer program I was telling you about?"

"No, I missed it," said Eustace.

Gus wondered how a man in Eustace's position could miss so much news that was happening in the world.

"It was a few weeks ago, in the March 17th edition of the paper. They ran a story about the Unity Stations with the volunteer people they are recruiting and that talked about how Crawford is running roughshod over the Constitution by using the Army as a police force."

"Yeah I hate that bastard," said the President.

"Me too, Mr. President, me too," said Gus, "Sir, do you recall that accident I had up in Connecticut before I joined you at Gettysburg?" asked Gus.

"How could I forget," said Eustace, "You got back at the police for killing Travis."

He didn't bother correcting the President that the two events were completely independent.

"Yes sir, do you remember how I let that other driver go?" asked Gus.

"Yeah, you said he didn't see anything right?" said the President.

"Well sir, he may have seen more than I originally reported. He has joined the Army as one of those volunteers," said Gus.

"Really, what makes you think he saw something?" asked the President.

"I don't know sir, he just joined up in the Army as the first volunteer and I think that might have been in response to what he saw at the accident," said Gus.

"Interesting. What do you want to do?" asked Eustace.

"I was thinking of assembling a team and making a trip up to Stratford to take him out and while we were at it, making a stab at the Army," said Gus, "If we used three trailer rigs, we could get a team and equipment up there to take out the facility and make our return by sea once again. I would insist on going to this one of course."

"Well we will have to talk about that Gus, I don't know if our senior military officer should be putting his boots on the ground," replied the President.

What the hell did he know about boots on the ground, thought Gus. I was killing Arabs when he was still pushing papers at his day job.

"Well sir, I wonder if we could have a meeting to discuss with some of the senior leadership? You did suggest I should get retribution as I recall?" said Gus.

"Major, I would love to, but I am booked this week. Can this wait until next week?" asked the President.

"Well sir, they have already fortified their position and are hardening their defenses every day sir. The longer we wait the harder this nut will be to crack," said Gus.

"Let me run this by a few others. Can you talk to Tanner, he's there with you, right? I will get back with you Major," said the President, "I'll call you later this week? Okay?"

"That would be fine sir. But I need to get a team ready to roll in preparation...I, "added Gus, but the phone had already gone dead.

What was he hesitating for, wondered Gus? It was a great target and Gus knew he could take it. Maybe the President really should have some military training, if he was gonna red light obvious tactical decisions like this.

Gus wanted to move on this now. What was the worst the brass could do? Yell at him? No one knew half of what he did about running the Army and it was HIS PLAN, after all.

He called Jamal and said, "Assemble the Third platoon, we are going to New England."

Jamal ran to assemble the Third platoon. Gus walked out back and Tanner was just pulling up to the tent city for food. He stopped the truck and got out to walk with Gus.

"Hey there, Major, where ya heading?" said Tanner.

"I'm going to brief the third platoon, want to join me?" asked Gus.

"Sure, what's going on?" asked Tanner.

"Well, I got this issue up in New England and I want your opinion," Gus said, "Do you remember that cop I killed up there?"

Gus enjoyed taking the opportunity to remind his Captain of his potential.

"Yeah, I remember that. Didn't you leave some loose ends up there as I recall?" Tanner said, trying to twist the knife a little.

"Yeah. One in particular who joined that new Army program," Gus explained, "He was written up in the New York Hour. Turns out, he is a bit of celebrity and sitting smack dab in the middle of a poorly guarded government target."

"So you're thinking of hitting the big fish and keeping a little of the bycatch for bonus eh?" Tanner said with a raised eyebrow.

Gus thought, leave it to a fisherman to use a metaphor on fishing for military action.

Gus said, "Exactly."

"I like the way you think Major, what do you need from me?" Tanner asked.

"I need your help convincing El Presidente to move on this thing before they harden up too much more," said Gus.

"I think that can be accommodated, but you're gonna owe me one, Major," said the Captain.

"Captain, I always like to butter my friend's bread," Gus said with a smile.

The two men walked into the cold setting sunlight and discussed how President Eustace might be persuaded to get on board with Gus' plan to take out Mr. Simon Gates of the Third Mechanized Brigade in Stratford, Connecticut.

## Chapter 27

Simon laid in his bunk and listened to the sound of Taps on the PA speaker. He hadn't spoken to his wife in a week and a half and he missed her painfully. The quiet hours after Taps was the time he missed her most. Just listening to the wailing horn blow, made his heart ache.

He savored the reverberation, as the last note played. He rolled over to look out the window. His view was of the two machine-gun nests in the parking lot and the line of traffic just beyond.

He heard his roommate, an enlisted guy from Ohio named Duhancik, snoring already. He missed his wife's arms, as they fell asleep and the quiet way she breathed when she was dreaming.

The barracks were quiet and the days were now becoming a habit. Up at 6, marching tours until 8, Breakfast at 830, colors at 9, guard duty until Noon, lunch break, cleaning and polishing until 4, another assembly at 4:30, dinner at 5, TV until 9, reading from 9 until tattoo. Text his wife from Tattoo until Taps. Taps at 10. Do it all over again the next day.

He just answered her last text of the day and hated how much she worried. He told her that he loved her and that he would be home soon, but he had no idea really when that might be.

While she worried, he was suffering another type of torture. Monotony.

The guns locked and loaded everywhere made him nervous at first. Now, however, he wasn't half as worried about the threat of violence, as he was about the boredom that was sure to kill him if they didn't let him out soon.

The enlisted guys let up a little bit, now that everyone was considered active duty. They still made jokes about his age and the senior citizen volunteers. The jokes translated into crap duties like KP and brass polishing, but at least they let him train with real weapons every once in a while.

His frustration about his situation ebbed from his mind and he felt himself drifting to more serene thoughts of home, thinking about his wife sitting by herself, less than three miles away. His eyes closed and he found himself sitting with her on his back deck, sipping a beer.

He smelled the freshly cut grass and the steak cooking on the grill. The steak started popping from the grease hitting the hot burners and the sound made his mind drift to that time when he was a kid and playing with fireworks. He lit the firework and stuffed it in the soda bottle and watched as the bottle exploded into a thousand pieces. The pieces landed all over him and he instinctively covered his face. He woke when he felt the glass cut into his palm. Opening his eyes to see where the pain was coming from, he saw his palm bleeding.

His blanket was covered with glass and the parking lot was on fire.

He hopped out of bed and that was when the general alarm went off followed by the PA announcement, "We are under attack, repeat we are under attack, all hands all hands....."

The announcement stopped with a loud bang.

He pulled his pants on and slid his bare feet into his boots. He grabbed a tee shirt and his helmet and ran toward the door, bumping into Duhancik in the dark doing the same thing. The two men tumbled to the floor and scrambled to untangle their legs in the darkness.

An explosion rocked outside the window and flung the rest of the broken window towards the back wall of the room, covering the men on the floor with glass. As Duhancik stood up, a bullet ripped through his throat.

He stood over Simon, who was still on the floor, clutching his throat in the dark. Simon could see his wild-eyed expression and the black ooze leaking from between his fingers. He gurgled and blood shot from his mouth and sprayed all over Simon. Duhancik collapsed to his knees and fell over. His face hit the concrete floor and his eyes stared straight at Simon without blinking. Duhancik was dead.

Simon pulled his legs free from the weight of the dead man's torso and crawled on his hands and knees toward the door. Another piece of glass wedged between his fingers and he winced in pain. He ripped the glass shard from his hand and watched his blood pool on the broken glass on the floor. He knew he needed to stop the bleeding so reached up and took a pair of socks from Duhanick's dresser and wrapped his hands in each and crawled to the door.

He stuck his head out the door and saw camouflaged legs running back and forth in the hallway. A layer of smoke above clouded their faces. The smoke alarm was going off and the smell of black powder filled the air while gunshots rang out from every direction.

He slid on his belly up across the hall and rolled against the wall, putting his back to the cinder blocks. He slid up to his feet and followed along the wall, to the back of the building where he knew he could find a weapon.

When he got to the armory, he jumped across the hall and saw a line of weapons and with only a half dozen or so missing. He grabbed a rifle and an extra clip and ran towards the front of the building where it seemed the most extreme fire was coming from.

Bob Richardson was on his knee, firing out the broken glass doors. Simon stood behind him and fired over his head, not sure what exactly they were firing at. The smoke and flames hid everything.

He saw a shape come running toward him through the flames, jumping over dead bodies. He did not recognize the uniform. He saw flashes of gray clothing but focused on the man's face covered in a ski mask.

Simon lowered his muzzle and aimed at the incoming man's chest and fired three rounds. The man flew backward and landed on top of the pile of bodies he had just vaulted.

Simon stopped firing and looked for movement but could detect nothing but fire and smoke. He became aware that Bob Richardson was screaming and now dry firing his weapon, having used up all his ammunition. Simon grabbed Bob's shoulder and yelled, "Bob Stop...stop...BOB BOB... BOB, stop!"

Bob Richardson lifted his finger from the trigger and collapsed on the floor. He looked like a child pouting with criss crossed legs. His eyes were filled with tears and his mouth agape, but he could make no sound.

Simon realized that voices were yelling outside and the fire alarm bell was ringing, but that the gunfire had stopped. He looked around and saw bullet holes covering the cinder block walls of the entry and noticed the flag that adorned the front entryway had fallen over. It was riddled with holes and smoldering.

He dropped his weapon and stamped on the burning corner of the flag. He looked around to see if anyone saw him stepping on the flag, but assumed it was ok to stop it from burning. When he saw it was extinguished, he picked it up and tried to set it upright. Broken glass bits made the base unlevel.

By the flickering light of the fires, he could see the floor was covered in glass. The weight of the base made the flag pole heavy, as he cleared a space on the floor of broken glass and debris with his boot. He placed the flag upright in the center of the space and scanned the atrium. All the glass was blown out of the doors and windows.

When he walked outside, he saw men in uniform and helmets running in every direction. His eyes fixed on the Lieutenant, who was sitting on the ground, propped against the wall talking on a cell phone. He walked over to check on him.

Altieri's chest seemed twisted and his legs seemed pointed in an unnatural direction. As Simon approached, he could hear Altieri say into the phone, "Sir I may not be here when you get here, but we need some help now."

His hand collapsed at his side and the phone fell to the ground. He swung and bobbed his heavy head toward Simon and looked up at him with tears rolling down his cheeks.

"Gates, I can't feel my legs," he said.

Simon fell to his knees beside his superior officer and saw Altieri's chest. He had a three-inch hole where his name tag used to be and it looked like charred meat with blood pouring out.

"I can't feel my legs,... Simon," slurred Altieri, "But I.... I called for help."

His neck went limp and his eyes lost focus. His head fell back hard against the brick wall and Simon saw his chest deflate without refilling. Altieri was dead. Simon reached over and closed the man's eyes and sat down next to him.

Soon he heard the sound of police sirens and fire trucks. An army truck drove in, crashing through the blown up humvee that was on fire that blocked the front gate. He noticed as it crushed the scattered sandbags that used to make up machine gun nests like soft marshmallows oozing sand beneath the tires.

The truck stopped and fifty men in tactical gear poured out of the back of the truck and ran toward the front door. Simon rose from the bushes and stepped toward the men.

One man stopped and stood beside him and the Lieutenant. He asked, "Was that your commanding officer?"

"Yes," was all Simon could say.

Simon walked toward the rocks where he had been talking to the reporter and had a seat. He wanted to call his wife but realized that he had left his phone on his desk in his room.

From the tree line, he tried to understand what happened. It looked like someone had fired a rocket into the humvee and blew up the two machine-gun nests. Several men in grey uniforms were laying by the front walk, including the man he shot, who was at least thirty feet from the door. When Simon fired, he thought that the man was ready to climb on top of him.

He examined the pile of bodies by the front door. There must have been at least a dozen men in Army green piled on the other side from the lieutenant, including Phil, who lay dead by himself, shirtless.

Another five soldiers were next to bushes where Altieri lay. It looked to him like the men filed out the door to their death. He told himself it was dark and that things would look different in the morning.

He sat looking at the wreckage of the building for several hours and realized that the birds had started chirping and the sun was coming up when another truck, this time with body bags, pulled in the lot. A man got out and said, "Hey you, Private, are you injured?"

Simon replied and said, "No, I'm a volunteer."

The man tilted his head and looked quizzically at Simon and said, "Well if you're not hurt, can you help me with some of these bodies?"

Simon got up and walked over to the back of the truck, where a man was handing out body bags to four other men. He got in line and waited to be handed a bag, when one of the men said, "Here, help me get this one."

Simon walked over and noticed the man's boot had been blown off one foot and a pool of blood had formed under his lower back. The soldier he was helping said, "You grab his feet and I'll get his head, let's put him in this bag," as he spread it open on the ground.

Simon grabbed the leg with the boot and was hesitant to touch the leg without the boot. He eyed it and saw the 'powersox' logo on the man's toe. It reminded him of when he was packing in basic and thought about the bureaucracy it must have taken to get those words allowed on a government-issued sock.

The soldier pulled him back from his thoughts saying, "he isn't gonna get much fresher and we got a dozen more to load."

Simon grabbed the man's leg and the other booted ankle and lifted the man into the bag. He helped load another six men and when it was all done, he had counted nine enemies and fifteen good guys.

The truck backed out of the driveway, bumping into the still smoking humvee, making a huge bang that made everyone jump. It pulled forward and backed out straight, this time onto the road that was closed with cops at either end.

Simon walked toward the building and wanted to go in to get his cell phone. His wife must be up now and she certainly heard about the attack he guessed.

As he walked through the shattered entrance, a sergeant was standing guard and asked him where he was going. He looked up and said, "Home. I want to go home."

Jessinia saw him and said, "Sarge he is one of us, let him pass." He walked up to his friend and she wrapped her arms around him. He broke into tears and she held him as he wept.

"Did you talk to your wife yet?" she asked.

"No," said Simon, " I was just going in to get my phone. I left it when I heard the gunshots."

She said, "I thought that was you, they pulled out your room until I saw you sitting outside on the rocks. I figured you would come in when you were ready."

"Did they get Duhanick out of there? I watched him get killed," said Simon.

"Yes they removed him an hour ago, but it's still a mess in there. You might want to wait until they clean it up," she advised.

He looked up at her and heard something snap in his heart when she said that.

"Are you kidding, *WE* are going to have to clean this up!" he yelled.

Her face went dark when she realized he was probably right. He pulled away from her arms and walked back to his barracks room. The floor was covered with glass and smeared blood. He saw the window that had been blown out and the smoke stains that funneled up to the ceiling.

His desktop was covered with glass and the room smelled of smoke and burnt flesh. He reached into his desk drawer and saw his phone light was blinking. He swiped it open and saw three missed calls and twelve messages. They were all from Sarah.

He was afraid to speak to her. She would ask him if he was okay. She would ask him to explain what happened and he wasn't sure he could even speak, let alone tell her what he had just witnessed.

He dialed the phone and waited for her to answer. She picked up on the first ring.

"SIMON, are you okay?" she cried.

He recoiled at her tone, but he wasn't sure why.

"I'm okay. Just a little confused," he said.

"My Christ, Simon. I was worried you were killed! The news said fifteen people were killed, but they didn't say who?" said Sarah

"Yeah. Altieri is dead," he said.

"Oh, My God? What happened?" she asked.

"He was shot in the chest and died," Simon began, "my roommate was killed too and there were shots and explosions everywhere..." he heard the words but it sounded like someone else's voice was talking, he thought.

"Oh, Simon. I am so sorry, when are you coming home?" she asked.

"I don't know. They haven't told us yet," he said.

A bugle call came over the PA and a voice told Simon it was time for assembly.

"I gotta go, I will call you when I know what's happening," said Simon.

"Wait don't hang up...Simon...Simon," she called.

"I gotta go, Sarah. They are calling for assembly. I'll call you later," he said and hung up the phone.

Eighty soldiers were assembled in the courtyard. Simon recognized a small fraction of the faces. A Captain stood in front of the cannon and the unit stood at attention.

"Good morning third battalion, my name is Captain Frank Battistini. I have been assigned as battalion commander to this unit, in the wake of last night's activities. We have about fifty new arrivals who have come in from New York. To those of you who were here last night during the attack, our hearts are with you.

"We have work to do. Our position must be secured and we need to get this place operational today. Volunteers are assigned to clean up detail and the first platoon will secure the entrance and work on getting the front passable. Second platoon, you are gonna take guard duty today and we will have sentries posted on the north and west sides of the property with a mobile security unit stationed at the front gate at all times.

"I know some of you need some time to get home to your families. For the soldiers who were here last night, you will be granted a three day leave beginning this evening at 1800 to spend time with your families and get your heads in order. That is all for now, Diss-Missed."

Simon wanted to ask questions, Simon wanted answers. Instead, he was given a mop and told to clean up the carnage that remained from the nightmare he awoke to the night before.

He walked into the barracks and saw Jessinia in the supply closet. She was donning hazmat gear and offered a set of goggles to Simon with a smile. He took them and said, "I told you so."

## Chapter 28

The hot shower water ran into his eyes and stung, but he held his head under the water and enjoyed the pain. He scrubbed his face and washed his hair and watched the small bits of dried blood wash down the drain. Simon took a long slug of beer and put the bottle back on the edge of the tub and allowed the water to wash away the images that flashed in his mind.

Sarah came in and said, "Do you need another beer, hun? You've been in there 45 minutes."

"Na, I'm okay. Thank you," he called from the shower. He stuck his head out and looked her in the eye and said, "I love you."

She tilted her head, squinted her eyes, smiled, and said, "I love you too."

"I have a steak for you downstairs. When you get out, you can eat, and maybe we can watch a movie later," she said.

"Thanks, I'll be down in a few minutes," he said.

She put a fresh towel on the toilet lid and closed the door.

When he got downstairs, he could hear the steak frying and saw the bottle of wine open on the counter. "May I pour a glass," he asked his wife.

"Of course honey, pour one for me too?" she asked

He poured the wine and handed a glass to his wife. He walked to the door and looked in the backyard. The sun had set, but he could see the grass was coming up again and the signs of the storm were disappearing.

She set the plate on the table and told him to come to sit down. They ate in silence.

When they were done, she cleared the table and Simon wandered into the living room and turned on the TV. A special report was coming on and he turned up the volume.

"Ladies and Gentleman, a message from the President of the United States."

He called to Sarah, "Sweet, the President is making an announcement. I thought this would happen. Come on in here."

Sarah walked in and refiled his wine glass and sat down.

"My fellow Americans. I speak to you this evening with a heavy heart and resolve to save our great Nation from forces that aim to do us harm.

"Last evening, while our American families slept with a notion of safety in their hearts and minds, a team of terrorists attacked a military installation in Connecticut and killed fifteen Army service personnel. They did so under the cover of darkness and without provocation.

"We believe these forces were part of a larger organization of rebellious factions that were responsible for the death of my friend and DNC Chair Cecil Mortimer earlier this month in his New Orleans home.

"The similarities in these attacks leave no question in my mind, that they are connected. The attire of the assailants' uniforms, the methods of their aggression, and the similarity of targets leads me to believe that this is a group of actors, who wish to do harm to America and its citizens.

"I have created and will send to Congress tomorrow, legislation calling for a declaration of war on seditious factions located within the United States borders. I have also authorized a state of emergency, effective at midnight tonight.

"These rebellious groups are identified by their attire, their racism, and their hate for America. They wear gray uniforms in honor of the racist forces that once tried to undo this Nation, that were resurrected by the irresponsible and hate-filled rhetoric of a dictatorial leader who evaded prosecution in the same way his Nazi predecessors did. We forced that leader out of our country but failed at removing its influence on our Nation.

"It was that divisive and racist ideology that fueled the violence last evening and was responsible for the death of one of America's most fervent patriots last month in New Orleans.

"I pledge to you, the good people of our Nation, that my administration will not abide by, nor tolerate the existence of such heinous ideologies. We will use the full might and power of the United States of America, to root out and destroy the groups and individuals who peddle in such vial beliefs and foster those belief structures through acts of violence and hate.

"And now I speak to the individuals who were responsible for the violence and death wrought upon our service members last evening. We will find you. We will capture you and we will punish you, for every life you have taken and every injury you have wrought. The United States of America is the land of the free and the home of the brave. You will not be successful in your attempts to undo our freedoms, through your cowardly and seditious actions. You are not safe within the borders of this Nation and you will be found and destroyed.

"My fellow Americans, the United States is under attack from within for the second time in our national history. We will weather this storm and accept nothing but complete surrender, just as we did on May 13, 1865, at an Appomattox Court House under the leadership of one of America's greatest leaders, Abraham Lincoln. And as he closed in his Gettysburg Address, where he consecrated the ground made hallowed by the death of young men in America's first Civil War, we too commit to those families who lost loved ones in recent days 'that we here highly resolve that these dead shall not have died in vain -- that this nation, under God, shall have a new birth of freedom -- and that government of the people, by the people, for the people, shall not perish from the earth.'

"May God bless you and may God bless the United States of America."

Simon clicked off the television and breathed deep. He looked at Sarah and she at him. He said, "I'm going to war my love, aren't I?"

She swallowed hard and nodded. They sat there in silence, neither wanting to move to the next minute for fear of what would come next.

Simon spoke again looking away from the black television screen, "You know something bothered me about last night."

"What's that?" she asked.

"I helped load the dead men who attacked us, into the trucks. When I was putting one of the bodies in a bag, I noticed that he had lost one of his boots in the fight. His socks were the same brand as mine."

"What?" Sarah asked.

"His socks were the same ones the Army gave me. I noticed because they had writing on the toe. I found it odd because they were branded and I didn't think the Government allowed that to happen. I mean they didn't allow branded clothing to be issued to soldiers."

"What do you think that means?" she asked.

"I don't know my love, but I think I should find out," said Simon.

---

Gus turned off the TV and yelled, "Jamal!!!!"

That mother fucker had just implicated them in an attack that he had nothing to do with. Crawford was a dirtbag, but did he know that Gus was behind *The Plan* and that he was building an Army? How could he know such a thing?

What about John? Did John have another force he didn't know about? Was there some other group that he didn't know about that dressed alike? Was that why he was dragging his feet on this target and why the very same target he wanted to hit was now burning?

"Jamal!!!!" he screamed again.

Jamal came running across the warehouse floor and was out of breath. "Yes sir?" he said, struggling to stand at attention before the Major.

"Where were you?" Gus asked.

"Ramirez was showing me the inside of an M117. I had to climb out sir," Jamal exhaled and tried to catch his breath.

"Aha, well we need to talk to the President now. Get him on the phone will you?" said Gus.

Jamal ran to get the cell phone from the office and dialed. He came back and said, "Sir he is coming on."

Gus waited and heard the president say, "Hawk what's up?"

Gus hung up the phone. He needed more information before he talked to the president.

"Jamal, there was an attack in Connecticut at the place I wanted to attack last night," said the Major, "I need to know who did it... _Now_. Find out, will you?"

Jamal said, "Yes sir," and ran out the door to head for a computer.

Gus got up from his desk and walked out of the hanger. He stepped into the afternoon sunshine and breathed deep. Clouds were building on the horizon and he thought he could smell a hint of snow on the breeze.

He heard a platoon of the soldiers drilling in the field as he walked back to his trailer and noticed a group of men laughing as they played cards next to a burn barrel outside one of the tents. The smell of smoke mixed with the snow and calmed his anger and the feeling that he had been betrayed.

He stepped into his trailer and kicked his boots off at the door. Stopping at the cupboard he pulled a glass down. He stopped at the freezer and grabbed two ice cubes from a bag of ice he remembered buying at the bodega in Florida.

He bent over and pulled a bottle of scotch from under the sink and poured two fingers over the ice in his glass.

Gus sat down in his dinette and sipped his scotch, thinking that someone would pay for this. It was time for war.

January 30, 2021
A Note From The Author

Hi there and thanks for reading this book. If this is the first book you have read that I have written, then you're doing it right, because it's my first, too. I am writing two more in this series and have another epic novel cooking in the back of my mind.

The second of this trilogy is called Governments of Men and it takes Gus and Simon through America's second civil war. It's not that I am laying out how I think we as a Nation should go by taking these men into war, but rather showing what that might look like if we ever got there, God forbid.

These times are scarier than anyone could ever imagine. Pandemics, armed assaults on our Government, and a Fascist who has just left the White House. If things weren't so dire, you'd think we were in a dystopian novel.

With healthcare skyrocketing in cost, the public education system collapsing, and the American Family unit dissolving before our very eyes, we would be well served if we all stepped back and took a deep hard look at who we are and whither we were tending. And that is what I hope you take away from this book, a different perspective.

If you like the way this book is written, I think you will love my most ambitious project that I hope to complete soon. It is a documentary called The Great Loop. Want to know what it's about? Turn the page and like us on Facebook.

Many thanks,
Capt. Chris German
www.thechartedlife.net

# The Great Loop

By Capt. Christopher German

When Ken Ransom came up with the idea to sail one continuous loop of the Eastern Seaboard in 1897, he could not imagine the history that brought him to that point in his life, nor the history he would set in motion for generations to come.

The Great Loop was never planned and it was by great happenstance that it came to fruition in the first place. A hodgepodge of canals and rivers, lakes and oceans, gulfs and sounds, some made by man, others made by God himself, all sewing one giant connected 6000 plus mile channel around the Eastern half of the US and Canada.

The first pieces of the Great Loop were envisioned by the founding fathers themselves before the ink on the Constitution was even set. They sought a way to secure shipping interests by creating a series of canals that would allow ships to travel between the North and South and establish an alternative route to fuel the newly minted US Economy and interconnect the several states and territories of the newly established nation.

Washington himself created many of the surveys that would be used to set out the inaugural public works projects. And thousands of slaves, immigrants, and natives would give their lives in the efforts to create such a vast network that over time would save Millions of dollars in shipping and fund the American experiment to this day.

But Ransom, the original "Looper," as they are known, living in Michigan in the late 19th century, saw the sailing ships of his day, sail parts of this loop to and from the Atlantic through the Erie Canal. And on those docks in his Michigan port town, he heard tales of how the ICW, the Mississippi River, and the Gulf of Mexico allowed for a complete connection if he left that very dock on which he stood and returned to it having made an entire loop in a sailboat that he would build himself.

What he could not possibly know, nor foresee at that time, would be the millions of vessels who would follow in his footsteps for the next 120 years and how this loop would become the holy grail of voyages for mariners from around the world.

It is with this eye to history and this enthusiasm for the holy grail of voyages, that we aim to create a docu-series where we select five teams of sailors to learn to sail, obtain a vessel and then set out to have their own adventures, sailing around The Great Loop. We will film every aspect of this voyage and share their adventures with an audience of viewers who no doubt share in the ambitions of Ransom himself, to complete a Great Loop of the Eastern Seaboard.

This project will require new techniques in storytelling and videography and will use the latest advancements in wireless and web-based programming to share the adventures of the five teams as they make their way around the Loop. Each team will garner support for their vessel by creating a team of followers on social media who will support them through various patronage platforms and in-kind donations delivered by the online marketplace.

After all five voyages, we will compile the footage obtained via onboard cameras and microphones, as well as video footage we shoot from a chase boat on the water and a bus on land, as we follow these boats around the Loop, With this compiled footage we will create a feature-length documentary series that is broken into four seasons as inspired by Antonio Vivaldi, Winter Spring Summer, and Fall. A fifth pre-season will be included showing the selection process and sail training as well as the construction of the vessels in Tampa Bay, Florida at the Catalina Sailboat Shop and Factory where we will train, depart and finish the voyage one year from the start.

This voyage will not just be challenging from a technical perspective but also from a human and spiritual perspective. When Ransom and his crew made the voyage, they suffered freezing temperatures, starvation, and deadly situations regularly. Our teams of voyagers will be made as safe as possible, but the fact that these people will live aboard a sailboat for one year will present a set of inherent challenges and risks.

They will be forced to endure long tiresome hours at the helm of a sailboat in some very challenging waters. They will give up many of the creature comforts afforded to land-based dwellers. Services like electricity on demand, limitless clean water, and climate control are some of the few things these sailors will be forced to live without that will be certain to cause some hardship for these sailors.

What's more, the environmental wear they will encounter is certain to spill over into their interpersonal relationships and become a challenge in itself when teamwork and togetherness are paramount for success in a voyage like this. The success of each team will be watched and supported by social media and so, therefore, the daily interactions and personalities of these sailors will be of utmost interest to the viewers. The team that best harnesses the support of their followers and translates that support into speed, comfort, and safety will be awarded certain perks provided by their patrons, as well as a cash prize at the close of the voyage and, will be given the title to their vessel so that they may continue their voyage funded by their followers around the world.

The first time we tried to plan this voyage and this project with one boat, we had great success with our number of viewers and candidates. We offered a 42' endeavor for this project and received 21 entries with over 200 thousand views. It was this overwhelming success, however, that convinced us to reexamine this effort and instead of selecting one team, expand the fleet to five boats and select five teams of sailors for this project with a fleet of newly constructed vessels.

By offering a brand new boat to the sailors, we can wire the boat for video and sound and can focus the story on the people and the places and history, instead of focusing on the restoration of the boat. We decided to change the format and come up with this format instead. The viewers and social media will be key in the development of this project with the teams relying heavily on the support of their friends, family, and followers just a Ransom himself did more than 120 years ago. And it is the power of social media that will begin this project as the entries will rely on their social media savvy to help them win a place on one of the five selected teams.

Each entrant will create a One minute video answering the question, "why do they want to sail the Great Loop?" and submit it to us at Info@thechartedlife.net. We will then add that video to our Youtube Channel and share that video on our social media feed and website. The top fifty videos submitted in terms of views calculated by Youtube on our channel will be submitted to our producers and of those fifty entries, twenty individuals will be selected to join one of the five teams of sailors. Entries may elect to submit four separate one-minute videos as entries for each member of an affiliated group of entries and link to each other as a team.

Alternatively, individuals may elect to submit an individual video, unaffiliated with any other entrant. Views will be calculated by dividing the total number of views of affiliated videos divided by the number of affiliates. (IE four videos are received as affiliated, all four view counts will be added together and divided by four). By using social media to decide the top 50, we hope to involve our enthusiastic followers of this project to assist in its creation.

As this project will require a massive collaborative effort of sailors, web gurus, and creative talent, we ask that anyone wishing to join in on this project send us a video resume explaining their interest in this project and how they might wish to assist. Questions about the planning, production, or rules of this project may also be sent to info@thechartedlife.net.